Law of Contract in Ireland

LAW OF CONTRACT IN IRELAND

By

CLAIRE-MICHELLE SMYTH

CLARUS PRESS

Published by
Clarus Press Ltd,
Griffith Campus,
South Circular Road,
Dublin 8.
www.claruspress.ie

Typeset by
Gough Typesetting Services,
Dublin

Printed by
SprintPrint
Dublin

ISBN
978-1-917134-05-7

A catalogue record for this book is available from the British Library

For Ed
You spin me like a hurricane

PREFACE

My interest in law, and specifically contract law began many years ago while still in secondary school. As part of the Junior Certificate cycle we studies Shakespeare's The Merchant of Venice which had a profound impact on my future career choices.

For those of you who have never read this, Antonio seeks a loan from notorious moneylender Shylock who, seemingly in jest, states that rather than charging interest, if the loan is not repaid within three months he requires a pound of Antonio's flesh. Antonio, confident that his ships will arrive long before this deadline agrees to the bond. Unfortunately for Antonio, his ships are lost at sea and the bond becomes due. Shylock refuses all requests to accept payment insisting that 'I will have my bond'. The matter goes to court where Portia, Bassanio's wife, dresses as Balthazar the lawyer to represent Antonio. Agreeing with Shylock, she says that the law is clear – he can indeed have his bond and take his pound of flesh. As Shylock is preparing to do this, Balthazar (Portia in disguise) points out that while he may take his pound of flesh, the bond makes no reference to spilling a drop of blood:

This bond doth give thee here no jot of blood. The words expressly are 'a pound of flesh'. Then take thy bond, take thou thy pound of flesh. But in the cutting it, if thou dost shed one drop of Christian blood, thy lands and goods are by the law of Venice confiscate unto the State of Venice.[1]

The outcome of this case sparked a lifelong fascination with contracts. Granted, this contract would not be upheld as valid in any court of law today for a variety of reasons, the notion that contracts need to be precise, specific and include all material terms whereas an oversight can render the entire contract unenforceable is nonetheless of the utmost importance. We enter into contracts on a daily basis, some of which are trivial and others which may have significant consequences to our lives. Thus, the law governing these contracts is of vital importance. From the formalities, to the terms, to the remedies, how we draft these contracts will have a bearing. It needs to be clear what the obligations, rights and responsibilities of each party to the contract is – where there is ambiguity there is room for argument.

1 William Shakespeare, *The Merchant of Venice*, Act 4, Scene 1, Lines 164-396.

For decades I have taught this subject to undergraduate and postgraduate students in both Ireland and England and my curiosity and interest in the area has not diminished. I hope that my enjoyment of the subject comes through in the following pages and that perhaps some of you are inspired, at least to read the Merchant of Venice.

Claire-Michelle Smyth
December 2024

TABLE OF CONTENTS

PART THREE
AVOIDING CONTRACTUAL LIABILITY

PART FOUR
DISCHARGING THE CONTRACT

PART FIVE
REMEDIES

TABLES OF CASES

TABLE OF LEGISLATION

EU Legislation

Statutory Instruments

UK Legislation

US Legislation

CHAPTER 1

INTRODUCTION TO CONTRACT LAW

1.1 What is a Contract?

There is no one case or piece of legislation that defines precisely what a contract is. A good definition comes from *Treitel on the Law of Contract* who says:

> A contract is an agreement giving rise to obligations which are enforced or recognised by law. The factor which distinguishes the contractual from other legal obligations is that they are based on the agreement of the contracting parties.[1]

At its most basic level, a contract is an agreement between two or more parties, but it differs from general everyday agreements in that it is legally enforceable. This means that if one of the parties to the contract does not comply with their obligations, the innocent party can enforce the agreement in court and may be awarded either performance of the contract or damages for breach of contract. This agreement is made where one party makes an offer which is accepted by the other, whereby they agree that they intend to be legally bound and provide 'consideration' which reflects the value of the exchange between the parties.

Generally, there is no prescribed way in which a contract must be created. In other words, there is no specific form or format that it must take. While there are dense legally drafted contracts that are formally signed, agreements written on a piece of notepaper or concluded orally have the same force of law. There are, however, certain types of contracts that must be concluded in a particular way. For example, the Land and Conveyancing Law Reform Act 2009 states that contracts in relation to the sale of land must be evidenced in writing. This means

[1] Edwin Peel, *Treital: The Law of Contract* (15th ed Sweet and Maxwell 2020) 3.

that in most cases an oral agreement to sell land will not be legally enforceable.[2]

1.2 Sources of Contract Law

Contract law originates from the common law (judge-made law) and is primarily still governed by common law rules today. There have been some recent legislative interventions, such as the Consumer Rights Act 2022, which apply to specific contracts. Much of this legislation derived from Ireland's membership of the European Union which required laws to be passed to facilitate cross-border dealings and harmonise the laws in the Union. Consumer rights are particularly important in terms of EU law, as are competition and employment law, which made EU legislation an important source of contract law. The reasoning behind the EU rules was to ensure that equivalent protection was given in each Member State. So, for example, it did not matter whether you bought a toaster in Ireland or Spain; your rights as a consumer were equal. This became particularly important with the advent of internet shopping and restricted 'jurisdiction shopping', ie seeking the best deals or terms in another country.

1.3 Freedom to Contract

The freedom to contract essentially represents the view that parties are free to enter into their own contracts and choose the terms upon which they are willing to be bound. The role of the court would be restricted to enforcing the contracts that the parties had entered into. This meant that even if a contract was fundamentally unfair, it would still be enforceable once freely entered into. It would only be in circumstances where this freedom was tainted with, say, duress or misrepresentation that the court would intervene. Otherwise, if the party enters into a bad bargain, that was their problem.[3]

Given that most contracts are business contracts, this meant that businesses were free to enter into contracts dictated by supply and demand. This was seen to encourage growth in markets and the creation of wealth in society overall. One of the reasons behind this approach was that if courts were interested only in holding parties to

---

2 A core principle of equity is that equity will not allow a statute to be used as a weapon of fraud. As such, where the strict application of legislation would cause an injustice, equity can depart from the provisions. See *Rochefoucauld v Boustead* [1897] 1 Ch 196.

3 Patrick S Atiyah, *The Rise and Fall of Freedom to Contract* (Oxford University Press 1979).

their bargain, it would create legal certainty.[4] However, this thinking was also based on the misconceived notion that the parties had equal bargaining power, which is not always the case and resulted in very unfair results.

This is illustrated in the US case of *Lochner v New York*.[5] The New York Bakeshop Act 1895 was enacted to limit the amount of hours that bakers could work in a bakery on the basis of a serious risk to health, and it made it a criminal offence for bakeries to employ workers for more than 60 hours per week. Lochner was charged with breaching this provision. It was argued by his lawyer that the legislation breached his, and the bakers', freedom to contract and that individual rights and freedoms ought not to be swept away by the legislature. Lochner was initially convicted, but appealed, and the US Supreme Court struck down the legislation as unconstitutional, stating that:

> The general right to make a contract in relation to his business is part of the liberty of the individual protected by the Fourteenth Amendment. Under that provision, no state can deprive any person of life, liberty or property without the due process of law. The right to purchase or to sell labor is part of the liberty protected by this amendment unless there are circumstances which exclude the right.

This case clearly shows that the freedom to contract was held in high esteem by the uppermost courts, despite a clear imbalance of power between the parties (the bakeries would have significantly more power than the bakers) which the legislation tried to ameliorate by creating added protection for the bakers. This case is clearly no longer good law, and the courts have moved away from this doctrine being all encompassing. There is now more of a recognition that in many relationships there is not equality of bargaining power, and legislation has been created to intervene and level the playing field, especially in areas of employment and consumer law.

1.4 Aspects of the Contract

Contract law is generally divided into several aspects, and this book, like most other contract law books, has followed a common structure. The first aspect when examining contract law is the formation of the contract and we look at this in Part I. Chapter 2 considers the issues of offer and acceptance: the agreement between the parties. We look at what is required to make a valid offer as distinguished from, say,

---

4 Richard Allen Posner, *Economic Analysis of Law* (7th Ed, Aspen Publishing 2007) Ch 4.

5 198 US 45 (1905).

an invitation to treat,[6] how this offer must be communicated to the other party, and when it can validly be revoked. We examine the rules around acceptance and distinguish it from a counter-offer or a request for further information. In Chapter 3 we move on to examine 'consideration'. As we have already seen, not all agreements are legally binding, and one of the core differences in making an agreement a contract is the provision of consideration. Consideration is the price paid or the service exchanged, the something given and something received, the monetary value of the contract which makes it legally binding and more than a mere moral obligations. We look at what the law deems to be appropriate consideration and when it must be provided in order for the contract to be valid. In Chapter 4 we move on to examine the requirement of an intention to create legal relations. This is a very important aspect as we enter into agreements on a daily basis but do not necessarily intend that we may be taken to court if we do not fulfil our obligations. For example, if you offer to drive a classmate home in exchange for €20 fuel money, and they agree and give you £20, we have an offer, acceptance and the provision of consideration. But what would happen if you did not turn up to bring them home? Would you end up in court? The answer is clearly no, because while you would have a moral obligation to uphold your end of the deal, neither party intended that the contract would have the force of law. Finally, in Part I, we look at what it means to have capacity to enter the contract in Chapter 5. This comes into play where all of the elements to form a contract are ostensibly present, but there may be some question about the person entering the contract. For example, the law prohibits minors from entering into contracts in most circumstances. Or indeed, a party could be suffering from a psychological impairment which renders them unable to understand the nature and consequences of the contract that they have entered into. In these circumstances, despite the formalities being present, no contract can be formed.

Once the contract has been formed, the second aspect to examine is the terms of the contract, which is the focus of Part II. Chapter 6 considers the issues of 'certainty'. As a contract is something that may be enforced by a court, its terms need to be certain and precise as a court order can never be vague. Chapter 7 then moves on to discuss how to determine whether a matter is in fact a term of the contract or not. For example, if a person makes a statement (as contracts may be concluded orally) in relation to the origin of a piece of furniture, would that be considered a term of the contract or merely some sales puff to try to entice you into the contract? It is important to distinguish such statements because only a breach of a term (express or implied)

---

6 Which is an offer to make an offer.

may result in damages or discharge of the contract, in some cases an innocent party will be able to claim for both discharge of the contract and damages. Chapter 8 then looks at exclusion clauses, whereby one party attempts to exclude any liability for loss or damage caused as a result of their breach of contract. We examine the rules surrounding how such clauses can be validly incorporated into the contract and in Chapter 9 we discuss the legislative interventions to ameliorate some of the harshness that these clauses cause, particularly in relation to consumer contracts. Finally in this section chapter 10 examines the rules of privity of contract and third party rights.

Once the contract has been formed, and the terms are clearly denoted, the court will generally enforce the terms of the contract. However, as we have previously said, a contract is an agreement in which parties freely assume their obligations. Therefore, there may be underlying reasons where it cannot be said that this has occurred, and in those circumstances the contract may not be enforced. Part III of this book examines those circumstances and begins in Chapters 11 and 12 with the issues of mistake and misrepresentation. Where a person is operating under a mistake as to, say, the identity of the person with whom they are contracting, or where some material facts of the contract have been misrepresented to them, we cannot say that there has been a meeting of the minds as one party is not getting what they believed they were contracting for. Chapters 13 and 14 discuss scenarios where a party has only entered into the contract due to external pressures such as duress or undue influence. In these cases, it cannot be said that they have entered into the contract of their own free will and volition and therefore such contracts may not be enforced. The final chapter of Part III, Chapter 15 looks at circumstances where the court will decide that a contract cannot be enforced due to illegality or public policy. For example, if you have entered into a contract to purchase illegal drugs, despite the fact that all of the above formalities may have been met, the terms are clear and there was no underlying pressure, the contract will still not be enforced as the subject matter of the contract is illegal. Again, there are circumstances where the contract itself may not be illegal, but enforcing such a contract would be contrary to public policy. For example, surrogacy contracts are not strictly illegal, but the court will not enforce a contract of this nature.

Part IV of the book follows the next aspect of the contract, examining how the contract may come to an end. In Chapter 16 we look at the straightforward aspects of agreement and performance. There is nothing controversial about these – a contract is one that the parties have freely entered into and they can also agree to end their obligations to each other. Further, once the contract has been performed, it will naturally come to an end. There are, however, other ways in which the contract may end. Chapter 17 examines the doctrine of frustration, when an intervening event outside of the control of either party occurs which renders the contract impossible to perform. For example, let us say that you hire a local pub for your birthday party, but two weeks before the event there is an accident and the pub burns down. This would be a frustrating event which means it is impossible to perform the contract – there is no pub for you to have your birthday party in. Chapter 18 then examines when a contract can be set aside on the grounds of breach. This is very closely linked with the chapter on terms, as the type of term that is breached will have an impact on the remedy available. In all cases, damages will be awarded, but where a fundamental term of the contract is breached, the court may set aside the contract in addition to or in lieu of damages.

Part V of this book then examines the remedies that are available to an innocent party when the contract has been breached. In all cases of breach, as a matter of law, the innocent party will be entitled to damages as considered in Chapter 19. The court will need to quantify the amount of damages, and we examine the rules surrounding this. Chapter 20 then looks to equity and the equitable remedies that can be ordered by the court, such as specific performance, rescission, rectification and injunctive relief.

At the end of each chapter in this book, there is a question designed to test your knowledge, together with an explanation of the correct answer, and a 'stretch and challenge' point for discussion.

PART ONE

FORMATION OF A CONTRACT

Chapter 2

OFFER AND ACCEPTANCE

2.1 Introduction

The existence of agreement is ascertained by the parties' words and actions. Blackburn J demonstrates in *Smith v Hughes* that the test for the existence of an agreement is objective:

> If, whatever a man's real intention may be, he so conducts himself that a reasonable man would believe that he was assenting to the terms proposed by the other party, and that other party upon that belief enters into the contract with him, the man thus conducting himself would be equally bound as if he had intended to agree to the other party's terms.[1]

To establish whether an agreement has been reached, the courts will generally look for an offer made by one party (known as the offeror) and determine that the other party (the offeree) has accepted it. This traditional approach can be referred to as the 'mirror image' rule of contractual formation in that the court must be able to find a clear and unequivocal offer which is mirrored by a clear and unequivocal acceptance.

Whilst this approach has the benefit of a degree of certainty, it is important to keep in mind that this traditional approach has been subjected to criticism as being excessively rigid. In *Butler v Ex-Cell-O Corporation (England) Ltd*[2] Lord Denning rejected the traditional approach, and in *Gibson v Manchester City Council* he said that 'to my

1 (1871) LR 6 QB 597.
2 [1979] 1 WLR 401.

mind it is a mistake to think that all contracts can be analysed into the form of offer and acceptance'.[3] In *G Percy Trentham Ltd v Archital Luxfer Ltd* Lord Steyn favoured prioritising the intention of the parties and the commercial reality over the strict determination of a valid offer and acceptance.[4] However, this is the exception rather than the rule and predominantly the tradition approach prevails.

2.2 Offer

An offer can be defined as a clear and unambiguous statement of terms upon which the offeror is willing to contract[5] or '[a]n expression of willingness to contract on specified terms, made with the intention that it is to become binding as soon as it is accepted by the person to whom it is addressed'.[6] Therefore the terms of the offer need to be precise and where such precision is lacking, no offer will have been made. In *Hoare v AIB Plc* a letter was sent by the defendant to its customers who had defaulted on certain loans stating that if certain actions were taken it would be 'willing to show a level of forbearance'.[7] The court held that this statement did not amount to an offer.

There are two types of contracts that can result from the kind of offer that is made, and it is important to distinguish between the two. A bilateral contract is one that is made between two or more *identifiable* parties. For example, if I said, 'I will give €10 to Stacey if she will make me a cup of coffee', this offer has been made directly to an identifiable party, Stacey, and only she can accept, resulting in a bilateral contract. A unilateral contract arises where an offer is made to a larger group of people and is capable of being accepted by anyone who fulfils the terms of the offer. For example, 'I will give €10 to the first person in the room who brings me a cup of coffee.' This is open to everyone in the room. The first person to bring me a cup of coffee has fulfilled the terms of the offer and can claim the €10.

2.3 Offer or an Invitation to Treat

An offer is a statement which is capable of being accepted whereas an invitation to treat is seen as an invitation to make an offer. Determining whether a statement is one or the other will come down to the words used and their interpretation by the court. In *Gibson v Manchester City*

---

3 [1978] 1 WLR 520, 523.
4 [1993] 1 Lloyd's Rep 25.
5 Robert Clark, *Contract Law in Ireland* (9th edn, Round Hall 2022) 9.
6 *Treitel on the Law of Contract*, (12th edn, Sweet and Maxwell 2007) 2-002.
7 [2014] IEHC 221.

Council Mr Gibson received a letter from the Council indicating that it 'may be prepared to sell' his council house to him at a particular price, but that the 'letter is not to be regarded as a firm offer of a mortgage'.[8] Mr Gibson was to fill in an application form and send it to the Council. Before the matter was concluded, there was a change in Council governance and the practice of selling Council-owned properties was reversed. Mr Gibson sought an order of specific performance (see Chapter 20) to force the Council to complete the sale. The House of Lords decided that there was no contract in existence in that there was no valid offer capable of acceptance. The wording of the Council's letter was an invitation to treat, inviting Mr Gibson to make an offer which could then be accepted or rejected by the Council. In contrast, in *Storer v Manchester City Council* the letter which stated 'I understand that you wish to purchase your council house and enclose the agreement for sale' was held to be a valid offer.[9]

The courts have developed rules that apply in specific circumstances which are considered below.

2.3.1 Advertisements

In Ireland, the Consumer Rights Act 2022 makes it an offence for anyone to invite offers on the basis of false or misleading information. In addition, The Consumer Credit Act 1995 requires that the terms of any credit facilities be made available to consumers prior to entering into the agreement.

Aside from this protection, as a general rule, an advertisement is to be considered as an invitation to treat and not an offer. In *Partridge v Crittenden* the defendant was not liable for the statutory offence of unlawfully offering wild birds for sale as his advertisement was not an offer but rather an invitation to treat.[10] In addition, in *Grainger and Son v Gough (Surveyor of Taxes)* the court found that the delivery of a price list does not amount to an offer that, as soon as there is an order, results in a binding contract.[11] The rationale behind this is to protect the vendor from multiple claims of liability in circumstances where it runs out of stock. Imagine a scenario where a company advertises a particular new mobile phone for €50, which is at an 80% discount from the normal price. There would be a considerable number of people who would want to buy this phone, and the company would quickly run out of stock. If the advertisement were to be seen as an offer, the

---

8 [1979] 1 WLR 294.
9 [1974] 1 WLR 1403.
10 [1968] 2 All ER 421.
11 [1896] AC 325.

company would have an obligation to provide every customer with a phone, which would be impractical and impossible. As such, an advertisement generally is an invitation to treat; an order resulting from that advertisement is an offer which can be accepted or rejected.

However, in certain circumstances an invitation can be deemed to be an offer, as seen in the landmark case of *Carlill v Carbolic Smoke Ball Company*.[12] This case involved an advertisement for a medicinal product. The company claimed that if the smoke ball was used correctly, the user would not contract influenza. So confident was the company in its claim that it offered £100 to anyone who used its product and contracted influenza. Further, it stated that, to show its sincerity, £1,000 would be deposited in a bank to meet the cost of any such claims. The plaintiff used the smoke ball, contracted influenza and claimed her £100 as per the advertisement. The company claimed that this was merely an invitation to treat and not an offer and refused to pay. The court found that the specificity of the statement made was such that the reasonable person would assume that they could rely on it and therefore it was an offer. The fact that the company had said it would lodge the money in a separate account meant that it intended for its statement to be relied upon. The plaintiff had accepted the offer made by performing the actions stipulated. Whether an advert is construed as an offer or an invitation to treat will depend on the context of the advert and its interpretation in light of the surrounding circumstances.

In *Tansey v The College of Occupational Therapists Ltd* the plaintiff attempted to rely on the principles of Carlill.[13] Here the plaintiff had enrolled on a course in St Joseph's College where she would, on successful completion of exams set by the defendant as the professional body, receive a diploma accredited by them. When the plaintiff enrolled, she was given a handbook that stated that if a student did not achieve a pass in their exam, they would receive two additional attempts. At some point this was lowered to one additional attempt. The plaintiff argued that she had a contractual relationship with the defendant on the basis of the handbook. The court disagreed and found that Carlill could not apply as the plaintiff was not aware of any offer at the moment she enrolled and that the purpose of the manual was merely to convey information.

The concept of reasonableness is key in cases involving advertisements. For example, *Leonard v Pepsico*, while a US case, demonstrates the

---

12 [1893] 1 QB 256.
13 Unrep, High Court, 27 Aug 1986.

principle well.[14] Here, Pepsi ran an advertising campaign whereby consumers of the drink Pepsi could collect tokens known as 'Pepsi points' and exchange them for certain goods such as t-shirts, hats, sunglasses etc. The advert ended with a young man arriving at school in a Harrier Jet, with the caption saying that it was had a value of 7 million Pepsi points. As part of the promotion, people could also buy points rather than collecting them. Leonard, determined to have the jet, raised US$700,000 and sent this to Pepsi with some additional Pepsi points. The company responded saying that the jet was not part of the promotion, and after some heated correspondence Leonard took the case to court. The question before the court was whether the advertisement could be construed as an offer. The court found that there was no way any reasonable person would determine that this was an offer, as the concept was ridiculous.

2.3.2 Goods Displayed for Sale

Many cases in this category arise not from the formation of a contract but from criminal proceedings which have been decided on the basis of contract law principles. In the case of *Minister for Industry and Commerce v Pim* a coat was displayed for sale with a notice stating the cash price and credit facilities.[15] It was an offence to offer credit without specifically setting out the terms of the credit, and the shopkeeper was prosecuted on the basis of this. The court found that the display was not an offer, but an invitation to treat, inviting offers from the public and therefore the prosecution failed.

In *Fisher v Bell* the defendant had displayed flick knives in his shop and was charged with the offence of 'offering for sale' an item contrary to the provisions of s 1(1) of the Restriction of Offensive Weapons Act 1959.[16] On appeal it was held that this was not an offer but an invitation to treat and therefore did not meet the test for the offence as set down in the legislation. The provisions of the legislation were subsequently widened as a result of this case.

The leading case in England and Wales is *Pharmaceutical Society of Great Britain v Boots Cash Chemists*.[17] Here the plaintiff alleged that the defendant had breached s 18 of the Pharmacy and Poisons Act 1933 which prohibited the sale of certain medicines without the supervision of a pharmacist. The question before the court was whether the display of the medicines on shelves was an offer which would be accepted

---

14 88 F. Supp. 2d 116 (SDNY 1999).
15 [1966] IR 154.
16 [1961] 1 QB 394.
17 [1953] 1 QB 401.

when the customer picked up an item and placed it in their basket; or whether the display was an invitation to treat, which became an offer when the customer brought the item to the checkout to pay, which could then be accepted or rejected under the supervision of a pharmacist and thereby complying with the legislative requirements. The court determined that it was the latter. This is clearly a common sense conclusion as if the alternative interpretation was accepted by the court, the customer could be seen to be bound to purchase an item simply by picking it up off the shelf. They would be unable to change their mind and choose a more suitable product.

Like advertisements, it is possible for a display to be construed as an offer. In *R v Warwickshire CC, ex parte Johnson* a notice placed in a shop window with the display of goods that stated 'we will beat any TV price by £20 on the spot' was held to be an offer.[18]

2.3.3 Websites

We have already noted that an advertisement of goods generally does not constitute an offer, so it would seem that a website advertising goods will be an invitation to treat and that the offer will therefore come from the customer at the checkout stage. An issue often arises in relation to pricing mistakes on a website. It can be argued in these situations that the advertisement is an invitation to treat, so that it is the customer making the offer, which can be rejected by the supplier where a pricing error has occurred. Problems can arise, however, where the supplier sends an automated reply confirming the order. For example, Kodak advertised a digital camera on its website for £100. This was a mistake, and the correct price ought to have been £329. The offer was only on the website for a few hours before it was rectified, but during that time several thousand cameras were bought at this price. One of the main issues in this case was that Kodak had sent a confirmatory email to the customers which could be construed as forming a contract. Once the mistake was notified, Kodak refused to honour these 'contracts' at the lower price. Customers threatened legal action and there was widespread media coverage of the issue, which led to Kodak eventually honouring the purchases at the lower price.[19]

2.3.4 Auctions

Under the Sale of Goods Act 1893 a sale under auction is complete

---

18 [1993] AC 583.

19 See Pinset Masons, 'Kodak Caves in to Customers over Pricing Error' (31 January 2002) Available at <www.pinsetmasons.com/out-law/news/kodal-caves-in-to-customers-over-pricing-error> accessed 20 August 2024.

when the auctioneer announces it to be, which is usually by the fall of the hammer. It is the bidder who makes the offer, and it is either accepted or rejected by the auctioneer.

The legislation puts on a statutory footing, principles previously espoused in case law. For example, in the case of *Payne v Cave*.[20] Here the claimant put goods up for sale by way of public auction with a reserve price. The defendant made the highest bid but changed his mind before the auctioneer's hammer fell. The claimant argued that there was a completed contract and therefore the defendant had to buy the goods. The court held that the auction was an invitation to treat; the defendant's bid was an offer which would have been accepted by the falling of the auctioneer's hammer. As it was revoked prior to acceptance, no contract was formed. The provisions have been somewhat enhanced where the buyer at an auction is classed as a consumer and in those circumstances the Consumer Rights Act 2022 applies.

The situation is different where there is no reserve price set. This is construed as a unilateral contract which is open to be accepted by the highest bidder no matter how low the offer. In *Barry v Davies* customs and excise auctioned without reserve two analyser machines which were worth in the region of £14,000 each.[21] The claimant bid £200 each – the highest offer – but the auctioneer refused to sell and withdrew the items. The claimant brought an action for breach of contract. The court here held that there was a breach of contract, stating that 'it would be the general and reasonable expectation of persons attending an auction sale without reserve that the highest bidder would and should be entitled to the lot for which he bids'.

It should be noted that online auctions do not conform to the same rules and participants are bound by the rules which are set by the service providers.[22]

2.3.5 Tenders

Generally, an invitation to submit a tender will be held to be an invitation to treat. In *Spencer v Harding* the defendants sent a notice stating, 'we are instructed to offer to the wholesale trade by tender the stock …'.[23] The claimant submitted the highest tender and alleged

---

20 (1789) 100 ER 502.

21 [2000] 1 WLR 1962.

22 See Ross Pearman, 'E-Bidding, Who Can You Trust?' (2002) 24 Contract Journal 9; Julia Hornle, 'Is an online Auction an Auction in Law' (2007) 8(12) Electronic Business Law 7.

23 (1870) LR5 CP 561.

that in refusing to sell to them the defendant was in breach of contract. It was held that the invitation to tender was not an offer to sell to the highest bidder. However, in *Harvela Investment Ltd v Royal Trust Co of Canada (CI) Ltd* the defendant sent a telex to two parties inviting them to submit a tender for the purchase of shares and stated, 'we bind ourselves to accept the highest offer'.[24] Harvela bid $2,175,000 while the other company bid $2,100,000 or $101,000 in excess of any other bid (this is known as a referential bid). The defendant accepted the other party's bid. The court held that the referential bid was invalid, and the defendant was in breach as the telex was a unilateral offer accepted by Harvela when it submitted the highest bid.[25] This principle has been upheld and applied in Ireland in the case of *Smart Telecom v RTE.*[26]

2.4 Request for Further Information

Where a request for information is made, this will not be held to be an offer. In *Harvey v Facey* Harvey sent a telegram to Facey saying, 'Will you sell us Bumper Hall Pen? Telegraph lowest cash price?'.[27] Facey telegraphed back, 'Lowest cash price for Bumper Hall pen £900.' The claimants then telegraphed, 'We agree to buy Bumper Hall Pen for £900.' Facey made no reply to that. Was there a valid agreement? The court held that there was no contract between the parties. Facey had not directly answered the first question as to whether he would sell, and stating the lowest price was merely responding to a request for information, which was not an offer capable of being accepted.

2.5 Terminating an Offer

An offer does not last forever and can be terminated in a number of ways. Of course, the offeree can simply say no and reject the offer outright which is the simplest way in which an offer may be terminated.

2.5.1 Lapse of Time

If the offer does not specify the time for which it will last, it can terminate through lapse of time. Where the offer expressly states that

---

24 [1986] AC 207.

25 For further analysis of this case see David R Percy, Radical Developments in the Law of Tenders: A Canadian Reformulation of Common Law Principles (1988) 4(3) Construction Law Journal 171; Martin Hogg, Liability for Improperly Rejected Contract Tenders: Legitimate Expectations, Contract, Promise and Delict (2012) 16(2) Edinburgh Law Review 246.

26 [2006] IEHC 176.

27 [1893] AC 552.

it is for immediate acceptance only, the offeree must comply with this requirement[28] and as in *Glencore Energy Ltd v Cirrus Oil Services Ltd* an offer may state that it will be incapable of acceptance once a specified deadline has passed, which again must be complied with.[29]

In the absence of specific requirements, *Commane v Walsh*[30] approving the English judgment of *Ramsgate Victoria Hotel Co v Montefiore*[31] states that an offer will remain open until it is withdrawn or until a reasonable amount of time has passed. This is judged at being a timeframe whereby it would be unreasonable for the offeror to hold the offer open any longer given the length of time taken by the offeree to accept.

2.5.2 Revocation

It is a generally accepted rule that an offer can be withdrawn or revoked at any time until it has been accepted. In *The Navan Union v McLoughlin* the defendant submitted a tender to the plaintiff who had agreed to accept the offer.[32] Before this acceptance could be communicated, the defendant revoked the offer. It was held that as the plaintiff had not validly accepted the offer, the defendant was entitled to revoke it.

This applies even where the offer states that it will remain open for a specified period of time, as seen in *Walker v Glass*.[33] Here the plaintiff wanted to buy the defendant's estate. A contract was drawn up in which the defendant offered to sell the estate for £400,000. The offer stated that it would remain open until 13th March and prior to that time the plaintiff was required to both sign an official acceptance and pay a deposit of £40,000. On 1st March the plaintiff expressed his intention to accept but did not pay the deposit until the 12th March. However, between the 1st and 12th March the defendant revoked the offer. The plaintiff sued for specific performance but the court held that the prescribed method of acceptance had not been complied with and as such the defendant was free to revoke the offer at any stage until acceptance had taken place. However, once the offer has been accepted, it cannot be revoked.

When it comes to unilateral offers, an offer cannot be revoked once performance of the terms has been commenced.[34] In order for

---

[28] See *Dooley v Egan* (1938) 72 ILTR 155.
[29] [2014] EWHC 87.
[30] Unrep, High Court, 2 May 1991.
[31] (1886) LR 1 Exch.
[32] (1855) 4 ICLR 451.
[33] [1979] NI 129.
[34] See Donald Clark, 'Revocation and the Unilateral Contract: A Reappraisal' (2000) New Zealand Law Review 17.

revocation to be effective, it must be communicated to the offeree; it is not enough that the offeror has silently changed their mind.

For example, let's say that Jacob has placed an advertisement in a local paper to sell his Guitar. He says that he is open to offers of €500 and above and that he should be contacted by email with any offers. (Remember as this is an advertisement it is an invitation to treat at this stage and not an offer). Darren sends an email to Jacob stating 'I am offering you €500 to buy your Fender Guitar'. Three days elapse and Darren has not yet has a response from his email. He then sees another similar guitar for sale and contacts the owner who responds immediately. Darren decides to buy this second guitar. The following day, Jacob contacts him accepting Darren's offer. Is Darren now bound by this contract? The answer is that yes, he is. The offer remains open and capable of acceptance until it has been revoked. Darren may have thought that the offer was not being accepted because of the length of time Jacob took to respond, but he did not specify any time limit in his initial offer. Before purchasing the second guitar, Darren should have emailed Jacob to withdraw the offer. Once Jacob has accepted the offer, Darren is bound by it.

2.5.3 Counter Offer

For a valid acceptance to exist, as seen in the next section, the offeree must accept the offer in its entirety. Where the offeree amends or changes any of the terms of the offer, this then becomes a counter offer which can either be accepted or rejected. In *Swan v Miller* the defendant offered to sell their interest in a lease for the sum of £4750 plus ground rent.[35] The plaintiff responded stating that they would pay the sum of £4450 for the interest. This response was held to be a counter offer which could not create a binding contract.

A counter-offer amounts to a rejection of an offer. This in effect terminates the original offer and replaces it with a new offer that is then capable of being accepted or rejected. If the counter offer is rejected, the initial offer cannot then be accepted.[36]

2.6 Acceptance

An acceptance is a final, unconditional and certain indication of agreement to the terms of an offer, communicated to the offeror, with the intention of accepting and being bound by the offer. If there

---

[35] [1919]1 IR 151.

[36] *Wheeler v Jeffrey* [1921] 2 IR 395.

are any alterations to any of the terms, then it will not amount to an acceptance.[37] The two key elements are acceptance of the offer made and communication of that acceptance.

2.6.1 Acceptance of the Offer Made

The mirror image rule states that the acceptance must mirror entirely the terms of the offer. Any variation, addition or detraction from the offer will not constitute an acceptance but rather a counter offer. However, the counter offer must be differentiated from a request for further information. This request will not terminate an offer. In *Stevenson v McLean* the defendant offered to sell iron to the plaintiffs for cash on delivery at 40 shillings.[38] The plaintiffs responded asking if they could buy the iron on credit to which they received no response. When they then accepted the offer, the iron had been sold to another party. Here it was held that the offer was not revoked, and the acceptance was valid.

In some circumstances, an offer can be validly accepted by conduct. In *Brogden v Metropolitan Railway Company* the two parties had been doing business for a number of years when they decided to formalise their arrangements by entering into a contract.[39] A contract was drafted which was signed and approved by one party and then returned to the other when it was forgotten about. The two parties acted in accordance with the agreement for a number of years until a dispute arose whereby it was claimed that there was no legally binding contract. The court found that the contract had been accepted by conduct as evidenced by the fact that they had abided by the terms therein. The leading Irish authority on this point is *Brennan v Lockyer*.[40] The plaintiff posted an offer requesting that certain benefits be made available to him via his trade union on enrolment. The trade union posted, from London, a certificate of enrolment which arrived in Dublin. The question arose as to where acceptance had taken place, in London when it was posted or in Dublin when it was received. The court distinguished between an acceptance which consists of a promise which must be validly communicated, and one that requests an action such as the posting of goods which does not.

A 'battle of forms' can arise where parties use standard forms and each tries to impose their own conditions on the other. The approach the courts have taken to this is that the last shot wins. This is illustrated in

---

37 *Bonner Properties v McGurran Construction Ltd* [2008] NI Ch 16.
38 (1880) 5 QB 346.
39 (1877) 2 App Cas 666.
40 [1932] IR 100. See also *Hamilton v Judge* [2009] NI Ch 4.

British Road Services v Arthur Crutchley & Co Ltd.[41] Here BRS delivered whiskey to the defendant for storage. The driver handed over a delivery note which contained conditions under which the contract would exist. The note was stamped by the defendant's employee stating 'received under our conditions' and handed back to the driver. The question arose as to which conditions were binding on the contract. The court found that the offer was made by the driver handing the note over, and the defendant's employee made a counter offer when the stamped note was handed back which was accepted by delivery of the goods. Therefore, it was the defendant's conditions that prevailed. In *Trebor Bassett Holdings Ltd v ADT Fire and Security Plc* the court reiterated that in such a case the traditional analysis based on offer and acceptance had to be adopted, unless the parties' conduct and the documents passing between them showed a common intention that some other terms were to prevail.[42] Under this logic, it is difficult to displace the traditional approach unless there is a clear course of dealing between the parties.

2.6.2 Communication of the Acceptance

As a general rule, an acceptance does not become valid until it has been communicated to the offeror. This means that an offer cannot be accepted by silence and there needs to be some outward indication of this acceptance. In *Felthouse v Bindley* there was a discussion between an uncle and nephew about the sale of a horse.[43] The uncle wrote to the nephew offering a price and saying, 'if I hear no more about him, I consider the horse mine at that price'. The nephew did not respond, and when an auctioneer sold the horse, the court had to decide if there was a valid contract between the uncle and nephew. It was held that in order for the contract to be binding, the acceptance needed to be communicated, and as the nephew did not respond there could be no contract. Further in *Russell Baird v Hoba*n the defendant requested a certain amount of oats from the plaintiff.[44] The plaintiff sent a note indicating that they could supply the oats and that 'if this sale note be retained beyond three days after this date, it will be held to have been accepted by the buyer'. The Court of Appeal held that there was no contract as there was a requirement that acceptance be communicated.

However, in *Re Selectmove Ltd* it was held that if it was the offeree who suggested silence as a means of acceptance, then this could be

---

41 [1968] 1 All ER 811.
42 [2011] EWHC 1936 (TCC).
43 (1862) 11 CB (NS) 869.
44 [1922] 2 IR 159.

valid.[45] So arguably, in *Felthouse*, if it was the nephew who said that if the uncle heard nothing more, he could treat the offer as accepted, there may have been a valid contract.

The leading case in relation to communication of acceptance is *Entores Ltd v Miles Far East Corporation*.[46] The offeror, a company in London, made an offer by telex to the offeree, a company in Amsterdam. The offeree sent its acceptance of the offer by telex back to the company in London. The question for the court was where the contract was made. It was held that the contract is only complete when the acceptance is received by the offeror, and the contract is made at the place where the acceptance is received (in this case it was received in London). Lord Denning MR gave this famous example:

> Suppose, for instance, that I shout an offer to a man across a river or a courtyard but I do not hear his reply because it is drowned by an aircraft flying overhead. There is no contract at that moment. If he wishes to make a contract, he must wait till the aircraft is gone and then shout back his acceptance so that I can hear what he says. Not until I have his answer am I bound ...

This decision has since been reaffirmed in *Brinkibon Ltd v Stalag Stahl GmbH*[47] and *JSC Zestafoni Nikoladze Ferroalloy Plant v Ronly Holdings Ltd*.[48]

This refers to the receipt rule – that the acceptance has to be received by the offeror to be valid. Its rationale was explained in *Carlill v Carbolic Smoke Ball Company* by Bowen LJ as follows:

> One cannot doubt that, as an ordinary rule of law, an acceptance of an offer made ought to be notified to the person who makes the offer, in order that the two minds may come together. Unless this is done the two minds may be apart, and there is not that consensus which is necessary according to the English law … to make a contract.

However, the question arises as to exactly when is a telex, fax or answer phone message communicated to the offeror? When it is received on the machine, or when it is read/heard by the offeror? In addition, what would be the position if, for example, a fax was sent outside of business hours?

In *Brinkibon* Lord Wilberforce's view was that no universal rule can

---

45 [1995] EWCA Civ 8.
46 [1955] 2 QB 327.
47 [1983] 2 AC 34.
48 [2004] EWHC 245 (Comm).

cover all cases. The House of Lords said, with regard to telex messages sent outside working hours, that the time and place in which the contract was completed would be determined by the intentions of the parties, standard business practice and, if possible, by analysing where the risk should most fairly lie.

The cases of *The Brimnes*[49] and *Mondial Shipping and Chartering BV v Astarte Shipping Ltd*[50] both reached the conclusion that a message sent outside of business hours was not communicated until the office re-opened for business.

An offeror who fails to receive an acceptance through their own fault may be prevented from claiming that the non-communication means they should not be bound by the contract. In *Entores* Lord Denning gave the example:

> if the listener on the telephone does not catch the words of acceptance, but nevertheless does not trouble to ask for them to be repeated: or the ink on the teleprinter fails at the receiving end, but the clerk does not ask for the message to be repeated: so that the man who sends an acceptance reasonably believes that his messages has been received. The offeror in such circumstances is clearly bound, because he will be estopped from saying that he did not receive the message of acceptance. It is his own fault that he did not get it.

A further example is provided in *The Brimnes* where the acceptance is sent by telex during business hours but is simply not read by anyone in the offeror's office. This is now also the case with emails sent during office hours. Essentially, where the communication is through instantaneous means and during normal business hours it will be deemed to be received as it is expected that these means will be monitored during said hours. However, where the communication is sent outside of working hours, receipt will be deemed to occur during the next working day. For example, if I send an email acceptance of an offer at 5.30pm on Friday evening, it will be held to be received at 9am on Monday morning.

2.6.2.1 The Postal Rule

There is one exception to the rule that an acceptance must be received before it is valid – this is known as the postal rule.[51] This rule was

---

49 [1975] QB 929.
50 [1995] CLC 1011.
51 PH Winfield, 'Some Aspects of Offer and Acceptance' (1939) 55 Law Quarterly Review 499.

developed in the case of *Adams v Lindsell*.[52] Here the defendant, whose business it was to sell wool, wrote to the plaintiff, who were manufacturers of wool, on 2 September 1817 offering to sell a large quantity of fleeces at '35s 6d per ton, to be delivered at Leicester, and to be paid for by two months' bill in two months, and to be weighed up by your agent within 14 days, receiving your answer in course of post'. It transpired that the defendant had addressed the letter incorrectly which resulted in the claimant not receiving the letter until 5 September. The claimant immediately accepted the offer which was received by the defendant on 9 September. In the ordinary course, had the defendant not incorrectly addressed the initial letter, they could have expected to hear back from the claimant by 7 September. When they had not heard by this date, they sold the wool to a third party. The question before the court was whether or not a contract had been formed between the parties and as such whether the defendant was liable to compensate the claimant for selling the wool to a third party. Lord Ellenborough held that if acceptance had to be received then 'no contract could ever be completed by post'. The court decided that acceptance took place when the letter was posted, rather than when it was received, provided that the letter was properly addressed and stamped, and therefore the contract was concluded on 5 September when the acceptance was posted.

The Irish Courts have also applied this rule. In *Sanderson v Cunningham* the plaintiff sent a proposal for an insurance policy through a broker in Dublin.[53] This constituted an offer. The insurance company issued a policy which it sent to the broker in Dublin. Later, the plaintiff wished to sue the company which he could only do if the contract was concluded in Dublin. The court, applying the postal rule, found that the contract had been accepted in London at the moment it was posted.

The rule holds true even if the postal acceptance never arrives.[54] However, where the reason for the loss of the letter is that it has been incorrectly addressed by the offeree, acceptance does not take place on posting.[55]

It is possible to avoid the postal rule by stipulating a different method of acceptance or ensuring the offer requires actual communication of the acceptance. In *Holwell Securities v Hughes* the defendant offered to sell property to the claimant, stating that the acceptance had to be

---

[52] (1818) 1 B & Ald 681. See Nicholas Sage, 'The Significance of Adams v Lindsell' (2020) 36(2) Journal of Contract Law 179.

[53] [1919]2 IR 243.

[54] *Household Fire Insurance Co v Grant* (1879) 4 Ex D 216.

[55] *LJ Korbetis v Transgrain Shipping BV* [2005] EWHC 1345 (QB).

'by notice in writing'.[56] The claimant sent a letter of acceptance, but the letter was lost in the post and never arrived. It was held that no contract of sale had been concluded because here the offer required notice in writing of the acceptance and that had not been given.

There is a body of English case law indicating that the postal rule does not apply to communication by email.[57] Further in *Greenclose v National Westminster Bank Plc,* Andrews J was also clear that 'email is not subject to the postal acceptance rule.[58] It is a form of near instantaneous communication' and therefore must be actually communicated.

If an offeror prescribes a certain method of acceptance, then only acceptance by that method or an equally effective one will be binding. To be equally effective, the mode of acceptance should not be slower or have any disadvantages for the offeror. In *Tinn v Hoffman* the offeree was asked to reply 'by return of post'.[59] It was held that any method which would arrive before return of post would be sufficient. In addition, in *Manchester Diocesan Council of Education v Commercial & General Investments Ltd* the claimant put out a request for tenders to buy land which said that 'The person whose tender is accepted shall be the purchaser and shall be informed of the acceptance of his tender by letter sent to him by post addressed to the address given in the tender'.[60] The defendant completed the tender and sent it to the claimant's surveyor. The claimant's solicitor accidentally wrote to the defendant's surveyor and not the defendant approving the sale. It was held that there was a valid contract because acceptance sent to the defendant's surveyor was no less advantageous to the defendant. The Irish Courts have followed this line of reasoning and in *Staunton v Minister for Health* where it was held that despite a requirement for signature, a verbal acceptance was adequate.[61]

2.7 Formal Requirements

It is generally accepted that for the vast majority of contracts, there is no specific requirement prescribed for the manner in which they come into existence. In other words, contracts can be agreed either orally or in writing. However, there are a number of specific types of

---

[56] [1974] 1 All ER 161.

[57] *Thomas v BPE Solicitors (a firm)* [2010] EWHC 306 (Ch) – where the judge reasoned that the receipt rule applies as per the telex decisions. See also Pang Wenn Ler, 'You've Got Mail! Examining the Postal Rule in the Technological Age' (2019) Singapore Comparative Law Review 35.

[58] [2014] EWHC 1156 (Ch).

[59] (1873) 29 LT 27.

[60] [1970] 1 WLR 241.

[61] Unrep, High Court, 21 February 1986.

contract that requires the contract either be in writing, or evidenced in writing. Before examining each of these, it is worth noting that adopting formalities in contracts can be beneficial for a number of reasons. First, if the contract has been reduced to writing, it can, in most cases, clearly identify the intention of the parties and the terms on which they intended to contract. Further, there can be no issue as to the identity of the parties or their respective obligations. Secondly, having the contract reduced to writing may encourage the parties to consider the contract that they are entering into and reduces the possibility of mistakes or uncertainty as to the terms. Finally, it may reduce the possibility that one party is entering into the contract under duress or coercion.

The Electronic Commerce Act defines writing so as to include electronic modes and further provides that information will not be denied legal effect solely on the grounds that it is wholly or partly in electronic form.[62]

Therefore, while it is only necessary in certain limited circumstances to evidence a contract in writing, and in all other circumstances an oral contract will carry as much weight and be as legally binding as a written one, to resolve any issues that may arise surrounding clarity, certainty, and intention, it may be beneficial to the parties to ensure that the contract is evidenced in writing.

2.7.1 Contracts that Must be Evidenced in Writing

Section 2 of the Statute of Frauds Act 1695 sets out a number of areas whereby the contract must be evidenced in writing and these are dealt with in turn:

2.7.7.1 Contracts to Pay for the Debts of Another

For a contract to fall within the scope of the Statute of Frauds it must be a guarantee. A guarantee is defined in the legislation as 'a promise to answer for the debt, default or miscarriage of another person'. This means that one person promises to pay for the liabilities that another might accrue. For example, let us say that Jacob wants to buy a new car on finance but his credit score is not that good. The finance company may ask for a guarantor. If his father then agrees to act as guarantor for this finance, and Jacob stops making the finance payments, his father is liable and contractually bound to make the payments. As this is the imposition of a serious liability, it is considered appropriate

[62] s 9.

that the guarantee be made in writing rather than trying to rely on an alleged oral agreement.

It is important to distinguish between a guarantee and an indemnity at this point. An indemnity is an express obligation to compensate someone for loss or damage. This is known as a primary obligation. If we go back to the example above, Jacob's father only has to pay under a guarantee where Jacob himself fails to keep up with the repayments. If his father provided an indemnity rather than a guarantee, he is agreeing to make all of the repayments on his son's behalf. It is irrelevant whether Jacob defaults on the payments. A guarantee is therefore a secondary obligation which will only apply where there has been some default on the obligations of another party. Section 2 of the Statute of Frauds 1695 applies only to the guarantee agreement and not to an indemnity. In *Yeomans Credit Ltd v Latter* the identical distinction in English Law as contained in s 4 of the Statute of Frauds 1677 was heavily criticised and appears to be illogical in terms of policy.[63]

The question of whether an email could satisfy the requirements of s 4 was considered in *J Pereira Fernandes SA v Mehta*.[64] In this case, Mehta was a director of a company which had not paid for goods supplied by the claimant. Mehta sent an email offering a personal guarantee of £25,000 together with repayment terms. However, the text of the email did not mention Mehta's name and there was no signature at the end of the email, although the sender was identified by the email address. In this case it was held that the email would constitute a memorandum as per the requirements of s 4 in that it was in writing, the terms were clear and there was evidence of an oral agreement accepting the terms. However, as there was no signature, the case failed. Had Mehta added his signature to the end of the email, it would have been binding. This issue has not arisen in Ireland as yet. The provisions of the E-Commerce Act 2000 make it clear that electronic communications will suffice as writing, however, the lack of identifying factors as in Mehta may make the difference.

2.7.1.2 Agreements Made in Consideration of Marriage

This provision relates to the old practice of family members transferring property and / or money to engaged couples in consideration or expectation of marriage was required to be evidenced in writing before it could be enforced. While it is of little relevance today, and its counterpart in England and Wales has been repealed, the provision ultimately remains law in Ireland.

---

63 [1961] 1 WLR 828.
64 [2006] EWHC 813 (Ch).

2.7.1.3 Contracts for the Sale of Land or an Interest Therein

This is the area which has generated the most case law and it is clear that the provision applies to situations well beyond the sale of a freehold estate to any sale which involves the transfer of an interest in the land. In *Mackie v Wilde and Longin* the allocation of fishing rights was held to fall within the statute and thus required evidence in writing.[65]

2.7.1.4 Contracts Not to be Performed Within One Year

If a contract is entered into, which will not be completed within one year, the Statute requires that it must be evidenced in writing. In *Naughton v Limestone Land Co Ltd* an oral contract of employment that was to last for four years was held to be unenforceable without a memorandum in writing.[66] However, where the parties have intended for the contract to be completed within one year, the statute is not engaged. In *Hynes v Hynes* an argument that a contract to transfer a business was unenforceable due to a lack of evidence in writing was rejected.[67] In examining the facts of the case Barrington J found that there was no evidence to suggest that the intention of the parties was for the agreement to take in excess of one year to implement.

2.7.1.5 Contracts for the Sale of Goods in Excess of £10

The Euro Changeover Amounts Act 2001 converts this figure to €12. S 13 of the 1695 Act provides that contracts for the sale of goods in excess of €12 must be evidenced in writing unless the buyer either accepts and receives parts of the goods sold, or he gives something in earnest to bind the bargain, or the buyer makes part payment.[68] Therefore, where there is no memorandum in writing, the enforceability of a contract for the sale of goods over €12 rests on the conduct of the buyer.[69]

2.7.2 The Requirements of the Statute of Frauds Act 1695 and s 51 of the Land and Conveyancing Law Reform Act 2009

Section 51(1) of the Land and Conveyancing Law Reform Act 2009 states that the contract must be in writing, or that there must be a note or memorandum in writing signed by the parties or their authorised

---

65 [1998] 2 IR 578.

66 [1952] Ir Jur Rep 19.

67 [1984] IEHC 48.

68 s 4 of the 1893 Act while not repealing s 13 of 1695 Act substantially repeated it.

69 See *Hopton v McCarthy* (1882) 10 LR Ir 266; *Tradex Ireland v Irish Grain Board Ltd* [1984] IR 1; *Kirwan v Price* [1958] Ir Jur Rep 56.

agent, or (as equity will not allow a statute to be used as a weapon of fraud) good reason as to why these formalities have not been complied with.[70] Barron J explains that 'where the agreement is a verbal one, the plaintiff must establish not only the concluded agreement but also the existence of a note or memorandum of the agreement signed by the defendant or his agent'.[71]

The concluded agreement ought to contain all of the terms and agreement between the parties, however where this is done orally, the memorandum or note need only contain 'material terms'.[72] What is material will be considered from the perspective of the parties and so what is material will vary depending on the facts of each particular case. If a term could be expressed as an implied term to the contract then there will be no need to expressly set it out in the memorandum.[73] However, it has been established that the memorandum must refer to the agreement concluded between the parties.

Given the risks associated with a potential action for specific performance (**See Chapter 20**), it became commonplace for lawyers to include the phrase 'subject to contract' in any correspondence, such was recognition that there was no concluded agreement. As explained by Lord Denning:

> It is everyday practice for a solicitor, who is instructed in a sale of land, to start the correspondence with a letter 'subject to contract' setting out the terms or enclosing a draft. He does it in the confidence that it protects his client. It means that the client is not bound by what has taken place in conversation. The reason is that, for over a hundred years, the courts have held that the effects of the words 'subject to contract' is that the matter remains in negotiation until a formal contract is executed.[74]

However, in the 1970's some doubt arose as to the legal status of this term in reference to the statute of frauds.[75] In Ireland the matter was considered by the Supreme Court in *Kelly v Park Hall School Ltd* where

---

70 Previously this provision was contained in s 2 of the Statute of Frauds (Ireland) Act 1695.

71 *Jodifern Ltd v Fitzgerald* [2000] 3 IR 321, 330.

72 There has been some debate as to whether agreement on the deposit and completion date are required in order to establish whether there has been a concluded agreement.

73 For example in *Supermacs Ireland Ltd v Katesan (Naas) Ltd* [2000] 4 IR 273 it was stated that if there is an implied term as to the deposit there would be no need to express it in the memorandum.

74 *Tiverton Estates v Wearwell* [1975] 1 Ch 146, 160.

75 In the UK *Tiverton* reversed a decision the year before in *Law v Jones* [1974] 1 Ch 112 where the court enforced the contract notwithstanding the fact that the correspondence contained the phrase 'subject to contract'

a contract was enforced despite the memorandum being expressed as 'subject to contract'.[76] The Supreme Court decided that the term meant 'a contract has been finalised subject to its being formalised in writing' and therefore was a sufficient memorial for the purposes of the Statute of Frauds.[77]

The most authoritative statement on the law of this area comes from the judgment of Keane J in *Mulhall v Haren*.[78] Fennelly speaks in the highest terms of the calibre of this written judgment, referring to it as 'an exemplar of common law judgments, imbued with the force and value of precedent'.[79] Keane J acknowledged that the rule could possibly produce some harsh results, and while acknowledging recent controversy in the area, recognised that this was a long standing principle and indicated that unless it had been expressly disproved of, he would follow the English decision in *Tiverton*. In assessing whether the Supreme Court of *Kelly* did in fact disprove Tiverton and whether the phrase was not inconsistent with a concluded contract, Keane J stated:

> If that were the effect of the decision, it would mean that the Supreme Court, by necessary implication was disapproving of the decision in the Tiverton case and also by implication was overruling or disapproving of the long line of authority on the 'subject to contract' topic to which I have already referred. I doubt very much whether the Supreme Court intended to disapprove of the decision in the Tiverton case or to disturb the authorities in question. Had that been their intention I think it would have been made clear in the Judgment of Mr Justice Henchy.[80]

In confining the decision in *Kelly* to the facts of that particular case, Keane J summarised his analysis thus;

> 1. A memorandum or note cannot satisfy the statute of frauds if, when it is read alone or with other documents which can properly be read with it, it does not contain a recognition, express or implied, of the existence of the oral contract sought to be enforced;
> 2. A letter, which expressly states that a transaction is 'subject

---

[76] [1979] IR 340.

[77] The final decision herein turned on the issue of delay on the part of the claimant, but the crucial element is that the phrase 'subject to contract' did not protect the defendant. This position was affirmed in *Casey v Irish Intercontinental Bank Ltd & Ors* [1979] IR 364.

[78] [1981] IR 364. It is interesting to note that Keane J was the legal counsel for the Defendant in *Kelly v Park Hall School* Ltd and *Mulhall v Haren* is his first recorded judgment.

[79] Niall Fennelly, 'A Fatal Rubric: Mulhall v Haren and "Subject to Contract"' (2011)33 Dublin University Law Journal 1, 5.

[80] [1981] IR 364, 388.

> to contract' cannot be a sufficient note or memorandum, since the use of those words is normally inconsistent with the existence of a concluded contract. It is only in certain rare and exceptional circumstances such as arose in *Kelly v Park Hall School* and *Michael Richards Properties v St Saviour's Parish* that the words 'subject to contract' can be treated as being of no effect.
>
> 3. In applying the two foregoing principles, it is immaterial whether the writing relied on itself contains the words 'subject to contract' or is part of a chain of correspondence initiated by a letter which makes it clear that any oral agreement already arrived at is 'subject to contract'.[81]

This decision was expressly approved of by the Supreme Court in *Boyle v Lee* where it was confirmed that a note or memorandum which contained the phrase 'subject to contract' could not, unless in exceptional circumstances, satisfy the requirements as set out in the Statute of Frauds.[82]

However, the case of *Jodifern Ltd v Fitzgerald* adds some additional complications.[83] Here Barron J found that if the words are placed in the document, rather than at the head of the document, then it is a matter of construction whether or not it denies the existence of a pre-existing agreement. He then states that there can be no valid note of an agreement where such a note denies the existence of an agreement. The two statements appear somewhat contradictory and it is unclear whether this undermines previous judgments.

It has been suggested that a simple way to ameliorate any issues in this area would be to legislate. In the UK under s 2(1) of the Law of Property Act 1989 the requirement of a 'note or memorandum' [84] now requires that in order for a contract for the sale of land to be valid, it must be in writing.

Occasionally there will arise circumstances where an oral agreement has been reached but there is no note or memorandum evidencing same. Here the court is faced with a particular dilemma, however it is well established that equity will not allow a statute to be used as a weapon of fraud and as such where to insist upon the statutory formalities would be to allow the defendant perpetrate a fraud, the court can depart from this requirement. Additionally, the plaintiff may be able to rely on the doctrine of part performance. In *Steadman v Steadman* the House of Lords determined that the action would

81 ibid, 391.
82 [1992] IR 555.
83 [2000] 3 IR 321.
84 Repealing s 40 of the Law of Property Act 1925.

have to be, on the balance of probabilities referable to some contract, and not inconsistent with the alleged contract.[85] The action required was considered by the Supreme Court in *Mackie v Wilde*.[86] Barron J considered the nature of the acts of part performance in order to determine their sufficiency. He summarised the essential elements of the doctrine as requiring:

> (a) A concluded oral agreement;
> (b) That the plaintiff acted in such a way which showed an intention to perform that contract;
> (c) That the defendant induced such acts or stood by while they were being performed; and
> (d) It would be unconscionable and a breach of good faith to allow the defendant to rely on the terms of the Statute of Frauds to prevent the performance of the contract.[87]

In this case, even if there were a concluded agreement as alleged the court found that there were no acts carried out by the plaintiff which evidenced an intention to perform the contract and therefore, he could not rely on the doctrine. The issue was again considered in *Liberty Asset Management Ltd v Gannon*.[88] Here the plaintiff sought specific performance of the acquisition of property which formed part of a wider transaction involving the plaintiff taking over a lease from the defendant. Applying the decision of *Mackie*, Laffoy J found that the plaintiff not only acted with intention to fulfil the contract, but had actually done so by entering into the lease and further had vacated the property in anticipation of the defendant taking possession. In the circumstances the court found that it would be unconscionable to allow the defendant to rely on the statute of frauds and awarded the order sought.

This matter has most recently been addressed by the Court of Appeal in *Keena v Coughlan*.[89] This case centred on a claim for specific performance to enforce the sale of a hotel and associated lands. The appellant in this case had agreed to purchase the property for €1.6 million and furnished a cheque for 10% which was non-refundable. The plaintiff was then informed through her representatives that she did not have a legally binding contract, and that the hotel was being sold to another party. One of the key pieces that the court was required to determine was whether a cheque for €160,000 which represented 10% of the purchase price, constituted a note or memorandum for the purposes of satisfying the requirements of the 2009 Act. Initially, the

---

85 [1976] AC 536.
86 [1998] 2 IR 578.
87 ibid, 587.
88 [2009] IEHC 468.
89 [2023] IECA 249.

High Court[90] found that this cheque did not meet the requirements as it did not clearly identify the purchaser and vendor, and that the words 'subject to title, freehold unencumbered' had the effect of creating additional terms meaning that there could not have been an agreement. The Court of Appeal disagreed with the findings of the High Court and held that above all, s 51 of the Act should not be used as a weapon of fraud and that the cheque, together with the emails sent and received shortly thereafter and the evidence adduced in court from witnesses was sufficient to determine that the appellant had a *prima facie* case and a contract which was capable of being specifically enforced. The Court of Appeal set aside the High Court decision to dismiss the case and remitted it back for a full hearing on the facts. At the time of writing it is unknown what the outcome of the substantive case is, however the Court of Appeal's interpretation as to what constitutes a memorandum is pivotal.

2.8 Issues with the Offer and Acceptance Model

The traditional approach to offer and acceptance has been criticised on the grounds of being artificial, in that there are some situations which do not easily fit with the offer and acceptance model.

In particular, Lord Denning in *Gibson v Manchester City Council* preferred to look at the negotiations as a whole rather than trying to fit the facts into offer and acceptance.[91] However, Denning's approach has not been widely accepted. On appeal in *Gibson*, Lord Diplock said that although there may be 'exceptional' cases which do not 'fit easily into the normal analysis of a contract as being constituted by offer and acceptance', there was no reason for departing from the conventional approach. In *The Eurymedon* Lord Wilberforce stated that 'English law, having committed itself to a rather technical and schematic doctrine of contract, in application takes a practical approach, often at the cost of forcing the facts to fit uneasily into the marked slots of offer, acceptance and consideration'.[92]

Besides being artificial, authors such as Elliot and Quinn have noted other problems with the offer and acceptance model, such as the difficulties surrounding revocation of a unilateral contract and problems relating to the objective approach.[93] In addition, McKendrick states:

---

90 [2019] IEHC 12.
91 [1978] 1 WLR 520, CA.
92 [1975] AC 154, 167.
93 *Contract Law* (12th edn, Pearson 2019).

> The offer and acceptance model has a core of well-established rules which are understood by lawyers, and which are capable of being understood by the business community. At the same time the model is applied with some degree of flexibility by the courts so that a conclusion can be reached which is consistent with the intention of the parties. The present state of the law cannot be said to be entirely satisfactory, but it is better than a system which imposes an unacceptable level of rigidity or a system which creates an unacceptable level of certainty.[94]

Test Your Knowledge

Jack sends Sarah a letter on 4 April stating that 'I am willing to sell you my collection of first edition books for the sum of £5,000'. Sarah responds on 6 April and asks 'will you accept a bank transfer or do you want cash?'. On 9 April Jack replies to Sarah and states that his preference is for a cheque. On 11 April Sarah posts Jack a cheque for £5,000 for the collection of books. On 12 April Jack sells his collection to Lucy for £5,500 and sends a message to Sarah that he is revoking the offer. The cheque from Sarah arrives on 13 April. In terms of the contracts, which of these is the accurate outcome:

- A The contract with Lucy is valid because Sarah's acceptance was not received.
- B The contract with Lucy is valid because Sarah made a counter offer and therefore rejected the offer.
- C The contract with Sarah is valid because there was valid acceptance.

The correct answer here is C. Under the postal rule, the acceptance is valid once the letter, properly addressed and stamped, is posted. This means that acceptance took place on 11 April and therefore Jack could not enter into a further contract or revoke the offer once it had been accepted. A is not correct as while generally the rule is that acceptance must be received by the offeror, the postal rule displaces this. If Jack did not want to be bound by this rule then he needed to have included in his offer specific instructions as to how acceptance would be valid, or at least state that the postal rule would not apply. B is incorrect as Sarah did not make a counter offer; she made a request for further information which does not terminate the offer.

Stretch and Challenge Question

Critically analyse whether the benefits of a more flexible approach of examining the contract negotiations holistically, as suggested by

[94] *Contract Law: Text, Cases and Materials* (10th edn, Oxford University Press 2022).

Lord Denning in *Gibson,* would outweigh the certainty provided by the traditional approach of offer and acceptance.

CHAPTER 3

CONSIDERATION

3.1 Introduction

Offer and acceptance, discussed in the previous chapter, represent the agreement part of the contract. However, a mere agreement is not legally enforceable. In order for the agreement to be legally binding and enforceable, consideration must be present. Consideration is the something provided in exchange for the promise, the quid pro quo. Traditional definitions focus on consideration as a benefit to the promisor or a detriment to the promisee. In *Currie v Misa* Lush J stated, 'A valuable consideration, in the sense of the law, may consist either in some right, interest, profit, or benefit accruing to the one party, or some forbearance, detriment, loss or responsibility, given, suffered, or undertaken by the other'.[1]

Atiyah argued that there is no coherent doctrine of consideration based upon reciprocity (A gives something, eg money, to B, and B gives something to A in return) but rather that 'consideration' is simply the 'reason' for enforcing a promise or obligation.[2] This view was sharply criticised by Treitel who argued that English law does recognise the existence of a 'complex and multifarious body of rules known as "the doctrine of consideration"'.[3]

3.2 Types of Consideration

There are two types of consideration which generally relate to the type of contract that is being entered into:

---

1 (1875) LR 10 Ex 153.

2 PS Atiyah, *Consideration in Contracts: A Fundamental Restatement* (ANU Press, 1971).

3 GH Treitel, 'Consideration: a critical analysis of Professor Atiyah's fundamental restatement' (1976) 50 Australian Law Journal 439.

- *Executory consideration.* In a bilateral contract, where a party agrees to pay for a service, both parties have not yet fulfilled the contract; however, they have agreed to mutual obligations in the future (an exchange of promises).
- *Executed consideration.* At the time of the formation of the contract, the consideration is performed simultaneously (a promise in return for an act).

To explain further, take an example: I say to Jane that I will give her €5 if she brings me a cup of coffee. This is a bilateral contract and is an example of executory consideration. At the time the agreement is made, the contract has not yet been fulfilled. The consideration is the €5 for the cup of coffee which Jane can claim if she accepts the offer and brings me the coffee. However, if I said that I will give €5 to the first person in the room who brings me a cup of coffee, this is an example of a unilateral contract and executed consideration. The offer is accepted, and consideration performed at the same time when the first person brings me a cup of coffee and claims the €5.

3.3 Consideration Rules

A number of rules have been devised by the courts in order to establish whether consideration is valid. Where consideration is held to be invalid, while there may be an agreement which is morally enforceable, it will not be legally binding and therefore cannot be enforced in a court of law.

3.3.1 Consideration Must Move

Traditionally, the position was that consideration had to move from the promisee to the promisor, and the contract could then only be enforced by the person who supplied the consideration, which effectively meant that third parties could not enforce the contract.[4] Where the traditional rule applies, it means that a person to whom a promise has been made (the promisee) can enforce the promise against the promisor (the person who has made the promise) where the promisee has provided consideration. To look at this in an example, let's say that Karl promises to wash Dave's car, if Dave promises to pay Emer £30. Karl then washes Dave's car, but Dave refuses to pay the money to Emer. In this scenario, Emer cannot enforce Dave's promise to pay as she has not provided any consideration. However, Karl may be able to enforce the promise as he was a party to the contract. It is

[4] MP Furmston, 'Return to Dunlop v Selfridge' (1960) 23 Modern Law Review 373.

now commonly accepted that in certain circumstances third parties can enforce contracts (see Chapter 21).

Consideration may be valid where the promisee suffers a detriment (by performance of an act or the payment of moneys) even where there has been no benefit conferred on the promisor.

This can occur where a contract is entered into with a third party at the request of the promisor. A practical example of this is the operation of credit cards. The card issuer promises the retailer, who accepts payment using the card, that the retailer will be paid.

3.3.2 Consideration Must Be Sufficient But Need Not Be Adequate

This rule effectively means that once the consideration provided has some monetary value (sufficient), it does not need to be of market value (adequate). This doctrine forms the basis of the freedom to bargain, even if it is at an undervalue. Therefore, if I want to sell my Porsche for €50, I can do so and the law will not intervene to set aside the contract (unless there has been some duress, misrepresentation, mistake or fraud) on the basis that the market value is far in excess of the sale price. The law allows for each person to bargain and enter into a contract regardless of whether it is at a fair price. This does assume that everyone in the marketplace possesses the same level of bargaining power, which is not necessarily true. For example, if I am desperate to feed my children, or pay my rent, I am more likely to accept a reduced price for any goods that I might be selling. So, once it can be shown that the consideration had some real value, the law will not investigate as to whether this was of equivalent or market worth.

In *Thomas v Thomas* a husband left his property to his widow in return for which she was to pay £1 in ground rent.[5] Notwithstanding that this rent was grossly inadequate as the property could fetch a much higher rent on the open market, it was found to be of actual value and therefore amounted to sufficient consideration.

Therefore, all we need to show valid consideration is that it has some 'actual value' in the eyes of the law and the contract will be enforceable. The case of *Chappell v Nestle* involved a promotional scheme run by the company where a customer could claim a music record for a reduced price with three chocolate bar wrappers.[6] The question arose as to whether the chocolate wrappers could be classed as consideration. The House of Lords found that the wrappers had some nominal and

---

5 (1842) 2 QB 851.
6 [1960] AC 87.

tangible value and could therefore constitute consideration, even if it could be shown that the defendant would just throw them away. In delivering his judgment, Lord Somerville stated:

> It is said that when received the wrappers are of no value to Nestlé's. This I would have thought irrelevant. A contracting party can stipulate for what consideration he chooses. A peppercorn does not cease to be good consideration if it is established that the promisor does not like pepper and will throw away the corn.

Thus, consideration must be something that is of actual value to the promisor, no matter how small in monetary value. This is supported by Irish Authority in *McDonnell v Ring* where Mahan J stated that 'adequacy of consideration is irrelevant'.[7]

However, it should be noted that this applies where the transaction is an honest one and a large disparity between the bargain struck and the market value will be an indication to the court of possible fraud or unconscionability. In *Noonan (A Ward of Court) v Connell* illustrates this principle well.[8] In this case the plaintiff who was suffering from dementia, sold his farmland to one of his relatives for the sum of 50p. In setting aside the transaction the court had regard to the fact that there was no equality between the parties and that the plaintiff did not fully understand the consequences of the action. Lynch J stated 'on its face it is a purely voluntary transfer and of course the reference to 50p consideration is a complete anachronism and does not constitute any consideration'.[9]

3.3.3 Past Consideration is No Consideration

As we know, there must be the agreement, or promise followed by the act, in order for the contract to be formed. If there is an act followed by a promise, this does not result in a legally binding contract.

For example, I say, 'I will give you €50 if you paint the wall in my garden' (promise). You then paint the wall in the garden (act). This is a legally binding contract that you can enforce, and I will have to pay you the €50. In contrast, if I come home to discover that you have painted the wall and I then say 'Thank you, I will pay you €50', this is not a legally binding contract that you can enforce as you acted without the promise to pay.

This is illustrated in the case of *Re McArdle* wherein the children were

---

7 [2016] IECA 16 [28].
8 Unrep, High Court 10 April 1987. See also *Hassard v Smith* (1872) 6 IR Eq 429.
9 ibid.

entitled to inherit a house after their mother's death.[10] One of the children paid for several repairs to be carried out on the property, and subsequently the rest of the children signed a document agreeing that £488 should be repaid from the estate for the work done. This was held to be unenforceable as it amounted to past consideration; the work was not carried out in exchange for the promise.

There is an exception to this rule, and that is where the work has been done at the request of the promisor and there is a legitimate expectation that payment will be received, although the precise details of the payment are unknown. The earliest example of this exception is seen in *Lampleigh v Brathwait.*[11] Brathwait was in prison for murder and he asked Lampleigh to obtain a pardon from the King, which he ultimately did. Brathwait then promised to pay £100. Technically this was past consideration as the act was carried out before the promise to pay. However, the court found that this case was different in that the act was carried out at the request of Brathwait and such request implied a promise to pay.

The case of *Pao On v Lau Yiu Long* set out the requirements for the exception to operate:

- The act must have been done at the promisor's request;
- The parties must have understood that the act was to be remunerated either by a payment or the conferment of some other benefit;
- The payment is legally enforceable.[12]

3.3.4 Performance of an Existing Duty is Not Good Consideration

Where you already owe a duty to perform a particular act, the performance of that act cannot be said to be consideration as that act has been induced by the pre-existing duty and not the promise. The duties tend to be divided into two categories: those imposed by law and those imposed by contract.

3.3.4.1 Duty Imposed by Law

In terms of the duty imposed by law, the leading case is *Collins v Godefroy.*[13] Here the plaintiff was promised payment in return for giving evidence at trial. He was, however, obliged to do this as he

---

10 [1951] Ch 669. See also *K v K* [2018] IEHC 615.

11 (1615) Hob 105, 80 ER 255. See also *Bradford v Roulston* (1858) IRCL 468; *ACC Bank v Mullee and Mullee* [2014] IEHC 553.

12 [1980] AC 614. See also *Morgan v Rainsford* (1845) 8 IR ER 299.

13 (1831) 109 ER 1040.

had been summoned by subpoena to do so. The promise to pay was therefore unenforceable as he was under a legal duty to attend.

The exception to this rule is where the person goes above and beyond their pre-existing legal duty. In *Glasbrook Brothers Ltd v Glamorgan County Council* the council was able to enforce a promise to pay where it provided police for a greater level of security during a mining strike.[14] As this was beyond the normal provision, it was in excess of the legal duty and therefore sufficient. Further, in *Harris v Sheffield United Football Club* the football club argued that it should not have to pay for police officers attending its home matches.[15] It was held that these services had to be paid for as they were over and above the regular duties. However, as seen in *West Yorkshire Police Authority v Reading Festival* it was confirmed that the person to whom the services were provides must have made either an expressed or an implied request for such services.[16] The court distinguished between policing services generally, and other 'special' services in *Leeds United Football Club v West Yorkshire Police*.[17] Police services for football matches that are held on private grounds will generally be deemed 'special' services except in the case where they are called to deal with actual or imminent violence. It is only where the services fall into the category of 'special' that additional payment will be enforceable.

The only Irish case to deal with this area to date is *McKerring v Minister for Agriculture*.[18] This case arose out of a dispute in relation to grant payments. The plaintiff was excluded because of non-compliance with the rules and one question which arose was that while the scheme was voluntary, was payment made under contract. O'Hanlon J in holding that compliance could be consideration in these cases stated: 'it appears to be that there is sufficient consideration involved in strict compliance with all the conditions, even though some of them may be a matter of legal obligation as well'.

3.3.4.2 Duty Imposed by Contract

When it comes to pre-existing contractual duties, this can be divided further into promises to pay more and a promise to accept less.

Promises to Pay More

When it comes to promises to pay more, these cases typically arise

14 [1925] AC 270.
15 [1988] QB 77.
16 [2006] 1 WLR 1005.
17 [2013] EWCA Civ 115.
18 [1989] ILRM 82.

where one party finds that they cannot complete their existing obligation under the current terms (either for the existing cost or within the existing time frame) and the other party agrees to pay an additional sum. This party then refuses to pay that additional sum and the question arises as to whether any additional consideration has been provided to enforce the extra payment.

Traditionally, the answer has been that performance of an existing contractual duty owed to the promisor does not amount to good consideration. In *Stilk v Myrick*, two sailors deserted a ship during a voyage.[19] The captain promised the eight remaining sailors extra wages for sailing the boat home. When they arrived back, the captain refused to pay the extra money. It was held that this promise to pay more was unenforceable.

However, as with the pre-existing duty imposed by law, the courts have recognised that if a party does more than their contractual duty, they have provided sufficient consideration. In *Hartley v Ponsonby*, half the crew deserted a ship and the rest were promised extra money.[20] As in *Stilk*, the captain then refused to pay. In this case, it was held that the promise to pay extra was enforceable as, with half of the crew missing, the contractual obligations on the remaining crew changed and they were required to perform over and above their existing contractual obligations. These views have been supported in the Irish courts in cases of *Farrington v Donogue*,[21] *Kenny v An Post*[22] and *McHugh v Kildare County Council*.[23]

This area of the law has been considered relatively recently in the English Court of Appeal in the important case of *Williams v Roffey Bros & Nicholls Contractors Ltd*.[24] Here Roffey Bros had a contract with a housing association to refurbish a block of flats. The contract stated that unless the work was completed by a specific date, Roffey Bros would have to pay a penalty to the association. Roffey subcontracted the carpentry work to Williams and agreed a price. Williams started work, but during the work realised that the price agreed was too low and he could not afford to pay his workers. Williams informed Roffey Bros who then promised to pay Williams an additional sum of money for each flat completed on time. Williams completed the job and then Roffey Bros refused to pay all of the additional money.

---

19 (1809) 2 Camp 317.
20 (1867) 2 El & Bl 872.
21 (1866) IR ICL 675.
22 [1988] JISLL 187.
23 [2006]1 IR 100.
24 [1990] 1 All ER 512.

The court held that there was consideration for the promise to pay additional money, and therefore the promise was binding even though Williams was merely performing his pre-existing contractual duty. This was because Roffey Bros received an additional practical benefit.

Glidewell LJ set out the test for when the promise to pay more will be enforceable:

> (i) if A has entered into a contract with B to do work for, or to supply goods or services to, B in return for payment by B; and
> (ii) at some stage before A has completely performed his obligations under the contract B has reason to doubt whether A will, or will be able to, complete his side of the bargain; and
> (iii) B thereupon promises A an additional payment in return for A's promise to perform his contractual obligations on time; and
> (iv) as a result of giving his promise B obtains in practice a benefit, or obviates a disbenefit; and
> (v) B's promise is not given as a result of economic duress or fraud on the part of A, then
> (vi) the benefit to B is capable of being consideration for B's promise, so that the promise will be legally binding.

While this reasoning has been followed (see for example *Adam Opel GmbH v Mitras Automotive (UK) Ltd*)[25] it has not been without its criticism. In *South Carribean Trading v Trafigura Bakeer BV* Colman J stated, 'but for the fact that *Williams v Roffey Bros* was a decision of the Court of Appeal, I would not have followed it'.[26]

Promise to Accept Less

As a general rule, a promise to accept less cannot amount to good consideration.[27] In *Foakes v Beer* Dr Foakes owed Mrs Beer a debt.[28] She agreed with him that he could pay part of the debt immediately and the rest in instalments. When Dr Foakes had paid off the debt, Mrs Beer asked for the interest too (which would usually be payable on this type of debt – a judgment debt). Mrs Beer sued. It was held that she was entitled to the interest.

The case of *Re Selectmove* established that *Foakes v Beer* remains good

25 [2008] EWHC 3205 (QB).
26 [2006] EWHC 2676 (Comm). See also Kevin Patel, 'Reconsidering Consideration – An Evaluation of Williams v Roffey Bros Thirty Years On' (2019) 8 Manchester Review of Law, Crime and Ethics 102.
27 Edwin Peel, 'Part Payment of a Debt is No Consideration' (1994) 100 Law Quarterly Review 353.
28 (1884) 9 App Cas 605.

law and that the *Williams v Roffey Bros* principle of identifying a practical benefit does not apply to part payment of debt and is only relevant to cases where there is a promise to pay more for goods and services.[29]

It would be different if the debtor did something different, such as making payment earlier. If a new element is introduced, this may amount to sufficient consideration.[30] This is known as the rule in *Pinnel's case*.[31] Here Pinnel sued Cole for a debt which became due on 11 November. Cole argued that he had paid a lesser amount on 1 October, which Pinnel had accepted in full settlement. Whilst Pinnel won the case on other grounds, the court said that it would have found in favour of Cole because he had made payment earlier than the due date and this amounted to fresh consideration. It is clear from this case that offering something different, like a chattel, could amount to fresh consideration. As Lord Coke opined, 'the gift of a horse, a hawk or a robe etc, in satisfaction is good'.

However, in *MWB Business Exchange Centres Ltd v Rock Advertising Ltd*, the Court of Appeal confirmed that, *in some circumstances*, a practical benefit obtained by a creditor in promising to accept a part payment of a debt *is* capable of amounting to good consideration.[32] This case concerned an agreement to accept less rent for a certain period, which MWB, who managed the premises, sought to revoke. On the issue of consideration, the court found that in continuing to have the premises occupied, the requirement of 'something more' (as in *Pinnel's case*) was satisfied. It was on this basis that *Re Selectmove*, which had followed *Foakes v Beer*, was distinguished, ie in *Re Selectmove*, the payment in itself had not been enough, but in *MWB* the additional benefit was the occupation of the property.

The appeal to the Supreme Court (*Rock Advertising Ltd. v MWB Business Exchange Centres Ltd*[33]), with Lord Sumption delivering the lead judgment, saw the judges declining to review the area of consideration and instead focusing on the issue of No Oral Modification clauses (NOMs).[34] Whilst the decision is welcome for bringing clarity to this area, meaning that such clauses are less likely to be disputed in the

---

29 [1995] 2 All ER 531.

30 See James Kane, 'The Rule in Pinnel's Case: The Case for Repeal, a Mistaken Preponderance and finding Consideration in Debt Renegotiations' (2014) 37 Dublin University Law Journal 79.

31 (1602) 5 Co Rep 117a. See also *Drogheda Corp v Fairclough* (1858) 8 IR CLR 98.

32 [2016] EWCA Civ 553.

33 [2018] UKSC 24.

34 This means that a contract cannot be modified orally and if there are any modifications to the contract as it has been agreed, this must be done in writing.

future, in failing to address the practical benefit distinction in promises to pay more/accept less, it was arguably disappointing. Given that the court declined to rule on this point, the Court of Appeal ruling that there was 'practical benefit' in the *MWB* case seems to indicate that cases will be decided on a fact specific basis, which, from a business perspective, may mean increased flexibility, but at the expense of commercial certainty.[35]

The Rule in *Pinnel's Case* is firmly established in Ireland with the court in *Barge Inn v Quinn* stating that 'it is beyond question that the Rule in Pinnel's Case still represents the law in Ireland and this Court is bound by it'.[36] The court did further note that the equitable doctrine of promissory estoppel (considered below) may 'obviate an inequitable outcome' which may be the result of a strict application of the rule.

Promissory Estoppel

One further matter to consider in relation to the promise to accept less is the operation of the doctrine of promissory estoppel. *Central London Property Trust Ltd v High Trees House Ltd* is the leading case in this area.[37] In 1940 the landlord agreed with the tenant to reduce the 'ground rent' for a block of flats by half, because many of the flats were empty due to World War II. There was no consideration for the agreement. By early in 1945, the block was full again and the landlord wanted to charge the tenant the full rent again and also required payment of the arrears. Denning J held that the full rent could be charged from mid-1945 onwards, but (obiter) the arrears could not be charged because the landlord was 'estopped' from going back on his promise.

There are a number of conditions that need to be met before promissory estoppel can be successfully relied upon:

(a) *The promise must be clear and unambiguous.* In *Woodhouse v Nigerian Produce Marketing Co.* the court reiterated that a promise to alter an existing contract must be unequivocal.[38] As Lord Hailsham opined, if the statement is ambiguous, a genuine misunderstanding of the meaning of the statement could result in the offeree obtaining something they cannot obtain under conventional contract law.

(b) *The promise must be one that varies an existing contract.* In

---

[35] Jeanette Ashton and Juliet Turner, 'Between Rock and a hard place? No consideration from the Supreme Court in *Rock Advertising Ltd. v MWB Business Exchange Centres Ltd.*' (2018) 29(10) International Company and Commercial Law Review 593.

[36] [2013] IEHC 387.

[37] [1947] KB 130.

[38] [1972] AC 741.

Combe v Combe a couple were getting divorced and the husband agreed to pay maintenance to his wife which he subsequently did not do.[39] It was held that this promise was unenforceable as the wife had not provided any consideration and estoppel could not be the basis of creating a new contract.

(c) *The doctrine can only be used as a shield and not a sword.* This means the promise can only be used as a defence to a claim (as in the *High Trees* case itself), the promise being not to enforce the promisor's strict legal rights. It cannot form the basis of a claim (as in *Combe v Combe*). So while it applies to a promise to accept less than the amount due (eg *High Trees*), promissory estoppel cannot be used to make a claim based on a promise to pay more – for that type of situation, the promisee would have to claim under *Williams v Roffey*.

(d) *The promisee must rely on the promise.* There must be evidence that the promisee relied or acted on the promise in some way. In *High Trees*, it was shown that the promise had been relied upon in that there was payment and acceptance of the lower amount of rent. It is not necessary that the reliance is detrimental.

(e) *It must be inequitable for the promisor to go back on their promise.* The issue of inequitability or unconscionability is one that will vary from case to case as it largely refers to the moral or ethical conduct of the parties. In *D & C Builders v Rees* R owed money to D & C for work done.[40] R's wife told them, in effect, that unless they agreed to accept part of what was owed, they would get nothing. It was held that promissory estoppel did not apply – the promise was not binding because the promisee had used intimidation to obtain it. Also, R and his wife misled D & C as to their financial position. It will not be inequitable for the promisor to go back on their promise if there is no prejudice caused to the promisee. In *The Post Chaser* the promise was withdrawn after two days so the promisee could be – and was – restored to his original position.[41]

(f) *Promissory estoppel suspends a right; it does not extinguish it.* So, in *High Trees*, while the promise lasted, the promisor could not charge the full rent, but when the promise came to an end (when the flats were full again), the full rent could be charged in the future. In *High Trees*, it was understood that the promise only lasted while the flats were empty.

The principles have been approved of and applied in the Irish Court in *Kenny v Kenny*.[42]

Here the applicant sought a declaration that she was entitled to a place as an undergraduate student in University College Dublin as a

---

39 [1951] 2 KB 215.
40 [1966] 2 QB 617.
41 [1982] 1 All ER 19.
42 [1988] IR 457.

transfer student from Trinity College Dublin. In applying High Trees, Barron J stated that 'the essence of promissory estoppel was said to be a promise intended to be binding, intended to be acted upon and in fact acted upon'.[43]

In *Healy v Ulster Bank*, the plaintiff had entered into a property development agreement with his then business partner, Dr Cullen.[44] The professional relationship between the plaintiff and his business partner broke down and it was clear that they could no longer continue with the property venture. At that juncture, the plaintiff, Dr Healy signed an agreement whereby he was indemnified against all liability to the bank. Dr Healy argued, inter alia, that the bank was estopped from pursuing him for any liability. The court referred to a more flexible definition of estoppel arising from the dicta of Charleton J in *National Asset Loan Management Ltd v McMahon* as one 'which takes into account all of the variations in the case law which have tended to make that defence more flexible and in accordance with an appropriate review of the fairness of the situation'.[45] Applying this definition to the instant case, the court found that the words used by the representative of the bank would, to any reasonable person in Dr Healy's position, be taken to mean that his obligations under any guarantee were at an end. Delving further into the requirements, the court affirmed that such a representation was insufficient to ground a defence of estoppel and that there was the additional requirement of reliance, which may or may not be detrimental, to persuade the court that it would be unconscionable to allow the promisor resile from his representation. In this case, Dr Healy had, on foot of the representation, lodged €2.2 million into the bank, which the bank then ultimately offset against liability which Dr Healy believed he was indemnified against. The court found that this was sufficiently unconscionable to allow Dr Healy's claim in estoppel to succeed.

3.3.4.3 Duty Owed to Someone Other than the Promisor

Performance of a duty owed to third parties is sufficient consideration. This arises in circumstances where party A pays for party B to perform an obligation that they already owe to party C. In *Shadwell v Shadwell*[46] and *Scotson v Pegg*,[47] the court found that the performance of an obligation already owed to a third party is good consideration. In *Shadwell*, the claimant was engaged to be married to a woman named

---

[43] See also Maggie Hemsworth, 'Contract: Consideration, Motive and Part Payment' (2022) 1 Journal of Business Law 66.

[44] [2020] IECA 332.

[45] [2014] IEHC 71. Also cited with approval in *Sheehan v Breccia* [2016] IEHC 67.

[46] [1860] EWHC CP J8.

[47] [1861] EWHC Exch J2.

Ellen Nichol. His uncle wrote to him and expressed his pleasure with the intended marriage. In that same letter he promised to pay his nephew £150 yearly during his lifetime, or until the claimant was earning six hundred guineas as a Chancery Barrister. The annuity fell into arrears and when his uncle died, the claimant sued his estate. The majority of the court found that there was a benefit to the uncle in that the marriage was 'an object of interest to a near relative' however the dissenting judgment by Byles J found that as the claimant was already engaged and therefore was already legally obliged to marry Ms Nichols, his marriage was no consideration for his uncles' promise.

The case of *New Zealand Shipping Co Ltd v AM Satterthwaite & Co Ltd, The Eurymedon* interpreted the law from these cases as established principal that performance of an existing duty to a third party can be sufficient consideration even in circumstances where there was no further detriment suffered to the promisee.[48]

One question that arises from this is whether different rules should attach depending on whether consideration is executed (performance of an existing duty) or executory (a promise to perform an existing duty). This was considered in *Pao On v Lau Yiu Long*, where the claimants agreed with a company (Fu Chip) to sell certain shares in return for an allotment to them of 4.2 million shares in Fu Chip. If all of the newly allotted shares had been sold, it would depress the value of all of the shares in the company. As such it was agreed between the claimants and Fu Chip that the claimant would not sell or transfer sixty per cent of the allotted shares for a period of one year. The claimant then refused to complete the agreement unless the defendant, who was the majority shareholder in Fu Chip, provided an indemnity to them against any fall in the value of the shares for that one year period. The defendants gave that indemnity and when the value of the allotted shares fell in value they pleaded that there was no consideration for their promise to indemnify. It was held in this case that the consideration was the promise of the claimant to perform their pre existing obligation to Fu Chip with Lord Scarman stating 'do not doubt that a promise to perform, or the performance of a pre-existing contractual obligation to a third party can be valid consideration.

Therefore, it is irrelevant whether the consideration is executory or executed, the consideration will still be held to be valid where it is either the performance or promise of performance to a third party.

[48] [1975] AC 154.

Test Your Knowledge

Dave's Builders have entered into a contract with Plough Ltd for Plough Ltd to prepare land prior to construction commencing. Construction on this land is due to commence in April, but by March the work is only half completed. If Dave's Builders do not start on time, they will be subjected to penalties from the local authority and other subcontractors. Dave's Builders speak with Plough Ltd, and agree to pay Plough Ltd an additional £10,000 to complete the works on time. In addition, Dave's Builders are owed £15,000 from a previous construction job that they worked on with Concrete Guys. Knowing that Dave's Builders have promised the extra amount to Plough Ltd and that they are short on cash, Concrete Guys offer to pay £10,000 in full and final settlement of their debt. Dave's Builders accept this, and the money is transferred. Plough Ltd have finished preparing the land on time and Dave's Builders have only paid them the original contract price. They are also initiating a claim against Concrete Guys for the remaining £5,000. In relation to the new agreements, what is the likely outcome:

- A Both of the new contracts are valid.
- B Neither of the new contracts are valid.
- C The contract to pay more is valid but the contract to accept less is invalid.
- D The contract to accept less is valid but the contract to pay more is invalid.

The correct answer here is C. Based on the rationale in *Roffey Bros,* Dave's builders are getting a benefit in that the land will be ready on time and they will not have to pay penalties. As they are receiving this benefit, the contract to pay more is valid and they will be required to pay the additional money to Plough Ltd. The contract with Concrete Guys is invalid as a promise to accept less is not valid consideration unless it is supported by something new – whether that is early payment, or an additional benefit.

Stretch and Challenge Question

Consider what the rationale is for applying different rules to the promise to pay more and the promise to accept less. Analyse whether the same rules ought to apply.

CHAPTER 4

INTENTION TO CREATE LEGAL RELATIONS

4.1 Introduction

The fourth essential element in the creation of a legally binding contract is that there must be an intention between the parties to create legally binding relations. Even in circumstances where there has been a valid offer and acceptance, supported by sufficient consideration, if the agreement was never intended to be enforced by a court, then it will not be legally binding. For example, if you ask your friend to drive you home after work in exchange for petrol money, and he agrees, we would have valid elements of offer, acceptance, and consideration. But if either your friend does not turn up, or you do not pay the petrol money, did you intend that this would be legally binding? There might be a moral obligation to adhere to the agreement made, but you would not be legally bound to it.

The law makes certain presumptions in relation to intention depending on the type of contract that is entered into or the relationship between the parties.[1]

4.2 Social and Domestic Contracts

For social and domestic contracts (generally contracts between family and friends) the presumption is that there is no intention to create legal relations.[2] In other words, it was not the intention of the parties at the time of entering the agreement that the matter would be enforceable

1 See Bhawna Gulati 'Intention to Create Legal Relations: A Contractual Necessity or Illusory Concept' (2011) 2 Beijing Law Review 127.

2 See Jeanette Ashton, 'A Contemporary Reimagining of the Intention to Create Legal Relations Doctrine' (2022) 4 Journal of Business Law 283.

in a court of law in the event that one party did not hold up their end of the bargain.

O'Sullivan J in *Leahy v Rawson* stated that the presumption 'appears to apply only to the closest family kinships such as parent and child and spouses'.[3] He went on to confirm that even in circumstances where it did arise, it was a presumption only and could be rebutted on evidence.

In *Balfour v Balfour*, the leading case in the English jurisdiction a promise by a husband to pay the living expenses of his wife during their marriage was unenforceable as there was no intention to create legal relations.[4] However, where maintenance has been agreed at the breakdown of the marriage rather than through its duration (as was the case in *Merritt v Merritt*[5] and *Soulsbury v Soulsbury*[6]), the court has found such agreements to carry the required intention. Balfour was distinguished in the Irish case of *Courtney v Courtney* where the court upheld an agreement between a husband and wife who had decided to live apart.[7] This case sets the precedent that the presumption will not apply where the parties have not been living together amicably. In addition, the agreement in Courtney was witnessed by a priest which also gave credence to the argument that it was intended to have legal effect.

The Supreme Court case of *Rogers v Smith* illustrates a further issue with agreements made between family members.[8] Here a mother promised her son that he would recover the cost of caring for her from her estate after her death. The court could not uphold any agreement as it was made in the vaguest of terms. As we see in chapter 6 for a court to uphold a contract the terms must be precise and unambiguous as a court order itself needs to be such. There was no way to precisely define what this promise specifically entailed. This principle recognizes that agreements with family members are often vague and imprecise as family members do not often bargain with the zeal that is applied to commercial contracts.

The English case of *Jones v Padavatton*[9] which was followed in Ireland

---

3 Unrep, High Court, 14 January 2003.
4 [1919] 2 KB 571. See also Prince Saprai, 'Balfour v Balfour and the Separation of Contract and Promise' (2017) 37(3) Legal Studies 468.
5 [1970] 1 WLR 1211.
6 [2008] EWCA Civ 969.
7 (1923) 57 ILTR 42.
8 Unrep, Supreme Court, 16 July 1970.
9 [1969] 1 WLR 328.

in *Hynes v Hynes*[10] determines that the test for establishing whether a family agreement is enforceable is that of an objective standard.

One of the most recent cases to look at this principle is *K v K*.[11] In this case a dispute arose over inheritance rights between two brothers. Their mother, the deceased, had fallen out with the plaintiff and consequently no provision was made for him in her will. However, the court found that there was sufficiently compelling evidence to show that he had been promised that a certain portion of the farm would be left to him, and that this was enforceable against his mother's estate.

These are merely presumptions, and as with all presumptions they can be rebutted with sufficient evidence. One way to rebut this presumption is to show that the matter is of considerable substance, and expressed in a manner which indicates an intention to bind the parties. The more substantial and specific the content of the agreement, the more likely it is to carry an intention to create legal relations. In *Parker v Clarke* an elderly couple entered into an agreement with their niece and her husband that if the younger couple sold their house, moved in and contributed to the household expenses then the elderly couple would leave them the house.[12] They did this and subsequently the two couples fell out, with the younger couple being told to find alternative accommodation whereupon they sought damages for breach of contract. The court found that the use of language and the precise details coupled with the seriousness of the act (the selling of their own property) indicated an intention to create legal relations, and thus rebutted any contrary presumption. Similarly, in *Simpkins v Pays*, there was an agreement between the claimant and her granddaughter to 'go shares' if they won the newspaper fashion competition which they regularly entered together and shared the cost of the entrance fee.[13] Here the court found that the presumption did not apply, as there was a long-standing agreement between the parties, mutuality, and the agreement was 'in the very nature of a very informal syndicate'. This line of reasoning appears to have been followed in *Horan v O'Reilly* where a member of a syndicate who had fallen into arrears was allowed to claim their share in a win on the grounds that the other members had allowed the defendant to be in arrears.[14] On appeal to the Supreme Court the decision of the High Court was overturned.[15] The Supreme Court's decision was based on the fact that at the time the agreement was entered into, it was clear that all of the members of the syndicate

---

10 Unrep, High Court, 21 Dec 1984.
11 [2018] IEHC 615.
12 [1960] 1 WLR 286.
13 [1955] 1 WLR 975.
14 [2004] IEHC 425.
15 [2008] IESC 65.

would contribute an equal amount and that should there be a win, that money would be split equally. If the terms of this were to vary, to allow the plaintiff to remain a beneficiary of any winnings, there would need to be an explicit agreement between all of the members of the syndicate to vary the terms of their initial agreement, which did not occur. In contrast, *Wilson v Burnett* involved a group of three work colleagues who went to a bingo night where one of them (Burnett) won a prize of £100,000.[16] It was claimed that there was an agreement to share any prize over £10. It was held that the evidence was not strong enough to rebut the presumption as there had not been any agreement (merely a discussion about sharing) and the event was a one off rather than a continuing agreement as per *Simpkins*.

4.3 Commercial Contracts

In contrast, contracts which are commercial in nature carry a presumption that there is an intention to create legal relations. The clear purpose of commercial contracts is to stimulate exchange and, as explained in *Dresdner Kleinwort Ltd v Attrill*, were this element required to be proven in each case it would become an additional hurdle for those seeking to enforce commercial contracts.[17] Therefore, contracts of a commercial nature, notwithstanding the relationship of the parties, are presumed to carry an intention to create legal relations.

The most recent restatement on this principle comes from the UK Supreme Court in *RTS Flexible Systems Ltd v Molkerei Alois Muller GmbH* where Lord Clarke explained:

> The general principles are not in doubt. Whether there is a binding contract between the parties, and, if so, upon what terms depends on what they have agreed. It depends not upon their subjective mind, but upon consideration of what was communicated between them by words or conduct, and whether that leads objectively to a conclusion that they intended to create legal relations and had agreed upon on the terms which they regarded or the law requires as essential for the formation of legally binding relations. Even if certain terms of economic or other significance to the parties have not been finalized, an objective appraisal of their words and conduct may lead to the conclusion that they did not intend agreement of such terms to be a pre condition to a concluded and legally binding agreement.[18]

---

16 [2007] EWCA Civ 1170.

17 [2013] EWCA Civ 394.

18 [2010] UKSC 14. See also Andrew Bowen, 'Intention to Create Legal Relations and the application of RTS Flexible Systems Ltd' (2013) 123 Business Law Bulletin 1.

In turn, it is possible even in the case of commercial contracts to specifically rebut the presumption of intending to create legal relations such that the agreement will not be legally binding. This can be achieved through the use of so-called 'honour clauses'. Such clauses inserted into the contract expressly state that it will have no legal effect and be binding in honour only. The leading case recognising this is *Rose & Frank Co v JR Crompton & Bros Ltd*.[19] Here the plaintiff was the defendant's agent to sell a certain type of paper in the United States, and the agency agreement contained an honorable pledge clause which said that the agreement was not to be viewed as a legal document subject to the jurisdiction of the courts. The plaintiff from time to time placed orders and the defendant would fulfil them. The defendant announced that it would no longer fulfil orders from the plaintiff who then sued to enforce the terms of the agreement. The court upheld the clause and found that there was no obligation on the plaintiff to submit the orders and there was no obligation on the defendant to fulfill any orders.

In the absence of specific clauses inserted into contracts, the onus of disproving that a commercial agreement did not carry a presumption to create legal relations will be a heavy one. In *Edwards v Skyways* the company offered a severance payment to a pilot on an *ex gratia* basis.[20] The company wanted to go back on the agreement, but the court held that while the interpretation of *ex gratia* meant that there was no obligation to make the payment, once the offer was made and accepted it was transformed into a legally binding contract.

4.4 Where the Category is Not Clear

Where it is not clear as to whether the contract falls into the category of social and domestic or commercial, the courts will tend to apply neither presumption and decide on the facts of the particular case. In *Blue v Ashley* the facts of the case bordered on both.[21] Here Ashley, the founder of the chain store Sports Direct, told Blue during a meeting in a pub, in which a lot of alcohol had been consumed, that he would pay him a £15 million bonus if the shares in the company rose to £8 per share. The shares did rise to £8 per share just over a year later and Blue sought to claim his bonus. The court held that there was no intention to create legal relations as, on the facts, no reasonable person present in the pub would have thought that this offer was intended to create a contract.

---

19 [1925] AC 445.

20 [1969] 1 WLR 349.

21 [2017] EWHC 1928 (Comm). See also Ryan Catterwell, 'The Limits on Intention in Contract' (2023) 139 Law Quarterly Review 571.

Test Your Knowledge

Alan is a law student who is not doing so well ahead of his exams. As he is going into his final year, his mother promises that if he passes all of his final year exams with at least 50%, she will buy him a brand new car. Alan, determined to get this new car, studies hard and passes all of his exams. Does his mother now have to buy him a new car?

A No, this is a social or domestic contract and there is no intention to create legal relations.

B Yes, Alan provided valid consideration by passing all of his exams.

C Yes, as there was a clear intention to rely on the promise and it would be unconscionable to allow the mother to go back on her promise.

The correct answer here is A. Notwithstanding that there has been a clear offer and acceptance, and Alan has provided valid consideration in the form of performance, as this is classed as a social or domestic contract there is a presumption that there is no intention to create legal relations. In the absence of any other evidence which would show that the mother intended to be legally bound by this promise, she is only morally bound and the agreement is not legally enforceable.

Stretch and Challenge Question

Should the presumptions based on different categories of contracts be dismissed in favour of a unified approach?

CHAPTER 5

CAPACITY

5.1 Introduction

The final element that is required to create a legally binding contract is that of capacity. That is that the person entering into the contract had both the legal capacity and authority to enter the contract and that they were capable of understanding the content and nature of the contract that they were entering.

The law limits the capacity of certain persons to enter into contracts. The effect of incapacity is not identical in every circumstance; some contracts will be void meaning that the law will hold that the contract never came into existence, others voidable meaning that one party can ask the court to have the contract voided. It is not automatically voided and requires action by one of the parties; and others unenforceable at the suit of one or both of the parties meaning that while the contract as a whole may not be treated as void, certain obligations under the contract may be unenforceable.

The underlying reason for the law on capacity is to protect those who may be vulnerable; however, this can sometimes cause unjust results for those who deal with an incapacitated person in good faith. This is why the law does not apply a 'one size fits all' response to issues of incapacity and has scope to determine the best outcome depending on the incapacity.

The Assisted Decision-Making (Capacity) Act 2015 came into effect in April 2023 and establishes a new framework for those who lack capacity to make decisions. The Act creates what it calls a 'functional test of capacity' where a person will be held to have capacity if they can:

i) Understand the information relevant to the decision
ii) Remember the information long enough to make a choice
iii) Use or weigh up information to made a decision
iv) Communicate their decision (although this may be with assistance)[1]

The legislation deals exclusively with mental capacity and has been criticised for its limited scope. Clark for example believes that a wider legislative framework ought to be adopted to protect vulnerable persons including minors.[2]

The guiding principles of the Act are set out in s 8 and are:

(a) A person is presumed to have capacity in respect of the matter concerned unless the contrary is shown;
(b) A person shall not be considered as unable to make a decision unless all practical steps have been taken to help him or her do so
(c) A person shall not be considered as unable to make a decision merely because the decision made or likely to be made is an unwise decision;
(d) Intervention should only take place on the basis of necessity and individual circumstances;
(e) Intervention must be made in accordance with human rights, be proportionate and limited in duration;
(f) The intervenor must make maximum efforts to been the wishes of that individual and take account of other specified requirements and interests

The legislation has only been fully in force since April 2023 and the impact that it will have in determining cases of capacity in contract law is not yet fully known.[3]

The areas where the law intervenes specifically in relation to limiting contractual capacity are considered in turn in this chapter.

5.2 Public Authorities

Public authorities whose powers are derived from statute are subject to the doctrine of *ultra vires*. This means that a public authority can only exercise powers which have been expressly conferred on it by statute.

---

1 s 3(2).
2 Robert Clark, *Contract Law in Ireland* (9th edn, Round Hall 2022) 665.
3 See Louise Ordinaire, 'Who Decides Now and To What Extent? A critical reading of the Assisted Decision Making (Capacity) Act 2015' (2017) 16 Hibernian Law Journal 61; Aine Flynn, 'Assisted Decision Making (Capacity) Act 2015: Matters Arising in Legal and Financial Services' (2021) 34(4) Irish Tax Review 141.

Where it acts outside of these powers, the act will be *ultra vires*. In terms of contracts, any contract that is entered into by a local authority which is *ultra vires* its powers will be void. In *Hazell v Hammersmith & Fulham LBC* the court stated that such contracts will be void unless they relate to the functions which the local authority is authorised (expressly or impliedly) to perform, or unless the acts are calculated to facilitate or are incidental to the discharge of those functions.[4]

The purpose of this rule is essentially to protect taxpayers and to ensure that money is being spent in a manner consistent with the duties of the local authority. However, it can cause hardship for those who enter into contracts in good faith with local authorities in ignorance of their lack of capacity. Cases such as *Hazell v Hammersmith & Fulham LBC,*[5] *Credit Suisse v Allerdale BC*[6] and *Credit Suisse v Waltham Forest LBC* provide examples where banks who had participated in housing or recreational schemes with local authorities, either as a joint venture or guarantor, could not sue on their contracts when they were held to be *ultra vires*.[7] The outcome of these decisions caused concern among private entities, making them reluctant to enter into contracts with local authorities.

The Local Government Act 1991 somewhat ameliorates the position. Section 6 of this Act gives the local authority the power to do whatever it deems necessary to 'promote the interest of the local community'. The provision essentially makes such contracts enforceable. However, this does not mean that all actions of the local authority will automatically be lawful. In *McDonagh v Galway County Council,* the Council were found to be acting *ultra vires* when the destroyed a horse that belonged to the plaintiff.[8]

The decision of the local authority may still be challenged by exercised Judicial Review under the Rules of the Superior Court.[9]

Further, local authorities do not have the capacity to enter into contracts which would be incompatible with the exercise of their powers or the discharge of their duties. In *York Corporation v Henry Leetham & Sons Ltd* the plaintiff entered into an agreement with the defendant which allowed the defendant to use two rivers, maintained

---

4 [1992] 2 AC 1.
5 [1992] 2 AC 1.
6 [1997] QB 306.
7 [1997] QB 362.
8 [2019] IEHC 717.
9 See *Mount Juliet Estates Residential Group v Kilkenny County Council* [2020] IEHC 128.

and managed by the plaintiff under statutory authority.[10] The plaintiff charged the defendant £800 per annum, rather than the tolls that it was authorised to collect under the legislation. It was held that this was not a contract that the plaintiff had capacity to make as it was incompatible with the statutory power to increase tolls as necessary to perform its duty of maintenance and management.

5.3 Unincorporated Associations

An unincorporated association has no separate legal personality, and it therefore cannot contract in its name. However, where such an association purports to enter into a contract, it will not necessarily be void. The person who enters into the contract on behalf of the association (such as the secretary or committee) may be held to have contracted personally and be personally liable. In *Bradley Egg Farm Ltd v Clifford* the plaintiff had its poultry negligently tested by an unincorporated association which caused loss.[11] The plaintiff attempted to sue for breach of contract. The court held it could not sue the association as it did not have separate legal personality, and its members' liability was limited to paying their subscriptions. However, where the committee members take on the role of an organisation and ratify contracts, they are personally liable. Ultimately, in this case, the committee members were personally liable in respect of the breach of contract. This principle has since been affirmed in cases such as *Artistic Upholstery Ltd v Art Forma (Furniture) Ltd.*[12]

5.4 Minors

At common law, the age of majority is 21 years. However, S 2(1) the Age of Majority Act 1985 reduces this to 18 years of age or younger if married. The rules relating to the contractual capacity of minors is governed by common law with modification in the Infants Relief Act 1874 (and the Minors Contracts Act 1987 in the UK). The area is a complex one with the law having two competing interests – the need to protect minors and the need to protect traders who enter into contracts with minors in good faith.

Generally, a contract is not binding on a minor unless it has been ratified within a reasonable time after reaching the age of majority. The only contract at common law that was not voidable at the option

---

10 [1924] 1 Ch 557.
11 [1943] 2 All ER 378.
12 [1994] 4 All ER 277.

of the minor was a contract for necessaries and beneficial contracts of service which are examined below.[13]

5.4.1 Contracts for Necessaries

Minors will be liable where they contract for goods which are deemed to be necessary, not only for the things necessary to life (food, clothing etc) but also for those things suitable to their status and circumstances in life at the time the contract was entered into. S 2 of the Sale of Goods and Supply of Services Act 1893 defines these necessaries as 'goods suitable to the condition in life of such infant or minor… and to his actual requirement at the time of the sale and delivery'.

Some things will be obviously out of the scope of a necessary purchase. For example, in *Ryder v Wombwell* a minor, bought a pair of crystal, ruby and diamond solitaires and an antique goblet; the court held that none of these items could be deemed as necessary.[14] Further, while the item itself could be deemed necessary, the quality or quantity may put it outside of this range. In *Nash v Inman* a tailor supplied an undergraduate student with clothing including several 'decadent' items. The court held that while clothing itself could be deemed a necessary item, the student already had an adequate supply of clothing, and the tailor could not prove that these items were suitable to the actual requirements of an undergraduate student.[15]

In determining whether the goods are necessary, the court will take into account a number of things including the nature of the goods supplied, whether the minor is in need of them or already has an adequate supply, and the actual circumstances of the minor.

At first glance, it would seem that this is inordinately harsh on the trader; the onus is on them to prove that the item was one that was necessary in order for their contract to be enforced (often to recover payment for the item). Thus, where the court finds that an item was not necessary, or was superfluous to the requirements of the minor, the contract will not be enforced against the minor and the trader has no recourse. However, where the minor is in actual need of the item, the contract can be enforced against them.

At common law, a loan for necessaries would not be recoverable, as per *Earle v Peale*: 'it may be borrowed for necessaries but laid out and

---

13 See Shivangi Gangwar, 'Minor's Contracts in the Digital Age' (2022) 43 Liverpool Law Review 237.

14 (1868) LR 3 Ex 90. See also *Skrine v Gordon* (1875) IR 9 CL 479.

15 [1908] 2 KB 1.

spent at a tavern'.[16] However, it was held in *Marlow v Pitfeild* that where the money borrowed to pay a debt for necessaries was actually spent to pay that debt, equity would hold that the lender stood in place of the creditor and was entitled to recover under the equitable doctrine of subrogation.[17] The Infant Relief Act 1874 confirms that 'all contracts .... For the repayment of money lent or to be lent, for goods supplied or to be supplied (other than contracts for necessaries)..... shall be absolutely void'.[18]

The Law Reform Commission's Report on Minors Contracts recommends removing the concept of necessaries and rather that the court, when making orders, ought to have regard to:[19]

- The subject matter and nature of the contract;
- The nature and value of property involved in the contract;
- The age, mental capacity and experience of the minor both at the time of the contract and at the time of the hearing;
- The experience and knowledge of the minor in relation to the subject matter of the contract;
- The economic circumstances of the parties;
- The circumstances surrounding the contract and the fairness of the contract;
- The actual benefits under the contract;
- The expenses or losses sustained or likely to be sustained;
- All other relevant circumstances.

5.4.2 Beneficial Contracts of Service

A minor may enter into contracts for employment and training and, provided that these contracts are beneficial to the minor, they are binding. The issue of benefit to the minor is key in deciding whether such contracts are binding. In *Clements v London and North Western Railway Company* the contract of employment contained a clause whereby the minor accepted the terms of an insurance policy against accidents in lieu of his right to take action under the Employers' Liability Act 1880.[20] It was held that the contract as a whole was for his benefit and he was bound by the terms. In contrast, in *DeFrancesco v Barnum* the defendant contracted to become the claimant's apprentice for a period of seven years.[21] She was 14 years old at the time she entered into the agreement. The terms of the agreement stated that she was required to obtain the consent of the claimant before agreeing to any professional engagement, and that she was not to marry during

---

16 (1711) 1 Salk 386.
17 (1719) 1 P Wms 558.
18 s 1.
19 LRC 15-1985.
20 [1894] 2 QB 482.
21 (1890) 45 Ch D 430.

the apprenticeship period. Further, she would receive payments for any performances that she might give during the time but there was no provision for general remuneration. In this case, the court found that the contract had the effect of placing the defendant entirely at the disposal of the claimant and was therefore not beneficial. It further stated that while there may be certain clauses that would not be beneficial, the court would look at the contract as a whole in determining whether or not the minor benefited from the agreement. In *Keys v Great Southern Railway*, the minor plaintiff was the holder of a season train ticket to allow her travel to and from school.[22] The terms of the ticket exempted the railway company from liability for any injuries which were caused as a result of their negligence. The plaintiff was injured as a result of negligence. The court held that the terms of the ticket were so harsh that the plaintiff could repudiate it. Hanna J stated:

> The contract in this case is very unfair to the infant because it deprives her of practically every common law right that she has against the railway company in respect of the negligence of themselves or their servants. For that reason, I think it is not to her benefit.

One of the most famous cases in this regard is the case of *Chaplin v Leslie Frewen (Publishers) Ltd*.[23] Here, the son of the famous actor Charlie Chaplin had agreed to write an autobiography to be published by the defendant wherein he would reveal certain facts about his father. The plaintiff was paid a substantial amount as a down payment and initially cooperated with the writers. When completed, the book painted the Chaplin family is a particularly poor light and the claimant sought to have the contract declared as unenforceable as it was not to his benefit, being potentially libellous. The Court of Appeal found that the advance payment and the royalties from the book outweighed any negative aspects and was therefore beneficial.

This issue was examined more recently in *Proform Sports Management Ltd v Proactive Sports Management Ltd*.[24] Here, the footballer Wayne Rooney entered into a player representation agreement at the age of 15 with the claimant that it would act as his executive agent and represent him exclusively. It alleged that the defendant had also entered into a player representation agreement and thereby procured a breach of contract with Rooney. The court found that the agreement was not enforceable against Rooney as he was a minor and the general

---

22 [1941] IR 534. See also *Harnedy v National Greyhound Racing Association* [1944] IR 160.

23 [1966] Ch 71.

24 [2006] EWHC 2903 (Ch).

rule applied. Further, it could not be classed as an apprenticeship as there was no training being provided. As the contract was voidable at Rooney's option, the defendant could not be liable for procuring a breach.

5.5 Mental Incapacity and Intoxication

The general rule is that a person who is lacking mental capacity or intoxicated will not be bound to a contract where it can be shown that they were unaware of the nature and consequences of the contract, and that the other party was aware of this. The principle was set down in *Imperial Loan Co v Stone* with Lord Esher MR stating:

> When a person enters into a contract, and afterwards alleges that he was so insane at the time that he did not know what he was doing, and proves the allegation, the contract is as binding on him in every respect, whether executory or executed, as if he had been sane when he made it, unless he can prove further that the person with whom he contracted knew him to be so insane as not to be capable of understanding what he was about.[25]

Even where a contract is unconscionable or unfair, it cannot be set aside unless the other party was aware of the mental incapacity. In *Hart v O'Connor* Lord Brightman confirmed:

> The validity of a contract entered into by a lunatic who is ostensibly sane is to be judged by the same standards as a contract by a person of sound mind, and it is not voidable by the lunatic or his representatives by reason of 'unfairness' unless such unfairness amounts to equitable fraud which would have enabled the complaining party to avoid the contract even if he had been sane.[26]

Therefore, the position in relation to incapacity can be distinguished clearly from that of minors examined above. It will be no defence for a party to argue that they were unaware of the age of the minor as the overarching policy is to protect the minor. With mental incapacity, the party will be protected if they can show that they were unaware of the incapacity at the time that the contract was entered into. It will only be voidable where the person who has full capacity can be shown to have, in some way, taken advantage of the other party who was lacking mental capacity. This is evident in the Case of *Hassard v Smith* where an action to set aside a lease failed.[27] Here the court accepted that for a contract to be upheld, the defendant would need to show that it was

---

25 [1892] 1 QB 599, 601.
26 [1985] AC 1000.
27 (1872) IR 6 EQ 429.

fair and bona fide and that a disparity between the price paid and the market value would infer that the seller had been victimised.

Contracts made with persons who are so intoxicated that they cannot understand the nature and consequences of their actions will be void. However, a person can choose to subsequently affirm the contract, at which point it becomes binding. In *Matthews v Baxter* the defendant, while intoxicated, bought property at auction.[28] When sober he then affirmed the contract but had second thoughts. When sued, he argued that he was drunk at the time, and the claimant knew of this. It was held that the defendant was bound by his affirmation of the contract and at the time of the affirmation he lost the right to avoid the contract.

Test Your Knowledge

Paul and Joe are two friends. Joe is 15 years old and Paul is 34. However, Paul has severe learning difficulties which gives him the cognitive age of 12. One day they decide to go into town and go to their favourite record shop. A power cut in the store means that payment cannot be taken electronically, and Joe sees an opportunity for the two to get lots of records that they have been wanting. They each take 10 records and bring them to the counter. They give details of the bank cards to the cashier and sign an authorisation that allows the shop to deduct the price of the records from their accounts once the power has been restored. Unknown to the cashier, both of these cards are restricted due to Joe's age and Paul's mental incapacity. The next day the shop is contacted by the bank which refuses to honour both transactions. Advise whether the shop may succeed in a claim to recover the cost of the records against

A both Joe and Paul
B neither Joe nor Paul
C Joe but not Paul
D Paul but not Joe.

The correct answer here is D Joe is a minor and does not have contractual capacity to enter into this contract. It is irrelevant whether the shop knew of Joe's age, and as the subject matter of this contract could not be deemed to be necessary, the shop will not be able to recover. However, Paul's incapacity relates to his learning difficulties, and unless the shop knew this to be the case then it will be able to succeed against him.

---

28 (1893) LR 8 Ex 132.

Stretch and Challenge Question

Consider whether the law goes far enough in protecting vulnerable persons from being exploited in contracts. What reforms, if any, would you suggest?

PART TWO

CONTRACT TERMS, PRIVITY AND THIRD PARTY RIGHTS

CHAPTER 6

CERTAINTY

6.1 Introduction

The general rule is that there is no contract unless the main terms are clear, despite the fact that the parties may have ostensibly complied with all of the formal requirements. In *Loftus v Roberts* it was held that all of the key terms must be identifiable, or the contract will not be enforced.[1] Further, in *Scammell v Ouston,* which concerned the sale of a van on 'hire purchase terms', it was not clear what was meant by hire purchase terms, and the court held that there was no concluded contract.[2] In *Baird Textile Holdings Ltd v Marks and Spencer Plc* the Court of Appeal held that the term 'Marks & Spencer would acquire garments from BTH in quantities and at prices which in all the circumstances were reasonable' was too uncertain to be part of a valid contract.[3]

However, in *Forstater v Dweck and Another* a case which concerned an oral agreement relating to commission payments, it was stated:

> Not to uphold a contract because it has been made orally and because every conceivable possibility cannot be shown to have been contemplated in discussion between the parties would be to deprive many agreements reached between ordinary people in ordinary language of their effect. The technicalities of the law do not compel me to reach that decision. The question, as it seems to me on the facts here, can only be answered by saying that there was an agreement.[4]

It seems therefore that there are somewhat differing approaches taken by the court as to whether or not the terms are certain depending on whether the contract is ultimately written or oral. Where the contract is

1 (1902) 18 TLR 532, CA.
2 [1941] AC 251.
3 [2001] EWCA Civ 274.
4 [2007] EWHC 191 (QB).

written, it is clear for the court to see what terms have been included, excluded or are particularly vague and uncertain. Where the contract is oral, the matter will come down, on the balance of probabilities, in favour of the person who the court believes more.

6.2 Ascertaining Terms

The court can ascertain uncertain terms in a number of ways as considered below

6.2.1 Past Dealing

Sometimes, a term may be ascertained when there have been past dealings between the parties. In *Hillas & Co v Arcos Ltd* Hillas agreed to purchase Russian timber of 'fair specification' from Arcos.[5] The contract allowed Hillas to purchase further timber the following year, but this option gave no specification as to the quality. When Hillas sought to exercise this option, Arcos argued that the clause was too vague and was merely there as an agreement to engage in further negotiations. The House of Lords held that given the previous dealings between the parties, there was sufficient intention to be bound and that the terms could be ascertained by reference to those in the original agreement.

6.2.2 Reasonableness

Where the intention of the parties is clear, uncertain terms may be subject to a standard of reasonableness applied by the court.[6] In *Hillas*, 'fair specification' was held to mean 'timber distributed over kinds, qualities and sizes in fair proportions having regard to the seasons output, a matter which, if the parties failed to agree, could be ascertained by the court'. A similar approach has been taken by the court to phrases such as market value (*Brown v Gould*)[7] and open market value (*Gillatt v Sky Television Ltd*).[8]

In *ESB v Newman*, Newman entered into a contract of indemnity to discharge the accounts of a Mrs Waddington for electricity supplied to her for a period not exceeding nine months.[9] It transpired that Mrs Waddington was receiving electricity supply at four separate

5 (1932) 147 LT 503.
6 See G Black, 'The Role of Contractual Intention and Email Disclaimers' (2011) Juridical Law Review 97.
7 [1972] Ch 53.
8 [2000] 1 All ER (Comm) 46.
9 (1933) 67 ILTR 124.

properties and the court had to determine whether the indemnity extended to all of these. By examining the contract through the lens of the intention of the contracting parties, the indemnity was held not to extend to all of the properties but was restricted to that which was specifically listed in the contract.

6.2.3 Executed Transactions

In these types of contracts, the court will have regard to what actions have been performed by the parties.

In *G Percy Trentham Ltd v Archital Luxfer Ltd* Lord Steyn said 'it will be difficult to submit that the contract is void for vagueness or uncertainty' in circumstances where the obligations have been wholly or partially performed.[10]

6.2.4 Agreements to Negotiate

The position of these types of agreements was considered by the House of Lords in *Walford v Miles.* In this case it was agreed on 17 March that provided Walford's bank confirmed that they had the resources to purchase Miles' business, Miles would 'break off any negotiations with any third party and would not consider any other alternative and would not accept a better offer but would deal exclusively with Walford with a view to concluding the deal as soon as possible after 6 April'.[11] Miles continued to talk with another interested party and on 27 March withdrew from negotiations with Walford, eventually selling to that other interested party. Walford sued for breach of contract and misrepresentation.

While Walford succeeded in their claim for misrepresentation as it was found that Miles had represented that they were not in negotiations with other parties, the claim for breach of contract failed. It was held that agreements such as these (agreements to negotiate) are akin to an agreement to agree and cannot be enforceable. The reasoning for this is twofold: first, that it would be impossible to tell whether it had been breached, and, second that quantifying damage for breach would be impossible as the court would not be able to determine whether the negotiations would have been successful or not, and thus what the overall result would be.

---

10 [1993] Lloyds Rep 25.
11 [1992] 2 AC 128.

6.3 Incomplete Contracts

If a contract is incomplete, the courts are reluctant to write the parties' agreement for them as this would undermine the principle of freedom of contract. The case of *Mackie v Wilde* confirms that the Court will not complete contracts or indeed re-write them to ensure certainty.[12] In *Central Meat Products v Carney* there was an agreement to 'supply as many cattle as possible to the plaintiffs' with a guarantee not to supply to any other competitor of the plaintiff.[13] When the defendant began selling to others without the consent of the plaintiff, they brought an action for breach of contract. The court held that there could be no contract as there were essential elements such as the number, quality and price of the cattle omitted from the agreement.

Further, in *Tolan v Connacht Gold*, the plaintiff and defendant signed a document at the conclusion of a meeting between them on the 16 July 2012.[14] The plaintiff alleges that this document constituted a binding contract and that the breach of its terms resulted in them sustaining substantial damages. In considering all of the surrounding circumstances, including the plaintiff's already substantial debt to the defendant, found that this document was not intended to be a binding agreement, but rather a note of ongoing discussions and agreements.

Difficulties particularly arise in circumstances where negotiations are protracted and involve multiple elements of correspondences wherein the parties negotiate various terms back and forth; one party insists that a contract has been made, but the other says it never went beyond the discussion of terms. Generally, in these circumstances, the correspondence will refer to a contract which will be entered into by the parties. In *Von Hatzfeldt-Wildenburg v Alexander* the court opined that it will be a matter of construction as to whether the execution of a further contract is a condition or a mere expression of the desire of the parties as to process:

> ... in the former case there is no enforceable contract either because the condition is unfulfilled or because the law does not recognise a contract to enter into a contract.[15] In the latter case there is a binding contract and the reference to the more formal document may be ignored.

This matter of construction will differ on a case by case basis and will take into consideration all of the facts of the particular case at hand. It

[12] (1997) WJSC-SC 1504.
[13] [1944] 10 IR Jur Rep 34.
[14] [2016] IECA 131.
[15] [1912] 1 Ch 284.

involves the court taking a holistic approach to the documents and the evidence adduced to determine the overall intentions of the parties.

However, if the agreement has been acted upon, ie performance has begun, the court may be more willing to imply terms based on the intention of the parties (*Foley v Classique Coaches*).[16]

More recently, we have seen the issue of certainty raised in relation to 'letters of intent'. These documents generally signal that negotiations have been concluded but the parties envisage a further formal document being signed. Whether or not these letters of intent can form the basis of a binding contract is a matter of construction and interpretation for the court. From *Chemco Leasing SpA v Rediffusion* it is clear that where the letter contains an express promise as to future conduct, this can have contractual effect.[17]

The matter was considered by the English Supreme Court in *RTS Flexible Systems Ltd v Molkerei Alois Muller GMBH & Co KG (UK Production)*.[18] The parties had entered into negotiations about RTS supplying and installing automated packaging machinery for Molkerei. Although they had intended that a written contract would set out the terms on which the work was to be carried out, work had in fact begun before the terms were finalised. For the purpose of enabling the work to begin, and while continuing to negotiate the full contract terms, the parties had entered into a contract formed by a letter of intent. By 5 July 2005, a draft final contract was produced, which provided that it would not become effective until each party had executed and exchanged a counterpart. That was never done. Rather, all the terms having been agreed, substantial works were carried out and, on 25 August, the agreement was varied in important respects. The issue was whether, after the expiry of the letter of intent, the parties had entered into a contract and, if so, on what terms?

It was held that the instant case demonstrated the perils of beginning work without agreeing the precise basis upon which it was to be done, and the moral was to reach agreement before work began. Where a contract was being negotiated subject to contract, and work began before the formal contract was executed, it could not be said that there would always, or even usually, be a contract on the terms that were agreed subject to contract. That was too simplistic and dogmatic an approach. The idea that there was no contract was unconvincing. It

16 [1934] 2 KB 1.
17 [1987] 1 FTLR 201.
18 [2010] UKSC 14.

was unrealistic to suppose that the parties had not intended to create legal relations. In this case it was held that there was a binding contract.

As we have seen in Chapter 2, agreements that are made 'subject to contract' give rise to no contractual liability. Even where it is clear that terms have been agreed, the effect of using these words means that there can be no contract. The contract will only come into existence once the contract has been signed by both parties. This has particular importance in relation to contracts for the sale of land in which agreements are often headed subject to contract, despite the fact that a deposit may have been paid. Up until such a time as contracts are signed and exchanged, either party is free to change the terms or indeed withdraw from the process altogether.

Test Your Knowledge

Jacob often buys art from a local gallery called Hughes. He has become well known to the owner of the gallery. At an exhibition Jacob finds a painting that he likes and decides to purchase it. He speaks to the owner, who is in a hurry to close and has just shut down the till. He tells Jacob that it will be purchased 'on the usual terms'. The next day Jacob receives an invoice via email which includes an additional cost that he has not paid before for 'packing, shipping and delivery' at a cost of £300.

Is the contract:

- A void for uncertainty
- B valid and Jacob has to pay the additional £300
- C valid and Jacob does not have to pay the additional cost?

The correct answer here is C. Normally 'usual terms' would be void for uncertainty, but as Jacob has a history of dealing with this gallery, the court can determine what the precise terms would be based on their course of dealing. When the owner said the 'usual terms', this would be taken to mean the terms that Jacob had previously contracted upon which did not include the additional fee.

Stretch and Challenge Question

Where a term is uncertain, the courts have devised ways, through interpretation or construction, to ascertain the term. Consider whether the courts should have the power to impose its standards of reasonableness onto a contract term.

Chapter 7

TERMS OF A CONTRACT

7.1 Introduction

Once it has been established that a contract has been created, it is necessary to examine the contents of that contract. Generally, a contract will contain a number of contractual clauses which establish the obligations on the parties. It is therefore important to establish what are the terms of the contract and whether they are of major or minor importance to the parties, as this will have an impact on the remedies available should there be a breach of any particular term.

Regardless of whether the term is expressed or implied, it must be sufficiently certain. This matter was considered in the case of *Glanbia Foods Ireland v E D and F Man Liquid Products Ireland Ltd*.[1] This contract involved the sale of molasses and the High Court was tasked with determining which of the parties terms and conditions governed the agreement. The court found that it was Glanbia's terms and conditions which governed the contract as they were incorporated by E D and F through their acceptance of purchase contract confirmations. There was insufficient notice given by E D and F to incorporate any further terms and conditions into the contract.

7.2 Express Terms

It is not always easy to identify whether a particular element is a clause of the contract. It could be that during the course of negotiations statements were made or assurances given which were not then subsequently included in a written agreement. These pre-contract statements can be divided into three categories: a puff, a term or a representation.

1 [2022] IEHC 666.

A puff is a statement which cannot give rise to legal consequences. It is not meant to be taken literally and is used as an advertisement tool. For example, if you saw a coffee shop advertising 'the best coffee in town' and it was not the best coffee you have ever had in that town, would you be able to sue for breach of contract? This is clearly a statement which is not meant to be relied on. In *Carlill v Carbolic Smoke Ball Co* the defendant argued (unsuccessfully) that its advertisement was a puff and not meant to be relied upon.[2]

Representations are statements which are made during the course of a negotiation. It may be that later the contract was reduced to writing or perhaps that the entire contract was concluded orally. The representation is not a term of the contract, and therefore where there is a breach the same remedies do not apply. This is the area which we focus on in the next section.

7.2.1 Terms or Representations

The difference between a term and a representation is that the person making the statement does not intend to make good on that statement. If a statement is deemed to be a term of the contract, then it forms part of the contract as if it were expressly included in the written document, and should there be a breach of that term, the wronged party can sue for breach of contract (the remedy available will depend on whether the term is classified as a condition, warranty or innominate term). Where the statement is seen as a representation, it does not form part of the contract. It is best to look at a representation as akin to an invitation to treat; it does not carry with it any legal intention to be bound. Should the statement, which is determined as a representation, be found to be false, fraudulent or negligent, the wronged party may have an action in tort for damages but cannot ground an action in breach of contract. This means that the contractual obligations will not be avoided for breach of a representation, but damages in tort may offset that liability.

The courts have devised certain guidelines to determine whether a statement is in fact a term or a representation. In making this decision, they have regard to a number of factors:

7.2.2 Intention of the Parties

The basic test in determining whether a statement is a term or a representation is one of intention, as recognised in *Heilbut, Symons &*

---

2 [1893] 1 QB 256.

Co v Buckleton.[3] This essentially looks at whether the party making the statement had intended for it to be a term or a representation. The test is not subjective and Lord Denning in *Oscar Chess Ltd v Williams* stated that it would depend 'on the conduct of the parties, on their words and behaviour rather than their thoughts'.[4] The objective nature of the test is clearly seen in the case of *Thake v Maurice*.[5] Here, Mr Thake underwent a vasectomy, and the surgeon, while explaining that the procedure was irreversible, failed to tell Mr Thake that there was a slight chance that it could naturally reverse itself. Subsequent to the surgery, Mr Thake's wife became pregnant and they argued that their contract contained a term that the operation would render Mr Thake sterile. The Court of Appeal found that there was no such term; however, the pair were awarded damages in tort for the surgeon's failure to warn of the possibly of natural reversal.

7.2.3 Importance of the Statement

If the statement is one which is so important that the contract would not have been entered into had the statement not been made, then it is likely the statement will be a term. In *Bannerman v White,* White was purchasing hops from the seller.[6] White asked if any sulphur had been used in the hops and stated that he would not even ask the price if sulphur had been used. The seller stated that sulphur had not been used, but in fact it had. White argued successfully that there had been a breach of a contractual term. In this case, the fact that White had specifically asked this question shows that it was of high importance to the contract and therefore the statement was held to be a term. In other words, White would not have entered into this particular contract had he known that the hops had been treated with sulphur.

7.2.4 Timing

It was held in *Inntrepeneur Pub Co v East Crown Ltd* that the longer the interval between the statement and the contract, the more likely it is that the statement was a representation and not a term.[7]

The nearer in time that the statement is made to the contract, the more likely it is that it is a matter of importance and should therefore be treated as a term. In *Routledge v McKay,* McKay was selling a motorbike and had told the plaintiff that the bike was made in 1942, whereas in

---

3 [1913] AC 30.
4 [1957] 1 WLR 370, 375.
5 [1986] All ER 497.
6 (1861) 10 CB NS 844.
7 [2000] 2 Lloyd's Rep 611.

fact it was made in 1930.[8] A week later the contract of sale was made. It was held in this case that the statement was not a term of the contract. The passage of one week was ample time for this to be classed as a representation. The fact that this contract was also later reduced to writing played a further part in the court's decision.

7.2.5 Expertise

The knowledge of the person making the statement is an additional consideration for the courts in determining if the statement is a term of the contract. The best illustration of this can be found in contrasting the following two cases. In *Oscar Chess Ltd v Williams* (see 7.2.2 above) the defendant sold a car to the plaintiff car dealer. He described the car as a 1948 model and the log book reflected the same. Unknown to the defendant, before he acquired the car, the log book had been tampered with and it was in fact a 1939 model worth £115 less than the 1948 model. When this fact was discovered some months later, the plaintiff sought to recover the difference in price. The court found that the statement was not a term of the contract; the defendant had simply relied on the date in the log book.

However, in *Dick Bentley Productions Ltd v Harold Smith (Motors) Ltd* the plaintiff asked the defendant to find him car.[9] The defendant found one and stated that since a new engine had been fitted, the car had only done 20,000 miles as evidenced by the odometer. The plaintiff bought the car, and in investigating faults it was discovered that the car had in fact done considerably more miles since the new engine had been fitted. The court found this statement as to the mileage to be a term rather than a representation based on the position of the person making the statement. Here, a car dealer was in a better position to establish the accuracy of such information.[10]

7.2.6 Reliance

The statement made is more likely to be a term if it can be shown that the statement maker intended for the other party to rely on it. In *Schawel v Reade* the plaintiff was examining a horse with a view to purchasing it for stud purposes.[11] Reade told the plaintiff, 'You need not look for anything – the horse is perfectly sound. If there was anything the matter with the horse I would tell you.' The plaintiff stopped the examination and took delivery of the horse, which was

---

8 [1954] 1 WLR 615.
9 [1965] 1 WLR 623.
10 See David Campbell, 'Oscar Chess, Dick Bentley and the abolition of Innocent Misrepresentation' (2024) 1 Journal of Business Law 1.
11 [1913] 2 IR 81, HL.

found to be unfit for the stated purpose. Did the statement amount to a term or a representation? It was held here that the statement was a term as it was intended that the plaintiff stop his examination of the horse in reliance on the statement.

In contrast, in *Ecay v Godfrey*, the seller of a boat said that the boat was sound but suggested that the buyer get a survey completed.[12] It was held that the statement was not a term of the contract but a representation. Here, the seller expressly stated that the buyer ought to get a survey to check the validity of his statement. There was no intention that the buyer should rely solely on the statement made.

7.2.7 Is the Contract Written

Where an agreement has subsequently been reduced to writing, the assumption is that all of the relevant express terms agreed between the parties will have been included in that written agreement.[13] This was part of the reason why the claim in *Routledge v McKay* (see 7.2.4 above) failed. Parties will often argue that there were additional terms agreed between them which were not included in the written contract, and the court will need to determine whether or not they form part of the contract. Generally, the parole evidence rule states that where there is a written contract, this is the document that establishes all of the obligations and rights of each of the parties, and all other evidence (whether oral or written) is ignored.[14] The reasoning behind the rule is that if the focus of the case is on the written contract rather than oral evidence, it will speed up trials and reduce litigation. In *Macklin and McDonald v Greacen & Co* the Supreme Court held that in the absence of a claim for rectification of the contract, it could not be varied by reference by reference to parol evidence.[15]

However, the rule is not absolute and there are a number of circumstances in which parol evidence may be admissible.[16] Firstly, it may be used to establish the limits of a contract. So, where a party is trying to show that either there was no contract at all,[17]or to show that there were a number of distinct contracts[18] parol evidence will

---

12 (1947) 80 Lloyd's Rep 286.

13 See Maire Ni Shuilleabhain, 'Formalities of Contracting: A Cost Benefit Analysis of Requirements that Contracts be in Writing' (2005) 27 Dublin University Law Journal 113.

14 See *Bank of Australasia v Palmer* [1897] AC 540.

15 [1983] IR 61. See also Geoffrey Marston, 'The Parol Evidence Rule: The Law Commission Speaks' (1986) 45(2) Cambridge Law Journal 192.

16 See D W McLauchlan, 'Parol Evidence and Contract Formation' (2005) 121 Law Quarterly Review.

17 *Pym v Campbell* (1856) 6 El & Bl 370.

18 *Carrigy v Brock* (1871) IR 5 CL 501.

be admitted. Secondly, it can be used to explain the circumstances surrounding an agreement. For example, in *Revenue Commissioners v Morony* evidence was admitted to show that an apparent sale was in fact a transfer by way of gift.[19] Third, it can be admitted to explain the subject matter of the contract as occurred in *Chambers v Kelly*.[20] Fourth, as per the *Macklin* case above, such evidence can be introduced where there is a mistake in the contract and the remedy sought is rectification (we examine this equitable remedy separately in chapter 20) Fifth, oral evidence can be introduced to show the price payable where the contract is silent on consideration[21] or to show that consideration is accurately reflected in the contract.[22] Finally, it can be used where the argument being made is that the written contract is not the entire agreement. In *Clayton Love v B&I Transport* it was held that details of a telephone conversation could be added to a written contract so as to form one contract, part written and part oral.[23] However, where there is a conflict between a written term and an oral one, the courts will prefer to rely on the written document with one small exception. Where the contract is a 'standard form' a promise which deviates from that may be given preference. The English courts have examined this issue in *BCT Software Solutions Ltd v Arnold Laver*.[24] Here a software company changed its standard terms to make all software licences integrated with support obligations. Prior to this, a customer could purchase the software without having to purchase a support package. The defendant here purchased the software after the commencement of the new terms, but staff on both sides agreed that this would be independent of any support obligations. It was held by the court that the expressly agreed term to waive the support obligations was valid notwithstanding that it was in direct contradiction with the standard business terms.

7.3 Implied Terms

There are certain circumstances where the parties to a contract will not have expressly included all of the terms in a contract. Depending on the nature of the contract, the court can, in certain circumstances, imply a term into a contract. This implied term has the same effect as it if were expressly agreed by the parties. The circumstances in which the court will imply a term (excluding statutory terms – see below)

---

19 [1972] IR 372. See also *Harries v Hardy* (1851) 3 Ir Jur 290; *Ulster Bank v Synnott* (1871) 5 IR Eq 595.
20 (1873) 7 IRCL 231.
21 *Jeffcott v North British Oil Co* (1855) ICLR 50.
22 *Black v Grealy*, Unrep, High Court, 10 Nov 1977.
23 (1970) 104 ILTR 157.
24 [2002] 2 All ER (Comm) 85.

are limited as it is not for the court to make contracts between the parties, but rather to interpret those contracts. There are four broad categories where terms are implied: by common law, by custom, by statute and by the Constitution. In *Tradex Ireland Ltd v Irish Grain Board Ltd* O'Higgins CJ observed that the power to imply terms 'must be exercised with care. The courts have no role in acting as contract makers, or counsellors, to advise or direct which agreement ought to have been made by two people, whether businessmen or not, who chose to enter into contract relations with each other'.[25]

Whether or not the duty of good faith is a term implied into commercial contracts has been considered by courts in *Flynn v Breccia*.[26] In this case, Breccia, a shareholder in the Blackrock Clinic acquired the overdue loans of another shareholder, Benray. Benray's loans were secured against their shareholding in the Blackrock Clinic. Breccia made a demand for payment and when Benray failed to comply, a receiver was appointed to Benray's shareholding. Benray sought to restrain this appointment arguing that each of the shareholders had an implied duty of good faith and fair dealing and that it was an implied term that they would not take steps to force the sale of any of the shareholders holdings outside of the terms of the initial shareholder agreement. The High Court initially agreed with the arguments of Benray, however this was overturned on appeal. The Court of Appeal categorically stated that there is no general principal of good faith and fair dealing in Irish Commercial Contract Law and cautioned against implying terms into a written contract.

7.3.1 Terms Implied by Common Law

Where parties have omitted to include a term, there are two tests that the court will use in order to determine whether it ought to be implied. These are the business efficacy test and the officious bystander test.[27] These two areas were expressly approved of by the Supreme Court in *Sweeney v Duggan*.[28]

7.3.1.1 The Business Efficacy Test

The business efficacy test applies to commercial contracts and relates to circumstances where a term ought to be implied to give effect to the core of the contract. The key case for the application of this test is *The Moorcock*, where a ship owner and the owner of a jetty contracted

---

25 [1984] IR 1.
26 [2017] IECA 74.
27 See Andrew Phang, 'Implied Terms, Business Efficacy and The Officious Bystander – A Modern History' [1998] Journal of Business Law 1.
28 [1997] 2 ILRM 211.

to allow the ship to be moored at the jetty.[29] At low tide the ship was damaged on the riverbed. The Court of Appeal held that it must have been intended that the area including the riverbed would be safe for the ship, and therefore this term was implied into the contract. The jetty owner was liable for breach of this term when the ship was damaged. This test is used where, without the implied term, the contract would simply be unworkable.

This test has been considered by the Irish Courts in a number of cases. In *O'Toole v Palmer* the parties agreed that if O'Toole was able to find a purchaser for a piece of land, then Palmer, an auctioneer, would agree to share the commission fee once that was paid by the purchaser.[30] O'Toole found a purchaser who did not agree to pay the commission fee and the sale was closed without any commission being paid. It was argued that in doing so, Palmer had breached an implied term that he would not prevent the claimant from earning his share of the commission. The court rejected the argument and held that 'I do not think there is any necessity to imply a term for the purpose of giving the contract a business efficacy. Here the terms are clearly expressed in writing and the plaintiff has undertaken an ordinary business risk'.

7.3.1.2 The Officious Bystander Test

The second test, which sometimes overlaps with the first, is applied by asking an 'officious bystander' whether or not this term ought to be in the contract. This comes from the case of *Shirlaw v Southern Foundries* where MacKinnon LJ said:

> … something so obvious that it goes without saying; so that, if, while the parties were making their bargain, an officious bystander were to suggest some express provision for it in their agreement, they would testily suppress him with a common 'Oh, of course!.[31]

In this case, Mr Shirlaw was appointed Managing Director of the Foundries for 10 years. Due to a change of ownership, the articles of association of Southern Foundries were changed to enable the removal of a director by two other directors and the secretary. Mr Shirlaw was then dismissed prior to the expiry of his 10 year contract and he brought a claim seeking damages for breach of contract. The company argued that it had the power to amend the articles under s 10 of the Companies Act 1929, and further as the articles had been appropriately adopted and the correct procedures followed, that the

29 (1889) 14 PD 64.
30 [1945] Ir Jur Rep 59. See also *Dakota Packaging v Wyeth Medica Ireland* [2005] 2 IR 54.
31 [1939] 2 KB 206.

court should not interfere. Mr Shirlaw argued that the articles could not amend a pre existing contract and that there was an implied term in his contract that such amendments would not occur prior to the expiration of his fixed term. Mr Shirlaw was successful in his claim. It was held that while the company had the statutory power to amend its articles, it would be liable in damages where doing so prejudices a pre existing valid contract.

The court will be reluctant to imply a term where the parties have concluded a carefully written contract. In *Shell UK Ltd v Lostock Garage Ltd*, Lostock Garage could only sell petrol supplied by Shell.[32] As a result of a petrol price war, Shell introduced a scheme which subsidised two Shell garages in that neighbourhood so that they could compete, but excluded Lostock Garage. Lostock obtained petrol elsewhere and Shell sought damages and an injunction. Lostock argued that there was an implied obligation on Shell not to discriminate against Lostock and that Shell was in breach of that implied term. The court refused to imply the term, holding that it was not necessary as the contract made business sense without it and further it was not obvious that Shell would have agreed to it.

In Irish Law, it would appear that the relationship between the parties is a core consideration when determining whether a term is implied into the contract. Despite prior cases to the contrary[33] the case of *Siney v Dublin Corporation* it was held that the local authority was liable in contract when they rented a flat to the plaintiff which was poorly ventilated and caused damp which damaged the plaintiff's possessions.[34] This case was extended further in *Coleman & Coleman v Dundalk UDC* which held that the local authority could not evade these responsibilities by executing a lease rather than a tenancy agreement and again implied the term that the premises be fit for human habitation into the contract.[35]

7.3.1.3 Distinguishing the Tests

Ashmore v Corporation of Lloyd's (No 2) suggested that a term may be implied in fact either on the basis of the business efficacy test or on the officious bystander test.[36] However, in *BP Refinery (Westernport) Pty Ltd*

---

32 [1976] 1 WLR 1187.

33 *Brown v Norton* [1954] IR 34.

34 [1980] IR 400. This case did turn on the fact that the Local Authority was under a specific obligation from the Housing Act 1966.

35 Unrep, Supreme Court, 17 July 1985. See also *Burke v Corporation of Dublin* [1991] IR 341.

36 [1992] 2 Lloyds' Rep 620.

v Shire of Hastings Ltd they were regarded as cumulative.[37] Sometimes both tests are applied to produce the same result.

When looking for the parties' intentions, one party's lack of knowledge of the subject matter of the proposed implied term may be relevant as to whether a term should be implied.[38] Another relevant factor is whether, at the time of contracting, both parties would have agreed to the term which one of them is contending should be implied.[39] Controversially, in *Dakota Packaging v Wyeth Medica Ireland* the court implied a notice period into a contract despite evidence from the defendant that it would not have agreed to a notice period at the time that the contract was entered into.[40] This ruling was overturned on appeal as it was found that there was no contract in place, and it is a well established rule that a term cannot be implied without a contract.[41]

The cumulative effect of the above is that the implied term must be reasonable. However, reasonableness alone will not be sufficient to imply a term into a contract,[42]nor because it will improve the contract,[43] and nor because it will make performance easier or more convenient.[44] As stated by Lord Edmund-Davies in *Liverpool City Council v Irwin* 'the touchstone is always necessity and not merely reasonableness'.[45] This was affirmed in *Equitable Life Assurance Society v Hyman*, in which the House of Lords held that it was necessary to imply a term into a contract to the effect that the directors were not to adopt a policy depriving certain retirement policies of the value inherent in their original purpose.[46] It was confirmed that a term would be implied in fact only if required as a matter of 'strict necessity'. In *Dear v Jackson* it was held that the implication of a term can only occur where the court is 'satisfied that it is what the contract actually means'.[47] Applying a 'sensible or reasonable commercial result' was not a proper basis for the implication of terms.

The case of *AG of Belize v Belize Telecom Ltd* concerned the articles of association of Belize Telecom and the rules within the articles about

---

37 [1977] UKPC 13.
38 *Spring v National Amalgamated Stevedores and Dockers Society* [1956] 1 WLR 585.
39 *National Bank of Greece SA v Pinios Shipping Co* [1989] 1 All ER 213.
40 Unrep, High Court, 10 October 2003.
41 [2005] 2 IR 54.
42 *Reigate v Union Manufacturing Co (Ramsbottom) Ltd* [1918] 1 KB 592.
43 *Trollope & Colls Ltd v NW Metropolitan Regional Hospital Board* [1973] 1 WLR 601.
44 *Russell v Duke of Norfolk* [1949] All ER 109.
45 [1977] AC 239, 266.
46 [2002] 1 AC 408, HL.
47 [2013] EWCA Civ 89.

the appointment of the board of directors.[48] The Privy Council held that the implication of a term (that a director appointed by virtue of a specified shareholding would vacate his office if there was no longer any holder of such shareholding) was necessary. Lord Hoffman in this case conflated the implication of a term and the construction (or interpretation) of a contract, arguing that the question for the court to answer is whether implying the term would 'spell out in express words what the instrument, read against the relevant background, would reasonably be understood to mean'. Lord Hoffman returned to this matter again in his judgment in *ICS Ltd v West Bromwich Building Society*,[49] where he said that the tests were ways that the courts have used to justify whether the proposed term spells out what the contract actually means, and that it would be dangerous to treat those tests as detached from the underlying principle which can only be achieved by examining the contract as a whole.

However, the Supreme Court in *Marks & Spencer v BNP Paribas Securities Services Trust Company (Jersey) Ltd* effectively reinstated the distinction between interpretation and implication and reiterated that it is the business efficacy and officious bystander tests that govern implication.[50] The current position would therefore seem to be as set out by Lord Neuberger (at [21]):

> First ... the implication of a term was 'not critically dependent on proof of an actual intention of the parties' when negotiating the contract ... but with that of notional reasonable people in the position of the parties at the time at which they were contracting. Secondly, a term should not be implied into a detailed commercial contract merely because it appears fair or merely because one considers that the parties would have agreed to it if it had been suggested to them. Those are necessary but not sufficient grounds for including a term. Thirdly... reasonableness and equitableness, will usually, if ever, add anything: if a term satisfies the other requirements, it is hard to think that it would not be reasonable and equitable. Fourthly, ... business necessity and obviousness ... can be alternatives in the sense that only one of them needs to be satisfied, although I suspect that in practice it would be a rare case where only one of those two requirements would be satisfied. Fifthly, if one approaches the issue by reference to the officious bystander, it is 'vital to formulate the question to be posed by [him] with the utmost care'. Sixthly, necessity for business efficacy involves a value judgment ... the test is not one of 'absolute necessity' ... but [rather] that a term can only be

---

48 [2009] UKPC 10.

49 [1998] 1 WLR 896.

50 [2015] UKSC 72. See also Joanna McCunn, 'Belize It or Not: Implied Contract Terms in Marks and Spencer v BNP Paribas' (2016) 79(6) Modern Law Review 1090; Richard Hooley, 'Implied Terms after Belize Telecom' (2014) 73(2) Cambridge Law Journal 607.

implied if, without the term, the contract would lack commercial or practical coherence.

7.3.2 Terms Implied by Custom

For a term to be implied by custom, it is only where the term is customary to a particular trade or profession that it can be implied into the contract.[51] It is not easy to establish such a custom, and it was held in *Cunliffe-Owen v Teather and Greenwood* that it needed to be 'certain, in the sense that the practise is clearly established, it must be notorious, in the sense that it is so well known in the market in which it is alleged to exist, that those who conduct business in the market contract with the usage as an implied term, and it must be reasonable'.[52]

This means that there are a number of elements that a claimant must prove to show that the term should be implied by custom:

- *Certainty.* The course of conduct which is alleged to form a custom in a particular industry must be identifiable and uniform, and it is this which proves certainty. It does not, however, require that all members of that trade adhere to the custom, and in *Sagar v H Ridenhalgh & Sons Ltd* 85% of Lancashire weaving mills adhering to a particular custom was sufficient to maintain it.[53] In *Gallagher v Clydesdale Shipowners* Co the court found that the essential issues to be established is whether the practice can be shown to exist in the trade or locality and that the parties relied upon it.[54] If these two elements are satisfied, then the term will be implied unless it has been excluded by an express term.
- *Notoriety.* It is not necessary for a custom to be notorious that everyone knows about it. It was held in *Strathlorne SS Co Ltd v Hugh Baird & Sons Ltd* that it must be well known in the market to which it applies and ascertainable to any person entering into a relevant contract.[55] In *O'Reilly v Irish Press* this element of notoriety must be present.[56] In this case it was unsuccessfully argued that there was a custom which entitled newspaper sub editors to a period of six months notice.[57]
- *Recognised as legally binding.* It must further be shown that the certain and notorious custom is intended to have a legally binding effect. In this sense, it must be distinguished from any course of conduct that is followed as a matter of

---

51 See Robert Clarke, 'Incorporation of Terms – Important Irish Developments' (2015) 22(11) Commercial Law Practitioner 272.

52 [1967] 1 WLR 1421, 1438.

53 [1931] 1 Ch 310.

54 [1908] 2 IR 482.

55 [1916] HL 134.

56 (1937) ILTR 194.

57 See also *Carroll v Dublin Bus* [2005] IEHC 278.

commercial convenience. The easiest way to show this, as per *Cunningham v Fonblanque*, is to demonstrate that the custom has been previously enforced.[58] In *O'Connail v The Gaelic Echo (1954) Ltd* a journalist was able to recover holiday pay on proving that others in the industry had also received this.[59]

- *Reasonableness*. The court in *Produce Brokers Co Ltd v Olympia Oil and Cake Co Ltd* defined reasonableness in this context to be 'fair and proper such as reasonable, honest and fair minded men would adopt'.[60]

7.3.3 Terms Implied by Statute

These statutorily implied terms are based on rules of law. There are multiple areas where legislation will imply terms into contracts, such as employment contracts and rental agreements, but one of the most important statutes which implies terms is the Consumer Rights Act 2022.[61] The scope of this legislation is considered in much more detail in chapter 9.

There are practical reasons for the implication of these terms into a contract. Imagine you are purchasing a toaster from your local appliance store. You will not expect a lengthy contract which sets out that the store has the legal right to sell you the item, that it looks like the display and the picture on the box, that it actually works and is fit for toasting bread etc. It would be excessive to expect every sale such as this to come with these lengthy terms and they are as such unnecessary. The relevant provisions of the legislation are implied into every contract of this nature.

Briefly, the 2022 Act provides that every consumer has the right to terminate a sales contract where the seller has no right to sell;[62] that the goods are in conformity with the sales contract;[63] that the goods are free from any charges;[64] that the goods meet the description and functionality of the contract and that they are fit for purpose;[65] that the goods apply to all standards set down by EU or other law;[66] and that the goods will be installed correctly either when installed by the

58 (1833) 6 C&P 44.
59 (1958) 92 ILTR 156.
60 [1916] 2 KB 296, 298.
61 This legislation overhauls and improves upon the previous legislation of the Sale of Goods Act 1893 and the Sale of Goods and Supply of Services Act 1980.
62 s 14.
63 s 15.
64 s 16.
65 s 17.
66 s 18.

trader or by the customer when following the traders instructions.[67] Under s 39, a trader who attempts to exclude any of these implied terms commits an offence. Further, the Act under s 82 implies further terms into contracts for services which are that the service will be supplied in accordance with the contract either at the time agreed between the parties or within a reasonable time frame; that the service will meet the subjective standards of the contract and that the objective requirements of the contract will be met.

7.3.4 Terms Implied by the Constitution

One key difference between implied terms in the English and Irish contexts is that the Constitution of Ireland of 1937 provides additional implied terms which are absent in English law. For example, Article 40.6 has been determined by the courts to include not only the right to form and join associations and unions, but an implied right to disassociate, or not to join such groups.[68] One of the leading cases in this area is that of *Meskell v CIE*.[69] In this case Meskell, a bus conductor employed by the defendant, was offered a new contract of employment which would make it compulsory for him to join a trade union. Should he refuse to do this, his employment would be terminated. Meskell refused, and following his termination he sued arguing that the condition in the employment contract breached his constitutional right to disassociate. It was held that despite such dismissal being permitted by common law, the constitution and any implied rights thereunder would take priority and that the use of the common law right to impede an individual from exercising a constitutional right 'must necessarily be regarded as an abuse of the common law'.[70]

Further, Article 40.3 has been held to include fair procedure rights which extends to allowing a party to be heard where he is accused of breach of contract. This is illustrated in the case of *Glover v BLN* where an employee was dismissed for misconduct.[71] The contract of employment provided that an employee could be dismissed without notice and without compensation for serious misconduct. However, it was held that:

> This procedure was a breach of the implied term of the contract that the procedure should be fair, as it cannot be disputed, in the light of so much authority on the point, that failure to allow a person to meet the charges against him and afford him adequate

---

67 s 19.
68 *Education Co of Ireland Ltd v Fitzpatrick (No 2)* [1961] IR 345.
69 [1973] IR 121.
70 Ibid [135].
71 [1973] IR 388.

> opportunity of answering them is a violation of an obligation to proceed fairly.[72]

The Supreme Court reiterated this position in *Gunn v An Bord Naisiunta Ealaine is Deartha* where it confirmed that dismissal must comply with the principles of natural and constitutional justice.[73]

Any investigation that takes place into alleged misconduct must take place as soon as possible[74] and conducted in a fair manner. This was held not to have occurred in *McAuley v Commissioner of An Garda Siochana* as the plaintiff had not been provided with the evidence against him.[75] It is clear that the process does not need to be uniform and identical in all circumstances, what is key is that in the circumstances, the procedure was fair and in compliance with constitutional justice.[76] This extends to a right to be heard by an impartial tribunal, where the tribunal can be shown to be biased this will offend the fair procedures implied by the Constitution.[77]

As with many rights under the constitution, these are not absolute. Where the parties are of equal bargaining power, they can agree to waive their rights.

7.4 Classification of Terms

Once a statement has been determined as a term of the contract, whether this is an express or an implied term, the next step is to classify that term. A term may classified in three ways: as a condition, a warranty or an innominate term. The importance in this classification comes when there is a breach of the term as different remedies are available to the wronged party.

Conditions are important terms which are said 'to go to the root of the contract'. If a condition is broken, the injured party is entitled to treat the contract as at an end, ie as repudiated, as well as claiming damages. Warranties are less important terms. If a warranty is breached, the injured party can only sue for damages, ie there is no right to treat the contract as at an end.

---

72 ibid [425].

73 [1990] 2 IR 168.

74 *Flynn v An Post* [1987] IR 68.

75 Unrep, Supreme Court, 15 February 1996.

76 See *Higgins v Bank of Ireland* [2013] IEHC 6.

77 *National Engineering & Electrical Trade Union v McConnell* [1983] ILRM 422. However, a person cannot use these provisions as a shield to prevent an employer from investigating allegations of misconduct: see *Maher v Irish Permanent Plc*, Unrep, High Court, 7 October 1997.

For example, if I am going to buy a car from a garage and we incorporate an additional two terms into the contract. One is that there are new tyres put on the car as the existing tyres do not meet the legal requirements, and the other is that the car will be valeted prior to collection. The term requiring the new tyres would be a condition, this is a term that is integral to the contract as without them it would not be legal to drive this car home. The second term is a warranty. It would be nice that the car is clean when I come to collect it, but it does not go to the root of the contract. If when I arrive to collect the car, there are no new tyres I will be entitled to treat the contract as repudiated. In other words, I can choose to treat the contract as at an end and not continue with it. I may also be able to sue for monetary compensation in addition to this. However, if when I arrive the tyres are there, but the car has not been valeted, I cannot treat the contract as repudiated as it is a minor breach. I may be able to obtain monetary compensation for breach of this term, but it will not be sufficient to end the contract.

The distinction between a condition and a warranty is demonstrated by contrasting the following two cases. In *Poussard v Spiers & Pond* a singer was under a contractual obligation to perform during the entire run of an operetta.[78] She did not arrive until after one week of the run, when a substitute had been taken on. It was held that the obligation to perform as from the first night was a condition, and the breach of it entitled the producers to dispense with her services (repudiate the contract). Whereas in *Bettini v Gye* a singer was under a contractual obligation to sing in a series of concerts and take part in six days of rehearsals before the first performance, but she was three days late.[79] The court held that the undertaking to take part in the rehearsals was a warranty and not a condition. The singer's breach did not allow the contract to be repudiated, but only entitled the other party to damages.

The Consumer Rights Act 2022 removes the distinction between conditions and warranties in relation to consumer contracts and determines that the remedy will be assessed on the specific facts and circumstances of the case. However, the distinction is still relevant in relation to commercial contracts.

7.4.1 Conditions

A condition is defined in *Anson's Law of Contract* as a promise as to a fact or as to future conduct which forms an essential part of the

78 (1876) 1 QBD 410.
79 (1876) 1 QBD 183.

contract.[80] If the fact is untrue, or the promise never comes to fruition, then the wronged party can treat this as a repudiatory breach and be discharged from the contract in addition to obtaining damages.[81] In *Behn v Burness* a ship was stated to be in the port of Amsterdam in a charter contract when it was not.[82] This untrue fact was sufficient to have the contract repudiated as it was an essential element to the contract.

In *Glaholm v Hays* a charterparty (a contract to hire a ship) provided that a vessel was to 'sail from England on or before the 4th day of February next' to Trieste to load cargo.[83] The vessel did not set sail for some days after 4 February, and when it arrived at Trieste the charterers refused to load the cargo. The court found that they were entitled to treat the contract as repudiated as the term was so vital to the contract.

However, even in circumstances where the parties have themselves identified the term as a condition, the courts will look at the seriousness of the breach. In *Schuler AG v Wickman Machine Tool Sales*, a term expressly stated to be 'a condition of this agreement' provided for weekly visits over a four-and-a-half year period to six named firms (1,400 visits).[84] The House of Lords did not believe that a single breach, eg the failure to make one visit, should entitle the other party to bring the contract to an end. This demonstrates that even where the parties have described a term as a condition, the court may hold that the parties could not have intended the term to have this effect.

This approach was applied more recently in *Kudos Catering (UK) Ltd v Manchester Central Convention Complex Ltd* where the English Court of Appeal concluded that a clause in a catering services agreement (buried in a section dealing with insurance/indemnities), and which purported to exclude liability for all direct loss (profits) and all indirect or consequential loss, did not reflect the parties' commercial intentions, since it could potentially result in there being no sanction for refusal to perform.[85] The Court therefore restricted the clause to defective performance, rather than refusal to perform, and justified this on the basis of where the clause was positioned in the agreement.

In commercial contracts (particularly mercantile contracts), time

---

80 (31st ed, OUP 2020) 140. William Bojczuk, 'When is a Condition not a Condition?' (1987) Journal of Business Law 353.

81 J W Carter, 'Breach of Condition and Express Termination Right: A Distinction with a Difference' (2017) 133 Law Quarterly Review 395.

82 (1862) 1 B&S 877.

83 (1841) 2 M&G 257.

84 [1974] AC 235.

85 [2013] EWCA Civ 38.

clauses are often treated as conditions, so that any breach entitles the other party to treat the contract as repudiated. *The Mihalis Angelos* concerned a charterparty which stated that the vessel was 'expected ready to load' on 1 July 1965.[86] The phrase 'expected ready to load' was held to be a condition, breach of which entitled the charterers to treat the contract as repudiated.

7.4.2 Warranties

A warranty has been defined in *Dawsons Ltd v Bonnin* as 'an agreement which refers to the subject matter of the contract, but not being an essential part of the contract either intrinsically or by agreement, is collateral to the main purpose of such a contract'[87]. Breach of a warranty entitles the wronged party to damages but not to have the contract discharged. As seen in *Bettini v Gye* (see 7.4 above), the failure of the singer to take part in rehearsals was seen as a warranty and not a condition and could be adequately compensated with damages. Had she not arrived for the performance itself, then the court would quite likely have come to a different conclusion.

7.4.3 Innominate Terms

The approach of the courts for decades was to follow the classification of terms into either conditions or warranties depending on whether or not they were judged as going to the root of the contract – of essential or collateral importance. There is some benefit to this in providing certainty, but it was not always clear into which of the categories the term would fall until after a breach. The new classification of 'innominate term' was introduced in the case of *Hong Kong Fir Shipping Co Ltd v Kawasaki Kisen Kaisha Ltd* where clause 1 of a contract for the charter of a vessel for a period of two years described the vessel as 'being in every way fitted for ordinary cargo service'.[88] However, the ship broke down on a number of occasions, and her engines were old. The question in the case was whether breach of the clause entitled the charterers to repudiate the contract or only entitled them to damages. The Court of Appeal found that the promise of 'seaworthiness' was not a condition but an innominate term, and breach of such a term would only allow discharge of the contract if the conduct of the parties and the consequences of the breach were so serious as to warrant it. This is a more flexible approach which is grounded not merely on the importance of the term, but also on the consequences of the breach of it.

[86] [1971] 1 QB 164.
[87] [1922] 2 AC 413, 422.
[88] [1962] 2 QB 26.

Lord Diplock explained the reasoning as follows:

> There are however many contractual undertakings of a more complex character which cannot be categorised as being conditions or warranties. Of such undertakings all that can be predicated is that some breaches will and others will not give rise to an event which will deprive the party not in default of substantially the whole benefit which it was intended he should obtain from the contract; and the legal consequences of a breach of such undertaking, unless provided for expressly in the contract, depend upon the nature of the event to which the breach gives rise and do not follow automatically from a prior classification of the undertaking as a condition or a warranty.

Whether a term is innominate involves the court effectively making a judgment call as to the 'commercial significance of the term in question'.[89] Where a term can be breached in a number of different ways, the court will look to the effects of the breach to determine the remedy. This was explained by Upjohn LJ in *Hong Kong Fir Shipping Case* (at 62):

> Why is this apparently basic and underlying condition of seaworthiness not, in fact, treated as a condition? It is for the simple reason that the seaworthiness clause is breached by the slightest failure to be fitted 'in every way' for service. If a nail is missing from one of the timbers of a wooden vessel or if proper medical supplies or two anchors are not on board at the time of sailing, the owners are in breach of the seaworthiness stipulation. It is contrary to common sense to suppose that in such circumstances the parties contemplated that the charterer should at once be entitled to treat the contract as at an end for such trifling breaches.

This more flexible approach has increased the level of uncertainty, and in modern contract law it is more likely that the starting point for a court will be to hold that a contract term is innominate, rather than a condition. This allows the court to take a more holistic approach, rather than just merely examining whether the term was one of high importance – it looks at the contract as a whole, the conduct of the parties and the effect of the breach.

The flexible approach adopted in *Hong Kong Fir* has found some judicial support in Ireland with Clarke J adopting the test in the High Court case of *Parol Ltd v Carroll Village (Retail) Management Services Ltd*.[90]

---

89 *State Trading Corp of India Ltd v M Golodetz Ltd* [1989] 2 Lloyd's Rep 277, 283.

90 [2010] IEHC 498. See also *Irish Telephone Rentals Ltd v Irish Civil Service Building Society Ltd* [1991] ILRM 880. See James C Fisher, 'Uncertainty, Opportunity and the Intermediate Term: The Hong Kong Fir Principle in English and Irish Contract Law' (2015) 14 Hibernian Law Journal 96.

7.5 Interpretation of Terms

Historically, terms would be interpreted literally, in accordance with their plain meaning and without any reference to any extrinsic evidence of the background[91] or consideration of the term in the wider context of the contract as a whole.

The modern approach, known as the contextual approach to interpretation, was articulated by Lord Hoffman in *Investors Compensation Scheme Ltd v West Bromwich Building Society*,[92] building on Lord Diplock's dicta in *Reardon Smith Line Ltd v Yngvnar Hansen-Tangen*: 'interpretation is the ascertainment of the meaning which the document would convey to a reasonable person having all the background which would reasonably have been available to the parties in the situation in which they were at the time of the contract'.[93] Further, that background includes 'absolutely anything which would have affected the way in which the language of the document would have been understood by a reasonable man' and that the literal meaning of words may be disregarded where the background makes clear that the parties used the 'wrong words or syntax' so that the courts do not impose upon the parties 'an intention which they plainly could not have had'.

In this case, a number of investors had been given some negligent advice and made claims in tort against their financial advisers, the building societies and solicitors. A central scheme was established (the ICS) to ensure that compensation was paid to those investors. In order to be entitled to compensation, the investors were required to sign a contract which assigned to ICS their claims against the advisers, building societies and solicitors with the one express exclusion of 'any claim (whether sounding in rescission for undue influence or otherwise)' against a building society which would abate sums otherwise owed to that society. The question raised by the plaintiff scheme in this case was whether that express exclusion meant that the investors had retained their right to claim in this regard against the building societies.

The House of Lords interpreted this clause to mean that 'any claim sounding in rescission (whether for undue influence or otherwise)' was retained by the investors. This construction meant that only claims for rescission (the remedy of rescission is considered in more detail

---

91 Goh Yihan, 'A Wrong Turn in History: Re Understanding the Exclusionary Rule Against Prior Negotiations in Contract Interpretation' (2014) 5 Journal of Business Law 360.

92 [1998] 1 WLR 896.

93 [1976] 1 WLR 989.

in Chapter 20 of this book) and not damages were excluded from the agreement.

Despite the fact that Lord Hoffman was clearly advocating for a wider approach to interpreting the contract, he expressly excluded the previous negotiations between the parties from the admissible background information. This exclusion was upheld by the House of Lords in *Chartbrook Ltd v Persimmon Homes Ltd* where a dispute arose as to how much was owed by the developer to the landowner.[94] The key phrase in the contract that was at issue was 'additional residential payment', and the developer argued that on proper construction of the contract it owed £897,051, while the landowner argued that it was owed £4,484,862. The landowner succeeded in the lower courts, but this was overturned with the House of Lords stating that this was a case where the background showed that something must have gone wrong with the language used.

While finding for the developer, the House of Lords rejected its argument to refer to pre-contract negotiations. While confirming that allowing this would not in itself contradict the contextual approach to interpretation, pre-contract negotiations themselves are usually irrelevant, and even if they were relevant, allowing them in evidence would create further uncertainty and add to the costs of litigation.

While all contractual terms are now subject to the contextual approach as set out by Lord Hoffman in English Law, there are a number of principles which are helpful (although must be read in light of the contextual approach):

(1) Words which may potentially have two meanings are given the meaning which will make the agreement valid rather than void.
(2) The document ought to be read as a whole, and the meaning of words or phrases are to be interpreted in light of the context in which they are used.
(3) Greater weight should be given to terms which parties have expressly agreed to, rather than generic or standard clauses.
(4) Where there is express mention of a particular 'thing' in a contract, this will naturally exclude all other 'things' of a similar nature.
(5) The words of a written document will be interpreted more harshly against the person who is seeking to enforce the agreement as there will be a presumption that this party looked after their own interests in its drafting.

The ICS judgment was approved of and applied by the Irish Supreme

---

[94] [2009] UKHL 38.

Court in the case of *Analog Devices BV v Zurich Insurance Co.*[95] However, they appeared to roll back a little on this position in *Marlon Homes v Walsh* where it was held that the starting point of interpreting contracts is to assume that sophisticated parties who have negotiated formal documents do not easily make mistakes, and therefore words should be given their ordinary and natural meaning.[96] In other words, 'context is apt to rewrite the contract'.[97]

The Supreme Court has had further opportunity to examine the position of ICS in *Law Society v MIBI.*[98] This case involved a motor insurance company called Setanta who went insolvent leaving motorists unable to obtain an indemnity. The dispute arose around who should be liable to cover the indemnity of these motorists, the MIBI or the Insurance Compensation Fund. The case in the lower courts turned on the interpretation of an Agreement made between the parties which only limited the MIBI's liability to uninsured and untraceable drivers. Therefore, the MIBI was liable to cover the loss. In the Supreme Court, O'Donnell J found that while the plain and ordinary meaning of words should be given considerable weight, it had no priority over the context of the agreement. He went on to state that plain appearances always depend on perspective or context. When interpreting the meaning:

> The Court must consider not just the words used, but also the specific context, the broader context, the background law, any prior agreements, the other terms of this agreement, other provisions drafted at the same time and forming part of the same transaction, and what might be described as the logic, commercial or otherwise of the agreement. [99]

On the facts of the case, it was held that the clause would make MIBI a 'blanket guarantor' and taking account of the commercial background allowed the appeal. While the decision was not unanimous, with a strong dissent from Clarke J, it appears that the contextual approach is steadfast within Irish law.

The Court of Appeal more recently addressed the issues of interpretation in the case of *Point Village Ltd v Dunnes Stores* where the entire case was centred on the proper construction of a single sentence in a written agreement.[100] The contentious issue was contained in clause

95 [2002] IESC 1.
96 [2009] IEHC 576.
97 Ronan R Condon, 'After Law Society v MIBI: Contextualism and Contracting in Irish Contract Law' (2019) 62 Irish Jurist 51, 58.
98 [2017] IESC 31.
99 ibid [12].
100 [2022] IECA 39.

1.38 of the Development Agreement which defines 'Fit Out Works' as 'such fitting out or other works as Dunnes may require to carry out in connection with the intended use and enjoyment of the store'. Dunnes argued that this clause meant that it has discretion as to when, if at all, it would carry out the fit out works. It argued that if it was a full obligation, then the word 'must' or 'shall' would be used rather than the word 'may'. Further, it argued that their interpretation is consistent with the fact that there is no 'keep open' clause in the agreement which would mean that they could close the store after one day with no breach of the agreement, but would have substantial fit out costs. However, the High Court, with whom the Court of Appeal agreed, found that the interpretation proffered by Dunnes was untenable and would defy common sense and logic as it was

> 'inconceivable that a commercial entity such as [Point Village] would have entered into an arrangement giving such discretion to Dunnes. The idea that two commercial entities would enter into an agreement which had the effect for which Dunnes contends is beyond belief and utterly implausible'.

The Court of Appeal further stated that it could not construe this one clause outside of the context of the rest of the agreement.

Similar issues have faced the court's scrutiny in light of the Covid 19 pandemic. For example, in *Hyper Trust Ltd (T/A The Leopardstown Inn) v FBD Insurance* the court was required to interpret the term 'closure' in an insurance policy to determine whether or not government mandated closures of public houses during the pandemic were covered by the insurer.[101] This was a test case taken by four publicans, but directly impacts over 1000 who had taken out insurance policies with the defendant. Specifically, FBD argued that it was not required to indemnify the companies as the government closure did not result from an outbreak on the premises or within a 25 mile radius. The court concluded that once the publicans can establish that the closure following outbreaks within a 25 mile radius was a proximate cause then their recovery under the policy will not be reduced regardless of whether or not there are additional proximate causes such as changes in societal behaviour. This was a significant case and resulted in the Central Bank warning that it will not hesitate to take action against insurers who refuse claims despite meeting the causation element set down by the court.

101 [2021] IEHC 279.

Test Your Knowledge

Donna is selling her tools on a local website. Phoebe contacts her and asks her specific questions about some of the tools, including whether the jack hammer is suitable for breaking up concrete in the garden. Donna says that she believes that it is, but she no longer has the manual. She suggests that Phoebe check to see if there is an online manual before she buys it. In addition, Donna has advertised one specific drill with the caption 'cobalt drill bits included – suitable for drilling on any type of surface'. Heather contacts her about this and asks whether they can be used to drill through glass to which Donna replies yes. Both Phoebe and Heather purchase the respective tools. Phoebe attempts to use the jack hammer in the garden and it immediately breaks. Heather uses the drill on her glass door which shatters. Neither of the tools were suitable for the jobs. Is Donna:

A liable to both Heather and Phoebe?
B liable to neither Heather nor Phoebe?
C liable to Phoebe but not Heather?
D liable to Heather but not Phoebe?

The correct answer here is D. Although both had asked Donna for further information, it is clear that the statement to Phoebe was not intended to be relied upon. She specifically suggests that Phoebe look up the online manual to make sure that it was the tool she required prior to purchasing. Therefore, the fact that the jack hammer is unsuitable for breaking up concrete in the garden cannot be seen as a term of the contract. In contrast, combined with the advertisement details and the simple 'yes' in response to Heather's question, it is much more likely that the use of the drill on glass will be held to be a term of the contract. It is likely that Donna will be held liable in damages (under an innominate term) for a refund of the purchase price and also for the damage caused to Heather's glass door.

Stretch and Challenge Question

Consider whether Lord Hoffman's contextual approach to contract interpretation creates too much uncertainty.

Chapter 8

EXCLUSION CLAUSES

8.1 Introduction

Exemption clauses are terms which attempt to exclude or limit a party's liability under the contract in certain circumstances. They can play a useful role in allocating the risks between the parties. Exemption clauses are usually found in standard form contracts. These are contracts frequently used in business which enable the same (ie standard) forms to be used for all customers. It enables the imposition of terms on the other party to the contract, especially if that other party is not in a strong bargaining position. Essentially there is a three-step test to determine whether the clause may be relied upon: Has it been incorporated into the contract? Is it worded in a manner sufficient to cover the breach? Is there any legislative provision that would render the clause invalid?

8.2 Incorporation

The effect of many exemption clauses is severely limited by statute, but regardless of any statutory provisions, the person seeking to rely on the exemption clause must show that it has been validly incorporated into the contract. There are a number of ways in which this may be demonstrated.[1]

8.2.1 Signature

If the contract is written and contains an exemption clause which has then been signed by the party, there can be little doubt that it has been validly incorporated into the contract. Thus, as illustrated in *L'Estrange v Graucob Ltd*, in the absence of fraud, mistake, misrepresentation or

1 RW Clarke, 'Exemption Clauses and Incorporation: Calling a Spade a Spade' (1979) Northern Ireland Legal Quarterly 39.

duress, a party will be bound to all of the terms contained within a written contract, and a lack of awareness of their presence is irrelevant.[2] In this case L'Estrange bought a cigarette vending machine from the defendant. She signed a printed contract of sale which contained an exemption clause in very small print on poor quality paper. It was held that as she had signed the contract, she was bound by its terms. It was irrelevant that she had not read it.

Where there has been misrepresentation as to the effect of the exemption clause, this may result in it being unenforceable. In *Curtis v Chemical Cleaning and Dyeing Co Ltd* the plaintiff was told that the clause excluded liability for damage to beads and sequins; however, it actually excluded all liability 'for any damage howsoever arising'.[3] Here the company could not rely on the wider clause as the contents of it had been misrepresented to the plaintiff.

In Ireland, the signature rule also still holds, however two cases have taken a more reasoned approach looking at the circumstances in which the contract was signed. In *Regan v The Irish Automobile Club Ltd* it was established that the plaintiff was aware that he was signing a document that was limiting his rights[4] and in *O'Connor v First National Building Society* an exemption clause excluding liability of the defendant should a property be defective was held to be valid where it was prominently displayed above the signature line.[5]

8.2.2 Notice

Where the contract is one that is not written, an exemption clause can still be validly incorporated into the contract where reasonable notice of the term has been given. There are a number of factors that are considered in determining whether or not the notice has been reasonable.

8.2.2.1 Timing of the Notice

If a term is to be binding, then it must be brought to the attention of the party either before or at the time that the contract is being entered into. If the term is only notified to that party after the contract has been concluded, it will not have been validly incorporated and will have no effect. This principle is illustrated in the case of *Olley v Marlborough*

---

2 [1934] 2 KB 394.
3 [1951] 1 KB 805.
4 [1990] 1 IR 278.
5 [1991] ILRM 208. See also Robert Clarke, 'When Rules Collide: The Interfoto Principle and the Signature Rule' (2023) 30(11) Commercial Law Practitioner 191.

Court Ltd where the plaintiff checked in and paid in advance for one week's stay at the defendant hotel.[6] When they went to their hotel room, there was a notice on the back of the door which read 'the proprietors will not hold themselves responsible for articles lost or stolen, unless handed to the manageress for safe custody'. Some of Olley's property was stolen from the hotel room and the hotel sought to rely on the clause. The Court of Appeal found that there was no legal effect to the notice as the plaintiff could not have been aware of this term prior to completing the contract. Here the contract was completed at the reception desk on check in, and a subsequent addition of a term could then not be included. Had the notice been placed at the reception desk it is likely that the outcome would have been different, but as this was not the case, the hotel was liable for the property stolen.

This matter was further considered in *Thornton v Shoe Lane Parking Ltd*.[7] In this case Thornton drove his car to a car park which had a notice outside stating the parking prices and that cars were parked at their owner's risk. At the barrier upon entry, Thornton received a ticket which in small print said that it was issued subject to conditions displayed on the premises. The notice inside the car park was that the owners would not accept liability for any injury that occurred on their premises. Thornton was injured and sought damages from Shoe Lane Parking, which sought to rely on the exclusion clause. It was held that this clause did not form part of the contract as the owner of the car park did not do enough to bring the clause to the attention of customers. In this case, the contract was concluded when Thornton drove into the car park, and the notice inside the car park was therefore unincorporated as it was not brought to his attention prior to or at the time of entering into the contract. In contrast, the Irish courts came to a different conclusion in a case with similar facts. In *Brady v Aer Rianta* the conditions were printed on a ticket and displayed outside the entrance to the car park.[8] It was held that the contract was concluded prior to the entrance and that the plaintiff had been given reasonable notice of the terms.

In *Noreside Construction Ltd v Irish Asphalt Ltd* the Supreme Court confirmed that additional terms contained within a delivery docket could not alter the central contract as it comes too late in time.[9] This ruling affirms and clarifies the position from two earlier cases *Knox v Great Northern Railway*[10] and *Slattery v CIE*[11] where the exemption

---

6 [1949] 1 KB 532.
7 [1971] 2 QB 163.
8 Unrep, High Court, 1974.
9 [2014] IESC 68.
10 [1886] 2 IR 632.
11 (1972) ILTR 71.

clause contained within the delivery documents were held to be valid as it was established that the plaintiff in both cases was aware that the contract had not yet been concluded. Thus, where there is a completed agreement, the court will not allow a delivery document or note to alter the previously concluded contract, however, where there is no complete agreement between the parties, the additional terms may be validly incorporated.

8.2.2.2 Sufficient Notice

This area examines the circumstances in which a person receiving a ticket, receipt or notice will be bound by the conditions that are contained therein. *Parker v SE Railway* set down three general rules as to when a person will be bound:

> (a) A person receiving a ticket who did not see or know that there was any writing on the ticket will not be bound by the conditions.
> (b) A person who knew that there was writing on the ticket, and knew or believed that the writing contained conditions, will be bound by the conditions.
> (c) A person who knew that there was writing on the ticket, but did not know or believe that the writing contained conditions, will nevertheless be bound where the delivery of the ticket, in such a manner that the writing on it could be seen, is reasonable notice that the writing contained conditions.[12]

It is the third of these conditions that has generated the most case law and effectively means that a person will be bound by an exemption clause, even if ignorant of it, where the party seeking to rely on it has done what is reasonable to bring it to the other party's attention. In *Parker*, the plaintiff had left a bag in the station's cloakroom. He was issued with a ticket. On the front of the ticket, it said 'see back', and the back contained a number of clauses including one which excluded liability for any bag with a value higher than £10. Parker's bag was lost and he claimed £24. He stated that he knew the ticket contained clauses but had not read them and therefore could not be bound. The Court of Appeal, in overturning the lower court's decision, held that the real question to be asked was whether reasonably sufficient notice had been given of the condition.

A very liberal, and somewhat unfair approach to incorporation was taken in *Thompson v LM&S Railway Co.*[13] Thompson, who was unable to read, travelled on a train. The ticket stated that it was issued subject to

---

12 (1877) 2 CPD 416, 421.
13 [1903] 1 KB 41.

the terms outlined in the company's timetable, one of which excluded liability for injury howsoever caused. Thompson was injured as a result of the company's negligence and sought to claim damages. It was held that the company had taken sufficient steps to bring the terms to her intention, and accepting the ticket for travel was acceptance of the terms, regardless of the fact that she could not read. This case shows that the test is an objective one and does not take into account any disability. The exception to this can be seen from the case of *Geier v Kujawa, Weston and Warne Bros (Transport) Ltd*.[14] Here the claimant was a passenger in the taxi and could not speak English, a fact which was known to the defendant. The defendant pointed out the exclusion clause inside the taxi and did so in English without translating. The claimant was then injured as a result of the defendant's negligent driving and sought to claim damages, while the defendant sought to rely on the exclusion clause. The court found that while normally this would be sufficient to incorporate the clause, the fact that the driver was aware that the claimant did not speak English meant that reasonable steps had not been taken to bring it to their attention.

Another consideration as to whether there was reasonably sufficient notice given of the clause is whether or not the clause was contained in a contractual document. In other words, would the person receiving this ticket or receipt reasonably expect it to contain terms? This was considered by the court in *Chapleton v Barry UDC*.[15] Here Chapleton hired two deck chairs from the defendant. He paid for these and received a ticket from the attendant. He took the chairs, set them up on the sand, sat on one and promptly went through the canvas seat causing injury. He sued the defendant for damages as a result, and the council sought to rely on an exclusion clause printed on the back of the ticket which stated 'the council will not be held liable for any accident or damage arising from the hire of the chair'. Chapleton acknowledged that he had glanced at the ticket but did not realise that it contained any terms. The court held that the defendant could not rely on this clause as it was not a 'contractual' document, and no reasonable person would expect to find terms on such a ticket.

Where the clause is one that is particularly onerous, what constitutes reasonable notice will be higher, and special measures may need to be adopted to ensure that the clause is brought to the other party's attention. In *J Spurling Ltd v Bradshaw* Lord Denning famously stated that some clauses would need to be 'printed in red ink on the face of the document with a red hand pointing to it before the notice could

14 [1970] 1 Lloyd's Rep 364.
15 [1940] 1 KB 532.

be held to be sufficient'.[16] Although not an exemption clause, the court examined the notice required for onerous clauses in *Interfoto Picture Library Ltd v Stiletto Visual Programmes Ltd*.[17] In this case Interfoto hired 47 photographic transparencies to Stiletto. On the delivery note was a clause which stated that they must be returned within 14 days, or a daily fee of £5 per transparency plus VAT would be charged. Stiletto returned the transparencies four weeks later and was met with a bill of £3,783.50. It was held that his particular clause had not been incorporated into the contract. Bingham LJ said that Stiletto would not be relieved of 'liability because they did not read the condition, although doubtless they did not; but in my judgment they are to be relieved because [Interfoto] did not do what was necessary to draw this unreasonable and extortionate clause fairly to their attention'.

The Irish Courts have not laid down precise standards which must be met. In *Early v Great Southern Railway* a passenger was injured during a train journey.[18] Text on the ticket referred the customer to the company's conditions which limited their liability. Notwithstanding the fact that these conditions were not available to view at the booking office, it was held that the company could rely on them. Similarly in *Shea v Great Southern Railway* the plaintiff's ticket referred to a notice excluding liability for theft.[19] The company was able to rely on this clause when the plaintiff's bicycle was stolen as the court determined that he was 'at liberty to get off the bus or remove his bicycle'.

8.2.2.3 Course of Dealing

When the parties have dealt with each other on a regular basis on standard terms, even if notice of the term was not given on the particular occasion, the term may be incorporated into the contract on the basis of the previous course of dealing. In *Spurling v Bradshaw* an exclusion clause was contained in a document which was received by the defendant after the contract.[20] It was held, however, that the exclusion clause was part of the contract because the defendant had received many of these documents before – the clause was part of the contract by a course of conduct. Further, in *Hardwick Game Farm v Suffolk Agricultural Poultry Producers Association* a farmer ordered feed three or four times per month for three years. This came with a note which had an exclusion clause on the back.[21] On one occasion, the feed was poisonous and the farmer suffered substantial loss. It was held

16 [1956] 1 WLR 461.
17 [1989] QB 433.
18 [1940] IR 414.
19 [1944] Ir Jur Rep 26.
20 [1956] 1 WLR 461.
21 [1969] 2 AC 31.

that the exclusion clause was valid as the farmer had had sufficient notice of the term. It was immaterial that the farmer had not read it.

However, there must be a consistent course of dealing, and this cannot be established if the parties have only dealt with each other on a few occasions (particularly if it is a consumer contract). In *Hollier v Rambler Motors* Hollier had used the defendant's garage to have his car repaired three or four times over the course of five years.[22] On at least two of these occasions, Hollier signed a document which included a clause stating that the garage would be excluded from liability where damage was caused by a fire on the premises. On the last occasion that Hollier took his car to the garage, he did not sign this form and the car was damaged by fire. The garage sought to rely on the exclusion clause which had been present on the previous forms, but the court held that three or four occasions in a five-year period was insufficient to establish a course of dealing and the exclusion clause was therefore not incorporated.

In *McCutcheon v David MacBrayne Ltd* the plaintiff had used a ferry service on several occasions in the past to transport his car.[23] In some instances, he had been asked to sign a note containing an exemption clause, but at other times he had not. In any event, he had not read the terms and claimed to have no knowledge of the clause. The ferry sank and on this occasion he had not signed the note. The defendant ferry service wished to rely on the course of dealing to incorporate the clause into the contract. It was held that the course of dealing could only incorporate an exclusion clause where the party had previous knowledge of the existence of such a clause.

The line of reasoning used by the English Courts has been adopted in Ireland in *Lynch Roofing Systems (Ballaghaderreen) Ltd v Christopher Bennett and Son (Construction) Ltd*.[24] In this case the parties were in dispute and the defendant sought to stay proceedings brought by the plaintiff on the grounds that they had agreed to an arbitration clause. Prior to the contract being entered into the defendant had informed the plaintiff of his intention to use a standard industry contract which contained an arbitration clause. The plaintiff argued that he was not bound by this clause as it had not been expressly explained to him prior to the commencement of the work. The court found that the standard contract terms would apply as the parties were engaged in the same business and of equal bargaining power and as such standard conditions would apply as there would be a common understanding

22 [1972] 2 QB 71.
23 [1964] 1 WLR 125.
24 [1999]2 IR 450.

of this. The reasoning here is designed to give effect to industry wide expectations that have been created through commercial practices.

8.3 Interpretation

Once it has been established that the exemption clause has been incorporated into the contract, the next step for the court is to determine how to interpret that clause.[25] There has been statutory intervention in this regard, which we examine in the next chapter, particularly in relation to consumer contracts. This section will examine the common law approach to interpretation.

8.3.1 Strict or Literal Interpretation

This approach essentially looks at the words that were used and gives them their clear and literal meaning, regardless of the intention of the parties. For example, a clause excluding liability for breach of a warranty will not exclude liability for breach of a condition. In *Wallis Son & Wells v Pratt & Haynes* Wallis bought seed from Pratt described as 'common English sainfoin'.[26] The contract contained an exclusion clause that the sellers 'give no warranty express or implied, as to growth, description, or any other matters'. The seed turned out to be giant sainfoin which is inferior in quality and of less value. Wallis was successful in his claim as there was a breach of condition (as to description) and the exclusion clause applied only to a warranty.

8.3.2 Contra Proferentem Rule

This rule states that where there is any ambiguity in the term, it will be interpreted in a manner less advantageous to the party seeking to rely on it. In *John Lee & Son (Grantham) Ltd v Railway Executive* the lease of a warehouse contained a clause which excluded liability for 'loss, damage, costs and expenses howsoever caused… (whether by act or neglect of the company or their servants or agents or not) which but for the tenancy hereby created would not have arisen'.[27] The warehouse was damaged, alongside goods stored within it by fire as a result of the alleged negligence of the lessor in allowing a spark to escape. The lessor argued that the exclusion clause exempted it from liability. In applying the *contra proferentem* rule, the court held that the words 'but for the tenancy hereby created' restricted circumstances to those which

---

25 See Mr Justice David Foxton, 'The Status of the Special Rules of Construction of Exemption Clauses in Consumer Contracts' (2021) 3 Journal of Business Law 205.

26 [1911] AC 394.

27 [1949] 2 All ER 581.

arose within the landlord and tenant relationship, and the lessor was therefore not protected by the clause.

In *Houghton v Trafalgar Insurance Co Ltd* a car insurance policy purported to exclude liability for damage if the car was conveying 'any load in excess of that for which it was constructed'.[28] An accident occurred whilst six passengers were travelling in a car which was only intended to provide seating accommodation for five. The court held that 'load' was ambiguous and construed it against the insurers to limit it to excess weight rather than excess passengers.[29]

8.3.3 Liability for Negligence

Where an exclusion clause seeks to exclude liability on the basis of negligence, the courts have taken a relatively strict approach to this, In *Gillespie v Bowles (Roy) Transport Ltd* Buckley LJ stated that it would be 'inherently improbable' that an innocent party would agree to exclude such liability.[30] The test was laid down in *Canada Steamship Lines v The King*.[31] In order to exclude liability for negligence, the clause would need to expressly extend to negligence liability, for example by using the word negligence. If there is not express reference to negligence, but the words would be wide enough to cover negligence liability, the clause will not cover negligence liability if there is some other liability to which the clause could extend.

This test has been adopted in English courts, and the House of Lords in *Caledonia Ltd v Orbit Valve Co Europe Ltd* that:

> Commercial contracts are drafted by parties with access to legal advice and in the context of established legal principles as reflected in the decisions of the court ... the parties to commercial contracts must be taken to know what those principles are and to have drafted their contract taking them into account; when the suggested result could have been easily obtained by an appropriate use of language but the parties instead used only general language, the result of the general principle is that the parties will not be taken to have intended to include the consequence of a party's negligence.[32]

However, the House of Lords subsequently opined in *HIH Casualty and General Insurance Ltd v Chase Manhattan Bank* that the *Canada*

---

28 [1954] 1 QB 247.

29 Edwin Peel, 'Contra Proferentem Revisited' (2017) 133 Law Quarterly Review 133.

30 [1973] QB 400.

31 [1952] UKPC 1.

32 [1994] 1 WLR 221, 228.

Steamship principles should not be treated as a rigid code, but rather as providing guidance.[33] Further, in *Persimmon Homes Ltd. v Ove Arup & Partners Ltd*, the Court of Appeal placed less emphasis on the *Canada Steamship* rule, noting that a party's acceptance of large risks under a contract will be reflected in the price and insurance cover and that there should be 'no need to approach [exemption] clauses with horror or with a mindset to cut them down'.[34]

8.3.4 Limitation Clauses

A limitation clause is one that limits the amount of compensation that will be payable on a breach, rather than excluding liability altogether. Interpretation of these clauses by the courts has been much more lenient.[35] In *Ailsa Craig Fishing Co Ltd v Malvern Fishing Co Ltd and Securicor (Scotland) Ltd* Securicor contracted to provide security cover for Ailsa Craig's fishing boat.[36] Through negligence and breach of contract on the part of Securicor, the vessel sank. Securicor's standard terms and conditions stated that its liability 'whether under express or implied terms of the contract, or at common law or in any other way' for loss or damage was limited to £1,000; however the loss to Ailsa Craig was £55,000. The House of Lords held that while the *contra proferentem* rule applied to such clauses, it was not to be applied to the same high standards as for full exclusion clauses. Lord Wilberforce justifies this position by saying that limitation clauses 'must be related to other contractual terms, in particular to the risks to which the defending party may be exposed, the remuneration which he receives, and possibly also the opportunity of the other party to insure'.

It is difficult to justify this stance in objective terms. One clause excludes all liability, and the other limits the amount the defendant would have had to pay for the breach. Much more judicial attention has been garnered by exemption clauses, but there is no logical reason why the two should not follow the same rules. In *Ailsa Craig*, it is difficult to see much practical difference in the claimant receiving £1,000 or nothing given the scale of its losses.[37]

---

33 [2003] UKHL 6.

34 [2017] EWCA Civ 373. See also Andrew Shaw-Mellors 'Negligence Construction: Does Anything Remain of Canada Steamship'(2017) 7 Journal of Business Law 610; Jeremy Cousins and Peter Dodge, 'Steaming away from Canada Steamship? The Interpretation of Exemption Clauses in Finance Documents' (2021) 36(5) Butterworths Journal of International Banking and Finance Law 325.

35 Paul Todd, 'Excluding and Limiting Liability for Misdelivery' (2010) 3 Journal of Business Law 243.

36 [1983] 1 WLR 964.

37 N E Palmer, 'Limiting Liability for Negligence' (1982) 45(3) Modern Law Review 322.

8.3.5 Fundamental Breach

Historically, the common law doctrine known as 'fundamental breach' provided escape from even some of the most carefully worded exemption clauses. This doctrine operated on the basis that there were some terms in a contract that were 'fundamental' (or core to the contract itself), and so a breach of such a term would amount to non-performance of the contract. Consequently, there arose the principle that a party could not exempt themselves from responsibility for a breach of a fundamental term. This rule of law operated in a manner which meant that the intentions of the parties were irrelevant and limited their freedom to contract as it meant that certain exclusions could never apply.

The rule of law approach to fundamental breach was rejected in *UGS Finance Ltd v National Mortgage Bank of Greece*,[38] a position unanimously endorsed by the House of Lords in *Suisse Atlantique Societe d'Armement Maritime SA v NV Rotterdamsche Kolen Centrale*.[39] In the latter case, Suisse chartered the vessel Silvretta to RCK for two years. It was agreed that should there be delays in loading or unloading the ship, RCK would pay the sum of $1,000 per day. There were lengthy delays which Suisse believed were the fault of RCK; however, it continued to allow RCK to use the vessel and did not seek to terminate the contract. On conclusion of the charter, Suisse sought damages in excess of the sum provided for in the clause above. It was argued that the breaches were fundamental and would have allowed Suisse to treat the contract as repudiated. As such, RKC could not rely on the clause which limited its liability.

This argument was rejected by the House of Lords. It held first that this was not a limitation clause but an 'agreed damages' clause. Secondly, if it had been a limitation clause, as a matter of construction it was wide enough to cover the breaches complained of.

The matter was once again considered by the House of Lords in *Photo Production Ltd v Securicor Transport Ltd*.[40] In this case Photo Production contracted with Securicor to provide patrol services at its factory. Within the contract was a clause which stated that 'under no circumstances shall the company be responsible for any injurious act or default by any employee unless such an act or default could have been foreseen and avoided by the exercise of due diligence on

---

38 [1964] 1 Lloyd's Rep 446.

39 [1967] 1 AC 361.

40 [1980] AC 827. Andrew Nichol and Rick Rawlings, 'Substantive Fundamental Breach Burn Out: Photo Production v Securicor' (1980) 43(5) Modern Law Review 567.

the part of the company'. During one of the patrols, an employee of Securicor deliberately lit a fire in the factory which spread causing serious damage. The Court of Appeal held that Securicor could not rely on the exemption clause as a fundamental term of the contract was to keep the building safe, and therefore the deliberate act of the employee would not be covered. This was overturned in the House of Lords, where it was held, in considering the contract as a whole, the small remuneration for the patrol (approximately 26p per visit) and the fact that the Photo Production could insure against fire, that Securicor had excluded its obligations. Importantly, in this context it was affirmed that exemption clauses relating to fundamental breach are a matter of construction of the contract and not a common law doctrine that applies automatically. Lord Wilberforce commented: 'I have no second thoughts as to the main proposition that the question whether, and to what extent, an exclusion clause is to be applied to a fundamental breach, or a breach of a fundamental term, or indeed to any breach of contract, is a matter of construction of the contract.'

This approach has been consistently followed, and *Wood v Capita Services* provides a more recent authority setting out the rules for the interpretation of contracts, including that for excluding liability for a fundamental breach.[41] The case follows the reasoning in *Photo Production* and sets to rest any thoughts of the doctrine's revival after *Internet Broadcasting Corporation & Ors v MAR LLC* where the High Court took the view that there was a strong presumption against an exemption clause which sought to exclude liability for a deliberate and fundamental breach of the contract, a presumption which could only be rebutted by strong language.[42]

The leading Irish case on fundamental breach is *Clayton Love v B&I Transport*.[43] This case involved a contract to transport deep frozen scampi from Dublin to Liverpool. The fish was not kept frozen and as a result, by the time it arrived in Liverpool it was completely spoiled and unusable. When the plaintiff claimed damages he was met with an exclusion clause which was drafted widely enough to potentially exclude liability for this loss. The Supreme Court however found that the failure to transport the fish frozen was something that was fundamental to the contract and that such a fundamental breach could not be excluded. Despite some obiter comments in High Court cases[44] the position as set down by Clayton Love remains the law and thus it

41 [2017] UKSC 24.

42 [2009] EWHC 884 (Ch). Michael Wagener, 'Fundamental Breach: Has the Baby gone out with the Bathwater?' (2005) 29 Tul Mar Law Journal 45.

43 (1970) 104 ILTR 157.

44 *Fitzpatrick and Harty v Ballsbridge International Bloodstock Sales*, Unrep, High Court, 25 February 1983.

is not unusual for a claimant to plead that an exclusion clause cannot be enforced as it covers a fundamental breach.[45] However, it is not a position that has been met with universal judicial agreement. In *ESL Consulting Ltd v Verizon (Ireland) Ltd* Geoghegan J reluctantly accepted that the decision in Clayton Love was binding on the case but stated:

> I would add, that if I was free to decide the issue in light of subsequent judgments in other jurisdictions, as has been observed already by a number of my colleagues in the High Court, there appears to be strong arguments in favour of the reconsideration of the application of the so called doctrine of fundamental breach to agreements between two commercial entities for the reasons outlined by the House of Lords in Photo Production.[46]

Test Your Knowledge

Paula owns a small boutique clothing shop in her village and has used the local dry cleaners approximately three times over the last four years. On her last visit, she left a very expensive handmade dress with hundreds of hand-stitched beads to be cleaned and was given a ticket. On the back of the ticket was a clause stating 'We do not accept liability for all damages which may occur as a result of dry cleaning. For full details of what is excluded, please visit our website.' And it provided a link to the website. When Paula went to collect her dress, many of the beads had fallen off as a result of the chemicals used. Paula says that she wants the dry cleaners to pay to have the dress repaired, but the dry cleaners have referred her to their terms and conditions on their website that specifically state that liability for damaged beads will not be covered. Is the exemption clause:

- A validly incorporated as the dry cleaners gave reasonable notice?
- B validly incorporated due to a course of dealing?
- C invalid as it has not been incorporated?

The correct answer here is A. Paula was aware that there were specific issues that would be excluded, and therefore she had the obligation to look at the website and see what they would be. The clause would not be incorporated by a course of dealing as, per *Hollier*, there would not have been a required consistency for the courts to hold this as valid.

---

45 See *Regan v The Irish Automobile Club Ltd* [1990] IR 278.

46 [2008] IEHC 369.

Stretch and Challenge Question

Consider whether the differing tests applied by the court to exemption and limited liability clauses cause injustice.

CHAPTER 9

UNFAIR TERMS AND CONSUMER PROTECTION

9.1 Introduction

Consumer protection law in Ireland has developed in somewhat of a haphazard manner. Some of the law has been influenced by the legislative developments in England and Wales, and others by membership of the European Union whereby multiple directives to protect consumers have been adopted into Irish law.

Some of the key provisions include the Consumer Protection Act 2007 (which implemented the Unfair Commercial Practices Directive 2005/29/EC into Irish law); Sale of Goods and Supply of Services Act 1980; European Communities (Unfair Terms in Consumer Contracts) Regulations 1995 and 2000 (as amended in 2013 and 2014) (which implemented the Unfair Terms in Consumer Contracts Directive 93/13/EEC into Irish Law) (the 'UTCC Regulations'); European Union (Consumer Information, Cancellation and Other Rights) Regulations 2013 (as amended) (which implemented the Directive on Consumer Rights 2011/83/EU into Irish law) (the Consumer Information Regulations); and The Consumer Credit Act 1995 and the European Communities (Consumer Credit Agreements) Regulations 2010 (which gave effect to the Directive on Credit Agreements for Consumer 2008/48/EC in Irish law).

The Consumer Rights Act 2022 was signed into law in November 2022 and represents a sweeping overhaul of the law on consumer protection. It amends some of the key legislation above and incorporates the various EU directives to create one comprehensive piece of consumer legislation. In addition to enhancing and consolidating existing legislation and directives, it also incorporates further EU directives which had not yet been transposed into Irish law including Directive 2019/770 on certain aspects concerning contracts for the supply of digital content and digital services (the 'Digital Content Directive'); Directive 2019/771 on certain aspects concerning contracts for the sale of goods (the 'Revised Sale of Goods Directive'); and the main provisions of Directive 2019/2161 on the better enforcement and modernisation of Union rules (the 'Omnibus Directive'), which itself amends the Unfair Contracts Terms Directive 93/13/EEC; the Unfair Commercial Practices Directive 2005/29/EC; the Consumer Rights Directive 2011/83/EU, and the Price Indication Directive 98/6/EC.

At the time of writing the new legislation has been in force for just over one year and as such there is very little information on precisely how it has impacted the consumer, particularly in terms of decided case law. It is likely that many cases decided under old legislation will remain good law, save for circumstances where the 2022 Act explicitly enhances the protection. As this book is concerned with contract law an in-depth analysis of consumer law is not warranted. This chapter will provide an overview of the key elements of the previous law and the new Act. What is important for students of contract law to remember is that the Act implies these terms into every consumer contract and from that perspective is relevant to contract law.

It should be further noted that the 2022 Act effectively creates two systems of protection. One where the 1893 Sale of Goods Act and the 1980 Sale of Goods and Supply of Services Act applies and one where the 2022 Act will apply. For the former, the law will apply to contracts in which one of the parties is not defined as a 'consumer'. These could include contracts between individuals or contracts between traders. In this chapter, we are concerned with consumer contracts only. Many of the provisions contained therein, as stated above, come from the existing legislation and various directives and are amalgamated in order to give comprehensive protection to consumers entering contracts.

9.2 The Old Law: The Sale of Goods Act 1893 and the Sale of Goods and Supply of Services Act 1980 (as amended)

Prior to the enactment of legislation, general principles of contract law governed contracts involving the sale of goods and supply of services. As we noted in the introduction chapter, historically the freedom to contract was a paramount consideration. The notion that contracts, regardless of their purpose, were not imposed by law, meant that individuals and companies were free to choose which contracts they entered into and on what terms. The law's role therefore ought to merely be to hold those parties to the promises which they had freely entered into. One issue with this premise is that the law is assuming that all parties are on an equal footing which is quite clearly not the case in a variety of situations. One very clear example of this is in consumer law. Here, the consumer, most often an individual, is at a significant disadvantage when trying to assert rights against a corporate body. Thus, legislation was enacted with the aim of protecting the weaker party in these types of transactions.

The primary legislation which governed the sale of goods was the Sale of Goods Act 1893 as amended by the Sale of Goods and Supply of Services Act 1980. This legislation initially evolved from mercantile practices between traders and sought to put these on a statutory footing. It was not an intention of the legislature to protect consumers, a concept that was alien in 1893. However, ss 12-15 of the Act (as amended) have represented significant impact to consumer law and can only be avoided by express agreement (ie, by way of an exclusion clause). In addition, to avoid the implication of these terms, it must be shown that the buyer is not a consumer and that the provision is fair and reasonable.[1]

9.2.1 Section 12

Section 12 of the Act establishes two distinct obligations in relation to the title of the property being sold, which can be summarised thus:

Section 12(1)(a) an implied condition in a contract of sale that the seller has the right to sell the goods and in relation to an agreement to sell, that the seller will have the right to sell the goods, at the time property is to pass; and

Section 12(1)(b) an implied warranty that the goods are and will remain free until the time when the property is to pass from any encumbrances not disclosed to the buyer and that the buyer shall enjoy quiet possession except in relation to encumbrances disclosed at the time of sale.

The first part of this section comes into force even where the seller believes he has good title to the property but does not. For example, perhaps the property has been stolen and the seller is unaware of this having bought the property in good faith.[2]

1 Sale of Goods and Supply of Services Act 1980, s 22.
2 *O'Reilly v Fineman* [1942] Ir Jur Rep 36.

Section 12(2) allows the parties to limit their obligations in circumstances where the seller is unsure of his rights to sell.[3]

9.2.2 Section 13

This clause states that where goods are sold by description, the goods must comply with the description given. This is incorporated into every contract of this nature by way of an implied condition. The fact that this is deemed a condition of the contract rather than a warranty is important in terms of the remedies that can be offered where there is a breach. Under S 13(3) this provision extends to the labelling of goods, allowing labels to form part of the description of the goods. This is illustrated in the case of *O'Connor v Donnelly* where the plaintiff was injured when consuming a tin of salmon.[4] In this case there was no reliance on the seller's skill or judgment, but the High Court affirmed that there can be a sale of goods by description even if the goods are shown to the buyer. In order to succeed, the buyer must rely on the description in establishing the 'essential characteristics' of the goods and not a mere quality attributed to the goods. This section is particularly important, and remains so, for those who are private sellers and who may exclude the provisions of the act by virtue of an appropriately worded exclusion clause where the buyer is not dealing as a consumer.

9.2.3 Section 14

Until the passing of the 2022 Act, section 14 of the 1893 Act (as amended) was seen as the 'cornerstone of Irish consumer protection law'.[5]

Section 14(2) of the 1893 Act (As Amended) makes it clear that there is an implied condition in every sales contract that the goods are of merchantable quality. There are some exceptions to this general implication under s 14(3) of where any defects have been brought to the buyer's attention or where the buyer has inspected the goods prior to contracting and the defects ought to have been revealed during this inspection.

Initially, the Act did not provide a definition of what would be considered to be 'merchantable quality', the amendment to the Act in 1980 did:

3 *Great Elephant Corp v Trafigura Beheer BV* [2012] EWHC 1745.
4 [1944] Ir Jur Rep 1.
5 Robert Clark, *Contract Law in Ireland* (9th Ed, Round Hall 2022) 321.

> Goods are of merchantable quality if they are as fit for purpose or purposes for which goods of that kind are commonly bought and are as durable as it is reasonable to expect having regard to any description applied to them, the price (if relevant) and all other relevant circumstances.[6]

In *James Elliot Construction Ltd v Irish Asphalt Ltd* the plaintiff purchased stone aggregate infill material from the defendants.[7] The material contained pyrite which expanded and caused bulging and cracking in the buildings in which it was used. It was held that the infill was not of merchantable quality.

Section 14(4) provides that the goods must be 'fit for purpose' and there is a considerable overlap between this provision and that of merchantable quality. The leading Irish case on this section is *Wallis v Russell*.[8] In this case the plaintiff's granddaughter sought to buy from the defendant 'two nice fresh crabs for tea'. The defendant informed her that he had no live crabs but did have boiled ones and selected two for her. Both the plaintiff and her granddaughter contracted food poisoning after eating the crabs. In finding for the plaintiff the court found that s 14 of the Act was not confined to manufactured goods, the disclosure made by the granddaughter that the crabs were 'for tea' was enough to signify the purpose for which they were to be used and there was no defence to say that the defect could not be discoverable by inspection.

A problem does arise when the 'purpose' for the purchase has not been disclosed. In other words, how can one argue that a particular item is not fit for purpose when the seller did not know what purpose you bought then item for. Initially, this created some harsh results. In *Brady v Cluxton* a woman purchased a fur coat without any disclosure of the purpose for which it was bought.[9] The coat caused a skin disorder on the woman and an action for damages was dismissed as she had not disclosed the particular purpose for which the coat was required.

This rule has now been somewhat relaxed in circumstances where the goods have only one purpose and are used for that purpose (shoes are meant to be worn on the feet, cakes are meant to be consumed, etc). However, where goods may have multiple purposes, disclosure may be needed.[10]

---

6 s 14(3) As Amended.
7 [2011] IEHC 269.
8 [1902] 2 IR 585.
9 (1927) 61 ILTR 89.
10 *Browne (BS) & Son Ltd v Craiks Ltd* [1970] 1 WLR 752.

The seller may avoid liability here if he can show that the buyer did not rely on the skill and judgment of the seller. In *Slater and Slater (a firm) v Finning Ltd* the defendant supplied a camshaft to be used in a fishing vessel, knowing that it would be used in that particular boat.[11] The defendant had not been aware that the boat in question was known to produce 'excessive torsional resonance' resulting in the camshaft becoming excessively worn. In finding for the defendants in this case the court noted that in the absence of the particular knowledge they were in no position to exercise skill and judgment.

9.2.4 Section 15

This section of the 1893 Act which was untouched by the 1980 Act creates three implied conditions. First, that where goods have been sold by reference to a sample, that the bulk will match the sample provided. Second, the buyer must be given a reasonable opportunity to inspect the sample. Third, if the bulk matches the sample in every way, but both the bulk and the sample suffer from a defect which would not be apparent from a reasonable inspection, the product will not be 'merchantable' as per s 14 and liability will attach to the seller.

9.2.5 Supply of Services

The 1980 Act created implied terms in relation to the supply of services which was not initially contained within the 1893 Act. The legislation does not state whether these terms are to be deemed as a condition or a warranty, however s 39 establishes that where a supplier is acting the course of business:

> (a) the supplier has the necessary skill to render the service;
> (b) that he will supply the service with due skill, care and diligence;
> (c) that where materials are used, they will be sound and reasonably fit for the purpose for which they are required; and
> (d) that, where goods are supplied under the contract, they will be of merchantable quality within the meaning of s 14(3) of the Act of 1893.

Section 39 of the 1880 Act as been of particular use within the package holiday context. In *O'Flynn v Balkan Tours Ltd* it was determined that this section applied and that there was a duty on the tour operator to provide information about ski runs within the resort[12] and in *McKenna*

---

[11] [1996] 3 All ER 398.
[12] Unrep, Supreme Court, 7 April 1997.

v Best Travel the tour operator was required to disclose information about the safety of an area or resort.[13]

The section also operates in circumstances where the contract operates over a period of time, as seen in *Irish Telephone Rentals Ltd v Irish Civil Service Building Society Ltd*.[14] Here the plaintiff contracted to install and maintain the telephone system of the defendant company. The system was installed in 1982 and at that time functioned well. However, by 1985 it was causing significant problems as it could not cope with the level of calls. Costello J held that the system was not adequately fit for purpose and therefore a breach of s 39.

9.3 The New Law: The Consumer Rights Act 2022

While the 1980 Act now clearly states that these provisions do not apply to areas which are governed by the 2022 Act, we can see from the comparisons below that the spirit of the protection remains the same. What this means effectively is that where a consumer is taking a claim against a trader under any of these provisions, they must do so under the 2022 Act and not the 1980 Act.

The 2022 Act began in earnest with the Sales Law Review Group report in 2011 which drew attention to the fact that Ireland's consumer law was somewhat haphazard and argued that there was a need for a comprehensive piece of legislation which would encompass all of the consumer rights.[15] Following the publication of this report, further EU Law Directives were introduced leading to further work by the Department of Jobs, Enterprise and Innovation publishing the 'Scheme of Consumer Rights Bill' in May 2015. While this Bill was never presented to the Oireachtas, it was highly influential in the drafting of the 2022 Act.

As previously noted, this legislation is now a comprehensive and all-encompassing piece of legislation for consumer law. However, it does not supplant the previous legislation when dealing with private contracts or with business to business contracts.

9.3.1 The Sales Contract

Section 16 of the 2022 Act now deals with issues relating to title for consumer contracts:

---

13 Unrep, High Court, 17 December 1996.

14 [1991] ILRM 880.

15 Sales Law Review Group, *Report on the Legislation Governing the Sale of Goods and Supply of Services*, 2011 (Pm.A11/1576).

Section 16(1): The Trader shall ensure that:

(a) At the time when the ownership of goods is to be transferred under a sales contract, the goods are free from any charge or other encumbrance (other than a charge or encumbrance which was disclosed to the consumer before the consumer entered into the sales contract) and
(b) The consumer shall enjoy quiet possession of the goods except so far as it may be disturbed by any person entitled to the benefit of any charge or encumbrance so disclosed.

Section 16(2): Where a sales contract shows, or the circumstances at the time the contract was concluded imply, that a trader and the consumer intend that the trader transfer only the limited title to the goods that the trader or a person other than a trader (a 'third person') may have:

(a) All charges or encumbrances known to the trader shall be disclosed by the trader to the consumer before the consumer enters the sales contract, and
(b) The consumer's quiet possession shall not be disturbed by
    (i) The trader or third person, or
    (ii) A person claiming through or under the trader or the third person unless that third person is claiming under a charge or encumbrance that was disclosed to the consumer before the sales contract was concluded.

Section 16(3): The consumer under a sales contract shall have the right to remedies specified in Chapter 3 where:

(a) The goods are not in compliance with subsection 1(a) or (b)
(b) The trader does not disclose all known charges or encumbrances in accordance with subsection 2(a)
(c) The consumers possession does not comply with subsection 2(b) or
(d) A restriction resulting from a violation of any right of a third person, in particular an intellectual property right, prevents or limits the use of the goods in accordance with subsections 17 or 18.

Section 16(4): In case of dispute, it shall be for the trader to show that

(a) The goods complied with the requirements of subsection 1(a) or (b)
(b) The trader disclosed all charges or encumbrances in accordance with subsection 2(a) and
(c) The consumers possession of the goods complied with subsection 2(b).

This new section provides a much more comprehensive protection for consumer contracts and importantly reverses the burden of proof – it is not for the consumer to show that the seller breached his obligations, but rather for the seller to show that he did not.

The provisions of sections 13, 14 and 15 above no longer apply to consumer contracts and instead the 2022 Act provides for a more extensive list of both objective and subjective conformity requirements under sections 17 and 18:

Section 17(1) the goods delivered under a sales contract shall

- (a) Be of the description, type, quantity and quality and possess the functionality, compatibility, interoperability and other features specified in the sales contract
- (b) Be fit for any particular purpose for which the consumer requires them
    - (i) That the consumer has made known to the trader at the time of, or before, the conclusion of the contract and
    - (ii) That the trader has accepted
- (c) supplied with all accessories and instructions including on installation of the goods specified in the sales contract and
- (d) be updates as specified in the sales contract

Section 17(2): The information that the trader is required to provide to the consumer in a distance contract or an off premise contract under ss 103, 104 or 106 shall form part of the contract

Section 17(3) Goods sold under a sales contract that is a distance contract or an off premise contract shall comply with any term of the contract deriving from the information referred to in ss (2) that is additional to the requirements of ss (1).

Section 17(4) Spare parts and adequate after sales service shall be made available by the trader

- (a) In such circumstances as are stated in the offer, description or advertisement by the trader on behalf of the producer or on the trader's own behalf, and
- (b) For such a period as is so stated, or if no period is stated, for a reasonable period.

Section 18 goes further in offering additional protection to consumers, these are classified as the objective requirements and include:

Section 18(1) The goods delivered under a sales contract shall-

- (a) Be fit for all of the purposes for which goods of the same type would normally be used, taking into account so far as relevant any enactment or rule of law, European Union

Law, technical standards or, in the absence of such technical standards, applicable sector specific codes of conduct.
(b) Be of the quality and correspond to any description of a sample or model that the trader made available to the consumer before the conclusion of the sales contract
(c) Be delivered along with any accessories, including packaging, installation instructions or other instructions, that the consumer may reasonably expect to receive, and
(d) Be of the quantity and possess the qualities and other features (including in relation to durability, functionality, compatibility and security) normal for goods of the same type that the consumer may reasonably expect given the nature of the goods and taking into account any public statement in relation to the goods made by, or on behalf of the trader or any other person constituting a previous link in the chain of transactions relating to the sales contract, including the producer, particularly in advertising or on labelling

Section 18(2): In subsection (1)(d) the reference to the durability of the goods is a reference to the ability of the goods to maintain their function and performance through normal use and to possess the ability to do so which is normal for goods of the same type and which the consumer can reasonably expect having regard to:

(a) The specific nature of the goods
(b) The possible need for reasonable maintenance of the goods
(c) Any public statement on the durability of the goods made by or on behalf of any person constituting a link in the chain of transactions and
(d) All other relevant circumstances, including the price of the goods and the intensity or frequency of the use made of the goods by the consumer.

Section 18(3): The trader shall not be bound by any public statement referred to in subsection (1)(d) or (2)(c) if the trader shows that:

(a) The trader was not, and could not reasonably have been, aware of the public statement in question
(b) At the time of the conclusion of the sales contract, the public statement had been corrected in the same way as it had been made (or in a compatible way) or
(c) The decision of the consumer to buy the goods could not have been influenced by the public statement.

Section 18(8) provides that there will be no lack of conformity in the sale contract where the consumer was informed of any deviations and expressly accepted them. Further, s 18(9) again provides that where there is a dispute, it is for the trader to show that he acted in compliance with the conformity requirements.

Section 19 states that incorrect installation of the goods shall be regarded as a lack of conformity with the sales contract where it has been installed either by the trader, or by the consumer following the instructions provided by the trader.

Section 20 expressly confirms that all of the foregoing sections (ss 14 and 16-19) are implied into every consumer contract.

The 2022 Act maintains the current approach regarding the delivery of goods, stipulating that unless otherwise agreed upon by the trader and consumer, the trader is required to deliver the goods within 30 days of the contract being finalised. If the trader fails to meet this deadline, the consumer may terminate the contract but only after providing the trader with an additional, reasonable period for delivery based on the circumstances (s 29(2B) of the Sale of Goods Act 1893, as amended by the European Union (Consumer Information, Cancellation, and Other Rights) Regulations 2013. However, the 2022 Act introduces changes concerning deliveries made in instalments. Under the previous law, if a trader delivers one or more defective instalments, whether this constitutes a repudiation of the entire contract or just a severable breach depends on the contract terms and specific circumstances. In the event of repudiation, the consumer has the right to treat the contract as cancelled, whereas a severable breach allows for a claim for compensation (s 31 of the Sale of Goods Act 1893). The 2022 Act, however, allows the consumer to terminate the contract if any instalment is not in accordance with the contract. This right can only be exercised concerning the non-conforming instalment(s) (s 37).

Significantly, the 2022 Act extends protection to recipients of a gift. Prior to the enactment of this legislation, Irish law provided no specific protection to those who received goods as a gift. In practice, may traders would allow these individuals to replace a defective product as a gesture of goodwill, but legally there was no entitlement to this as the recipient to the gift was not a party to the initial contract. Under s 46 of the Act the recipient of a gift is given all of the rights and remedies as if they were party to the sale contract.

9.3.2 Digital Content

Traditionally, consumer law in Ireland has focused on protecting consumers who purchase goods and services. However, the 2022 Act expands this scope, extending protection to contracts involving the supply of digital content, digital services, and goods that include digital elements. Importantly, the 2022 Act's safeguards also apply in situations where the consumer does not make a monetary payment but instead provides personal data, which is then used for purposes beyond what is strictly necessary to deliver the content or service.

The term 'digital content' refers to data produced and supplied in digital form, such as games, e-books, music downloads, and apps. 'Digital services' include services that enable consumers to create, process, store, access, share, or interact with data in digital form, such as social media platforms. The protections provided under these contracts include:

Supply Rights: Where digital content or a digital service is to be supplied under contract, the trader must ensure that it has the right to supply the digital content or service to the consumer at the time of supply. If not, the consumer will have the right to terminate the contract (s 50).

Where a digital content or digital service contract provides for continuous supply over a particular period, the trader must ensure supply is maintained throughout that period (s 51). Similarly, where a contract provides for supply of the digital content or service on a number of occasions, the trader must ensure supply on each of those occasions.

Conformity Requirements: The 2022 Act imposes stricter conformity obligations on traders, requiring them to ensure that the goods, content, and services they provide to consumers meet the contract's standards in terms of quantity, quality, functionality, interoperability, and suitability for their intended purpose. The 2022 Act outlines both objective conformity requirements, such as suitability for the typical purposes of goods, content, or services of the same type (s 54), and subjective conformity requirements, such as suitability for the specific purpose the consumer has in mind (s 53). For digital content or service contracts, the trader must ensure that the digital content or service possesses the qualities and performance features specified in the contract such as functionality, compatibility, accessibility, continuity, and security as well as those typically expected for digital content or services of the same type. If the contract provides for 'continuous supply' over a period, conformity must be maintained throughout that period. Any interruption in supply that is more than negligible will be considered a lack of conformity.

The digital content or service must be delivered with any accessories and instructions, including those related to installation or integration, as specified in the contract, as well as any additional instructions the consumer might reasonably expect. Additionally, the trader is required to provide the consumer with any necessary updates, including security updates, to ensure the digital content or service remains in conformity with the contract throughout the relevant period. Unless otherwise agreed, the digital content or service must be supplied in its most recent available version.

Consumer Remedies: The 2022 Act includes a number of specific remedies for consumers in relation to digital content.

A. The right to terminate the contract if the trader fails to supply the digital content or service (s 60(1)).
B. The right to have the digital content or service brought into conformity with the contract at no cost, within a reasonable time after the lack of conformity is reported, and without significant inconvenience to the consumer (s 61). If it is not possible to bring the digital content or service into conformity, or if doing so would impose disproportionate costs on the trader, the consumer can request a proportionate price reduction or contract termination (s 62(2)). The consumer may only terminate the contract if the lack of conformity is more than minor (s 62(3)).
C. The right to terminate the contract without charge if the trader modifies the contract in a way that negatively impacts the consumer's access to or use of the digital content or service (s 64(3)).

Additionally, the 2022 Act extends several familiar redress options to consumers of digital content and services, including the right to a full refund, exchange, or repair if the content or service is not as described or fails to meet its intended purpose. Consumers may withhold any remaining payments to the trader until the trader fulfils their legal obligations. This right can be exercised through a written notice to the trader.

9.3.3 Service Contracts

The provisions of s 39 of the 1980 Act are mirrored in the 2022 Act with the addition that s 80 for the first time in law, specifies a requirement that a service supplied under contract must be reasonably fit for its purpose. An implied statutory condition for fitness for purpose has long existed in respect of contracts for the sale of goods, resulting in an implied condition in all contracts for the sale of goods to consumers requiring that those goods be fit for all purposes for which such goods are commonly supplied.

The introduction of a statutory fitness for purpose requirement for the supply of services in the 2022 Act marks a significant change from the previous legal standards governing service provision. Before the 2022

Act came into effect, service providers were only obligated to exercise due skill, care, and diligence. However, it is important to note that the fitness for purpose requirement introduced by the Act is more limited in scope and is subjective. This requirement only applies if (i) the consumer informed the trader at the time of contracting that the service was needed for a specific purpose, and (ii) the trader agreed that the service would fulfil that purpose.

Despite its limited scope, there is concern about how this requirement might affect certain types of insurance. Some insurance policies only cover claims related to the failure of the insured to use reasonable skill and care when providing a service. Since a fitness for purpose obligation imposes a higher duty than the standard obligation to act with reasonable skill and care, many insurance policies specifically exclude coverage for any acceptance of or guarantee of fitness for purpose by the insured. If an insured person makes a non-negligent mistake after accepting a fitness for purpose obligation, and fails to meet the assumed standard, their insurance might not cover the claim. As a result, service providers who frequently supply services to consumers must be very aware of any exclusions in their insurance policies regarding fitness for purpose and should carefully consider the implications of the 2022 Act.

It is crucial to understand that the fitness for purpose provisions in the 2022 Act only apply when the trader has accepted that the service will meet a particular purpose or result. If a consumer requests that a service be fit for a specific purpose, the trader should proceed cautiously and clearly communicate to the consumer that they cannot guarantee the service will meet that specific purpose.

Maintaining thorough records and having clear contract terms are essential in this context, as s 80(5)(a) of the 2022 Act requires the trader to demonstrate that they did not accept any purpose communicated to them by the consumer regarding the service.

Section 81 of the 2022 Act separately specifies some objective requirements of a service contract, including that a service must comply with any public statement (such as an advertisement) in relation to the service.

The 2022 Act also introduces a limit on the price that can be set for services in circumstances where the parties have not agreed to a price either under contract or by way of oral or written statements. In such circumstances, the price payable for the service 'shall be a reasonable price and no more' (s 83(1)). What is a reasonable price for a service will be a question of fact.

9.3.4 Unfair Terms

The 2022 Act revokes and replaces the existing legislation on unfair terms, the UTCC Regulations. Under the UTCC Regulations, a consumer is not bound by a standard term in a business to consumer contract if that term is 'unfair'.[16]

This principle is retained in the 2022 Act, however, it is extended to all 'consumer contracts' under s 129. Section 130 states that a contractual term is regarded as 'unfair', and consequently unenforceable, if contrary to the requirement of good faith, it causes a significant imbalance in the parties' rights and obligations under the contract to the consumer's detriment. A consumer contract is defined under s 126 as 'any contract between a consumer and a trader' and s 127 specifically provides that a consumer contract will not be excluded by reason only that the contract or a term therein has been individually negotiated.

In addition, if the governing law applicable to the consumer contract is that of a country or territory other than an EEA State, Part 6 will still apply if the contract has a close connection with the State.[17]

The UTCC Regulations contain an indicative and non-exhaustive list of terms, commonly referred to as a 'grey list', which may be regarded as 'unfair'.[18]

The 2022 Act retains the concept of a 'grey list' but provides that terms on that list shall be presumed 'unfair'.[19]

Below are some examples of the terms appearing on the 2022 Act's 'grey list' include those which have the object or effect of:

— requiring any consumer who fails to fulfil his or her

---

16 European Communities (Unfair Terms in Consumer Contracts) Regulations, 1995, r 6(1).

17 s 127(5).

18 European Communities (Unfair Terms in Consumer Contracts) Regulations, 1995, r 3(7) and sch 3.

19 r 133(1)–the UTCC Regulations provided that they 'may' be regarded as unfair but it did not state that a presumption of unfairness arose. While the Bill proposes retaining much of the existing 'grey list' from the UTCC Regulations, it significantly adds to it and there is also the possibility of Ministerial Regulations being enacted, in the future, to specify further terms that shall be presumed "unfair' (r 133(4)).

obligations under the contract to pay a disproportionately high sum in compensation;
- enabling the trader to terminate a contract of indeterminate duration without reasonable notice except where there are serious grounds for doing so;
- irrevocably binding the consumer to terms with which they had no real opportunity of becoming acquainted before the conclusion of the contract;
- enabling the trader to alter the terms of the contract unilaterally without a valid reason which is specified in the contract;
- enabling the trader to alter unilaterally without a valid reason any characteristics of the goods, digital content, digital service or service to be delivered or supplied;
- giving the trader the discretion to decide the price payable under the contract after the consumer has become bound by the contract, where no price or method of determining the price has been agreed prior;
- requiring a consumer to pay a fee in order to exercise a statutory right;
- preventing, without a valid reason, the consumer from obtaining repairs or spare parts from another trader; or
- requiring a consumer to restrict his/her rights as a data subject under data protection law.

Significantly, the 2022 Act includes, for the first time in s 132 the introduction of a 'black list' of contractual terms which shall always be regarded as unfair if its object or effect is to:

- exclude or limit the trader's liability for the death or personal injury of a consumer arising from the trader's act or omission;
- require a consumer to pay for goods that have not been delivered or a service that has not been supplied, including a digital service;
- impose on a consumer a burden of proof that, according to the applicable law, would otherwise rest with the trader;
- exclude or hinder a consumer's right to take legal action or exercise a legal remedy (including by requiring the consumer to resolve a dispute through an arbitration procedure that is not governed by law);
- require a consumer to bear its own costs in respect of arbitration;
- give a trader the exclusive right to determine whether goods are, or digital content, a digital service or a service is, in conformity with the contract;
- grant the trader a shorter notice period to terminate the contract than the notice period required of the consumer; or
- confer exclusive jurisdiction for disputes arising under the contract on a court in the place where a trader is domiciled unless the consumer is also domiciled in that place.

The first case to test the provisions of the 2022 Act in relation to unfair terms came before the High Court in *Flatley v Austin Newport Group Ltd*.[20] This case centred around the plaintiff's dispute with an insurance company. He engaged the services of a specialist insurance broker to secure insurance on his home which he had spent €30 million renovating. The plaintiff agreed that he would pay the sum of €69,285 as an annual premium for this insurance and further agreed that should a dispute arise, it would be resolved by arbitration. Despite agreeing to this term, the plaintiff argued that he entered into this agreement as a consumer and that requiring arbitration for disputes in a consumer contract amounts to an unfair term contrary to s 129 of the 2022 Act. The plaintiff argued that the reason this is an unfair term is that the policy does not make it clear that he would have to bear his own costs for arbitration. The thrust of his interpretation, as noted by the court, is that in order for this to be a fair term, the arbitration must never be at a cost to the consumer therefore the consumer would never be liable for any costs (their own or another's) even in circumstances where they lose their case at arbitration. It is worth noting that if a claim is brought in litigation the plaintiff would almost certainly be liable for the costs accrued to the other side if he lost his case under the 'loser pays' principle. In examining the legislation, the court determined that this interpretation is not what the Oireachtas could have had in mind as the practical effect of this would be to potentially encourage unmeritorious claims to be pursued in arbitration as the legal fees would be recoverable against the trader in all circumstances.

Turning to the 2022 Act itself, the court found that if the arbitration clause made it a requirement that the consumer pay their own costs it would be unfair as this would mean that even in circumstances where the consumer wins his case, he would still be responsible for his own costs. However, as the clause itself in the agreement makes no reference whatsoever to costs, it could not be deemed to be unfair. Therefore 'the fact that an arbitration clause does not state that Mr Flatley will never be liable for legal costs is not basis for Mr Flatley claiming that the clause is unfair'.

9.3.4.1 Increased Transparency

The UTCC Regulations require the supplier to ensure that written terms are drafted in plain, intelligible language.[21] The 2022 Act strengthening this by requiring traders to ensure that the terms of a consumer contract are 'transparent'. Section 134 states that in order to satisfy the transparency criteria, a term must be:

---

[20] [2024] IEHC 359.

[21] European Communities (Unfair Terms in Consumer Contracts) Regulations, 1995), r 5(1).

- in plain and intelligible language;
- written terms must be legible and presented clearly;
- made available in a manner that gives the consumer a reasonable opportunity to become acquainted with it before conclusion of the contract;
- if a term is novel or onerous, it must be specifically brought to the consumer's attention;
- the costs of any other financial consequences of the term are understandable; and
- the term complies with such other requirements as may be prescribed.

In assessing transparency, the 2022 Act requires various other matters to be taken into account, including:

- the nature and subject matter of the contract;
- the means by which the contract is communicated to the consumer;
- the other terms of the contract or any other contract on which it may be dependent;
- compliance with any obligations imposed under an enactment relating to the provision of information before a consumer contract is concluded; and
- all the circumstances relating to the conclusion of the contract.

Under s 134(4) the onus rests with the trader to show that a term is 'transparent' should a dispute arise.

9.3.4.2 Cancellation Rights

The 2022 Act extends the statutory 14-day cancellation right, commonly known as the 'cooling-off' right, provided under the Consumer Information Regulations.

Under the 2022 Act the 14-day 'cooling-off' right will continue, however, if the contract is concluded in the context of an unsolicited visit to the consumer's home or an excursion organised by the trader with the aim or effect of promoting a service or supply of digital content, or water, gas or electricity (that is not supplied in a limited volume or set quantity) then the cancellation period is extended to 30 days.

9.3.4.3 Payment Fees

Section 48 of the Consumer Protection Act 2007 provides that where a trader makes a representation that it will accept payment by any one of two or more payment methods or where its practice is to accept a different payment methods, it is not permitted to impose a surcharge for using one method in preference over another and such constitutes a criminal offence. This provision, however, was never commenced so traders are currently permitted to charge consumers for using debit cards for transactions instead of cash for example.

Section 122 of the 2022 Act prohibits traders from charging fees/ surcharges for using a particular payment method and where a trader does so, it will be required to reimburse the consumer for the excess paid. The Act also makes this practice an offence. For the avoidance of doubt, traders are permitted to charge the consumer the cost borne by it for use of a particular payment means (e.g. processing fees).

9.3.4.4 Prohibited Practices

Section 55(1) of the 2007 Act sets out a list of prohibited commercial practices, such as falsely representing that the trader or product has a particular approval, endorsement or authorisation, making a false representation that a product is available for a limited time in order to elicit an immediate decision from a consumer, failing to disclose that editorial content used to promote a product is a paid promotion and creating the impression that the trader is a consumer and running fake competitions.

Section 157 of the 2022 Act bolsters these provisions by prohibiting the following actions:

- providing search results to a consumer online search query without clearly disclosing any paid advertisement or payment made in order to achieve higher ranking of products within the search results;
- reselling event tickets where the trader acquired them by using automated means to circumvent any limit on the number of tickets that a person may buy or any other rules applicable to the purchase of tickets;
- stating that reviews are submitted by consumers who have actually used or purchased the product without taking reasonable and proportionate steps to check that the reviews originate from those consumers; and
- submitting or commissioning false reviews or endorsements, or misrepresenting reviews or social endorsements by consumers, in order to promote products.

9.3.4.5 Obligatory Disclosures

Section 155 of the 2022 Act provides that where a trader hosts an online marketplace, it must state clearly whether the third party offering the products is a commercial trader or not, on the basis of a declaration made by that third party to the trader.

Where a trader's website enables consumers to search for products offered by different traders, general information relating to the main parameters determining the ranking of products in search results and the weighting of those parameters, must be made available in a directly and easily accessible section of the online interface. This obligation does not apply to online search engines, such as Google.

9.3.5 Remedies

Chapter 3 of the 2022 Act sets out the position in relation to the remedies that the consumer may have against a trader.

Section 23 states that where the goods in a sales contract are not in conformity with the contract, the consumer has the right to cancel the contract, or to have the goods brought into conformity by way of repair or replacement. Section 23(2) further says that repair or replacement will not be possible for the trader to repair or replace; or where the remedy chosen would impose a disproportionate cost on the trader. Section 24 provides that this short term right in relation to sales contracts expires after 30 days, or sooner depending on the subject matter of the contract. Where the consumer elects to have the goods replaced or repaired, s 25 states that the trader must do this free of charge, within a reasonable time period (having regard to the nature of the goods, the severity of the lack of conformity and the effort needed to repair or replace) and without significant inconvenience to the consumer.

Section 26 provides that where the consumer has exercised their rights under s 23 and the trader has failed to comply with their obligations under s 25, the consumer is entitled to a price reduction or to terminate the contract. Section 26(3) however states that where the defect is minor, the consumer will not have the right to terminate the contract and will only be entitled to a price reduction. In the case of a dispute, it will be for the trader to show that the lack of conformity is minor and further, the consumer is required to allow the trader a further attempt to bring the goods into conformity before finally exercising the right to terminate the contract.

Where the consumer is entitled to a price reduction as a result of the lack of conformity, s 27 requires that such a reduction be proportionate to the decrease in value of the goods that the consumer actually received versus the goods that the ought to have received.

Where the consumer is exercising their right to terminate the contract they must communicate this decision to the trader, and return the goods to the trader, at the trader's expense as per s 28. Where the consumer fails to do this, he may be liable in damages to the trader.

Section 29 specifically refers to digital content and provides that where the digital content does not conform to the sales contract, the consumer will have the right to either terminate the contract or to obtain a price reduction. There is no express provision in this section to allow the trader to repair or replace digital content.

Section 30 imposes obligations on the trader once the contract has been terminated and the consumer has complied with their obligations under s 28. At this stage the trader must reimburse the consumer for the price of the goods (if they have paid) and also for the cost of returning the goods, if any. If the consumer has failed to return the goods, the reimbursement may be reduced. In addition, where the goods have been used, the trader may reduce the reimbursement amount in a proportionate matter. Section 31 gives the trader 14 days to reimburse the consumer from the date on which the returned goods were received (or proof of postage if the trader wishes). If the trader fails to reimburse within this time frame, damages will be payable.

Section 34 of the Act does not restrict or affect the rights of the consumer to pursue other remedies. The legislation here is intended to provide a speedy resolution to relatively minor consumer rights issues and where large amounts of damages has occurred as a result of a breach of the legislation, the consumer may opt to take a case seeking damages, injunctions, or specific performance. As such, the law on damages and their quantification is still very relevant to consumer contracts, as is the law on implied terms considered in chapter 7.

Test Your Knowledge

Paul is refurbishing his kitchen. He contracts with a local trader Willard's Kitchens to install his new kitchen. He tells Willard's that in an attempt to keep costs down, he will provide all of the materials needed and he requires Willard's to only install the kitchen. Willard agrees to this and gives Paul a list of certain items that they will require in order to complete the job.

Paul then goes to his local hardware store to buy the materials that Willard's have listed. On the list is a specific type of wood glue. At the store Paul sees that this glue is really quite expensive but that there is another bottle of 'wood glue' for a fraction of the price. Conscious of his desire to keep the costs down, Paul opts to buy the cheaper glue.

With all of the equipment purchased, Willard's kitchens then install the kitchen as agreed. Two days after, while cooking dinner, all of the cupboards above the cooker fall down causing damage to the kitchen. It transpires that the glue that Paul bought was not suitable for the job and would come unstuck when met with steam. In terms of liability, who is liable for damages under the 2022 Act?

A. Both the hardware store and Willard's Kitchens
B. Willard's kitchens only
C. The hardware store only
D. Neither of the parties.

The correct answer here is B. As Paul did not disclose to the hardware store what specifically he required the glue for they cannot be liable under the 2022 Act. Willard's Kitchen's would argue that they used the materials that Paul provided, however Paul did not provide the specific glue that they required. In using the substandard glue they did not comply with their duties under s 39 of the 2022 Act to supply the service with due skill, care and diligence.

Stretch and Challenge Question

Should the same level of protection be given to businesses and consumers, or does the law strike a fair balance?

Chapter 10

PRIVITY OF CONTRACT AND THIRD PARTY RIGHTS

10.1 Introduction

The general rule at common law is that only the parties to the contract can be bound by it. This is known as the doctrine of privity. However, it is not inconceivable that a contract is created where the benefit is going to a third party. In those circumstances, can the third party who is not privy to the contract enforce it? For example, Adam is contracting to sell his car to Sarah, but the car is put into John's name as it is being purchased for him. If the car is faulty, does John have any remedies against Adam as he did not enter the contract himself? This is the type of scenario that arose in the famous tort case of *Donoghue v Stevenson* where a decomposed snail was found in a bottle of ginger beer.[1] The claimant suffered illness as a result, but she could not recover compensation in contract law. The beer had been purchased by her friend, and as the claimant was not privy to the contract she could not recover. Instead, she took her case in tort, and the modern test for negligence was established. Indeed, tort law has long picked up the slack where contracts have failed to provide remedies for an injured party.[2]

10.2 Privity and Consideration

A much quoted passage by Viscount Haldane in *Dunlop Pneumatic Tyre Co Ltd v Selfridge & Co* summarises the position in relation to privity:

1 [1932] AC 562.
2 BS Markesinis, 'An Expanding Tort Law – The Price of a Rigid Contract' (1987) 103 Law Quarterly Review 354.

> My Lords, in the Law of England certain principles are fundamental. One is that only a person who is a party to a contract can sue on it. Our law knows nothing of a jus quaesitum tertio [a right on account of a third party] arising by way of contract. Such a right may be conferred by way of property as, for example, under a trust, but it cannot be conferred on a stranger to a contract as a right to enforce the contract in personam. A second principle is that if a person with whom a contract not under seal has been made is to be able to enforce it consideration must have been given by him to the promisor or to some other person at the promisor's request.[3]

Thus, there are two parts to this: first, a person needs to be a party to the contract, and, secondly, they need to have provided consideration.

The rule that consideration must move from the promisee originates in the early privity case of *Tweddle v Atkinson*, where a married couple's respective fathers entered into an agreement where they would each pay a sum of money to the husband.[4] The agreement further gave the husband the right to sue for the money promised. After the death of the wife's father, the husband sued the estate to recover the amount promised. It was held that he could not recover as, despite not being privy to the contract, he had not provided any consideration. Thus, the application of consideration resulted in lots of complex issues and applications in order to avoid the strict application of the doctrine of privity. It could therefore be argued that the doctrine of privity is really no more than the application of the doctrine of consideration. Lord Haldane in *Dunlop Pneumatic Tyre Co Ltd* distinguished between the two in that privity relates to who can enforce the contract, and consideration relates to the types of promises that can be enforced. However, as noted in *Anson's Law of Contract*, if consideration here is interpreted such that consideration must move from the claimant, the two are indistinguishable. [5]

In Ireland, the courts have readily adopted the doctrine of privity with Monahan CJ stating that 'it has been decided that where the foundation of the right of action is rested upon contract, no one can maintain an action who is not party to the contract'.[6]

10.3 Privity and Burdens

It is generally well established that a third party cannot have any burdens from a contract imposed upon them. However, there are some

---

3 [1915] UKHL 1.
4 (1861) 1 B&S 393.
5 (31st edn, OUP 2020).
6 *Murphy v Bower* (1868) IR 2 CL 506, 512.

common law exceptions to this rule. The first exception is known as bailment, which involves the delivery of goods for some purpose (dry cleaning, repair etc) and then their return. In some cases, the terms of a sub-bailment will be enforceable. In *Morris v CW Martin & Sons Ltd* the owner of a mink stole (the bailor) sent it to a furrier (the bailee) for cleaning.[7] The bailee then sent it to a sub-bailee for cleaning and the conditions of this were 'at the customer's risk'. Could the sub-bailee rely on this clause when sued by the bailor for damages? Lord Denning stated that because the bailor had agreed that the stole be passed to the sub-bailee for cleaning, she had consented to all of the terms including the exclusion clause.

As such, the bailor will be bound by the terms of a contract that they have not entered into where it can be said that they gave their express or implied consent. In *KH Enterprise v Pioneer Container* the claimant had entered into a contract for the carriage of goods, which allowed for the carriers to subcontract, which they did to the defendant.[8] In the contract between the original carriers and the subcontractor, there was a clause which stated that any disputes should be dealt with in the jurisdiction of Taiwan and the question was whether the claimant was bound by this clause. The court held that the claimant was bound as it consented to the subcontracting on the defendant's terms.

The second exception comes from the case of *Tulk v Moxhay* which states that third parties can be subject to restrictive covenants affecting land.[9] This means that there are covenants that can attach to land and bind every successive purchaser. It was argued that this rule ought to be extended to contracts involving the use of chattels in *Lord Strathcona Steamship Ltd v Dominion Coal Co Ltd*.[10] However, Lord Diplock in *Port Line Ltd v Ben Line Steamers Ltd* stated that *Strathcona* had been wrongly decided.[11] Despite this, *Strathcona* was followed in *Swiss Bank Corporation v Lloyds Bank Ltd* on the basis that it was the equitable counterpart of the tort of knowing interference with contractual rights.[12] There has been no concrete resolution as to whether the rule in *Tulk v Moxhay* does in fact extend beyond land, with conflicting decisions of the court.

The rule in *Tulk v Moxhay* has been approved of in Ireland in *Whelan and Whelan v Cork Corporation*,[13] affirmed by the Land and Conveyancing

---

7 [1966] 1 QB 716.
8 [1994] 2 AC 324.
9 (1848) 2 Ph 774.
10 [1926] AC 108.
11 [1858] 2 QB 146.
12 [1979] Ch 548.
13 [1991] ILRM 19.

Reform Act[14] and discussed in great detail by Wylie on Irish Land Law.[15]

10.4 Statutory Intervention in England

As far back as 1937, the Law Commission in England proposed that a third party should be able to enforce a contract where that contract was specifically and expressly for the benefit of that third party.[16] However, this was not acted upon, and the courts were critical of the government's lack of response to these proposals. In *Woodar Investment Development Ltd v Wimpey Construction (UK) Ltd* Lord Scarman lamented the fact that nothing had been done to address what he called an 'unjust rule',[17] feelings that were echoed by Lord Goff in *White v Jones*.[18]

The core case for reform was set out by Lord Steyn in *Darlington Borough Council v Wiltshier Northern Ltd* as follows:

> The case for recognising a contract for the benefit of a third party is simple and straightforward. The autonomy of the will of the parties should be respected. The law of contract should give effect to the reasonable expectations of the parties … there is no doctrinal, logical, or policy reason why the law should deny effectiveness to a contract for the benefit of a third party where that is the express intention of the parties. Moreover, often the parties, and particularly third parties, organise their affairs on the faith of the contract. It is therefore unjust to deny effectiveness to such a contract. I will not struggle with the point further since nobody seriously asserts the contrary.[19]

In the early 1990s, the debate over reform concerned how best this could be achieved. Should it be judicially led on a case-by-case basis, or should there be legislative intervention? The Law Commission advocated strongly for legislative intervention as there were numerous issues with a judicially led reform, including the fact that one would need to wait for an appropriate case to challenge the rule and further it would result in a significant level of uncertainty, particularly within the commercial context.

---

14 s 60.

15 (6th Ed, Bloomsbury Professional 2021). See also John Mee and Alan Murphy, 'Reform of the Law of Covenants' (2007) 12(4) Conveyancing and Property Law Journal 100.

16 Andrew M Tettenborn, 'Third Party Contracts – Pragmatism from the Law Commission' (1996) Journal of Business Law 602.

17 [1980] 1 WLR 277.

18 [1995] 2 AC 207.

19 [1995] 1 WLR 68.

The proposals of the Law Commission were broadly accepted in the Contracts (Rights of Thirds Parties) Act 1999 in England.[20] The Act does not abolish the doctrine of privity but rather sets out certain exceptions where third parties can enforce rights under the contract.[21]

Section 1 of the 1999 Act states that a third party can enforce a benefit under the contract where the test of enforceability is satisfied. Further, once this is satisfied, the third party will have all rights to remedies as if they were a party to the contract.[22]

Under the 1999 Act, there are two ways in which the third party may satisfy the test. The first is that the contract expressly provides that a specific third party has the right to enforce the contract. The second is where the third party is expressly identified in the contract and the 'term purports to confer a benefit' on that particular person. The scope of this second element was considered by the court in *Dolphin Maritime & Aviation Services Ltd v Sveriges Angfartygs Assurans Forening.*[23] In this case the claimant was a recovery agent for the insurer in relation to a ship which had been involved in an accident. The claimant entered into an agreement with the defendant club whereby sums recovered from the owner of the ship at fault would be paid to it (Dolphin). The insurer then settled directly with the club and refused to pay commission to the claimant. The court found that Dolphin was not entitled to bring the claim as a third party. The agreement was only made in relation to how the sums would be paid as the insurer was always the intended beneficiary, although it would have benefitted Dolphin as its fees would have been deducted before transferring the remainder to the insurer. As it was not 'an agreement by A and B that A will pay C' but rather a 'provision for payment of a sum to an agent on his principal's behalf', it was not covered by the scope of the Act.

The second part of the enforceability test does not apply where it appears, on proper construction of the contract, that the parties did not intend for the third party to be able to enforce the contract (s 1(2)). This was considered in *Nisshin Shipping Co Ltd v Cleaves & Co Ltd* where Cleaves had negotiated a number of time charters on behalf of the

---

[20] Meryll Dean, 'Removing a Blot on the Landscape – Reform of the Doctrine of Privity'(2000) Journal of Business Law 143.

[21] See Robert Stevens, 'The Contracts (Rights of Third Parties) Act 1999' (2004) 120 Law Quarterly Review 292.

[22] Neil Andrews, 'Strangers to Justice no Longer – The Reversal of Privity Rules Under the Contracts (Rights of Third Parties) Act 1999' (2001) 60(2) Cambridge Law Journal 353.

[23] [2009] EWHC 716 (Comm). This case is commonly referred to as 'The Swedish Club' case.

owners.[24] Each of these contained a provision that Cleaves would be paid commission and further contained an arbitration clause. Nisshin claimed that Cleaves was in repudiatory breach of the contract and was therefore not entitled to commission. Cleaves sought to refer the matter to arbitration, arguing that it satisfied the second aspect of the enforceability test, although not party to the time charters. It was held that the clause purported to confer a benefit on Cleaves. Further, Coleman J held that in order for s 1(2) to apply, it needed to be demonstrated that the parties' intention was that the third party would *not* have a right to enforce the contract. As the contract was silent on this, and there was nothing to suggest that the parties did not want Cleaves to have the right of enforcement, the test was met. This application was further affirmed by the court in *Laemthong International Lines Co Ltd v Artis, The Laemthong Glory*.[25]

For either aspect of the enforceability test to apply, the third party must be expressly identified by the contract. This imposes particular limitations, specifically within the commercial context. In *Avraamides v Colwill*, A employed C to refurbish his bathroom.[26] C's work was defective and he was liable to A. C then sold his business to B, with B agreeing to complete any outstanding customer orders and to pay any liabilities incurred by A up to a certain date. The Court of Appeal was required to determine whether A would be able to enforce this agreement. The Court of Appeal held that as A was not expressly identified in the contract between B and C, it could not be said that the intention of the parties was to transfer the enforceability of A's rights against C to B.

This clearly imposes a significant limitation on who can access these third party rights and requires careful drafting.[27]

Of concern with this section is the possibility that a third party may be able to enforce a right under this section where the contract does nothing to rebut the presumption that the contract purports to confer a benefit. In *Chudley v Clydesdale Bank Plc*, Arck LLP opened an account with the defendant through a letter of instruction which was held to be a binding contract.[28] The account was described as 'segregated client account' for the 'sole purpose of the development of the Paradise Beach Resort Sal Cape Verde'. The bank agreed to hold monies in that account until a specified date and to release withdrawals only on

---

24 [2003] EWHC 2602 (Comm).
25 [2005] EWCA Civ 519.
26 [2006] EWCA Civ 1533
27 See Timothy Liau, 'Privity: Rights, Standing and the Road not Taken' (2021) 41(3) Oxford Journal of Legal Studies 803.
28 [2019] EWCA Civ 344.

receiving an unconditional undertaking from a named solicitor. The bank never set up this account and the funds paid by various investors were paid into the Arck LLP's general account with the bank. It was later discovered that the scheme was fraudulent and Arck LLP went into liquidation. The investors sought to recover their money from the bank as they had failed to set up the required account and released the funds without the undertaking from the solicitor. Despite the fact that they were not privy to the contract between the bank and Arck LLP, they argued that the 1999 Act applied, an argument which was successful in the Court of Appeal. Davies argues this case evidences a scenario where a benefit has been conferred to the investors despite the fact that it would clearly not have been the intention of the parties to the contract to do so and therefore drafters should be careful to ensure that they exclude the provisions of s 1.[29]

One of the key considerations in reform of this area of law is whether or not the parties to the contract can vary or cancel the third party rights. Section 2 of the 1999 Act provides that the contracting parties cannot vary or cancel the third party rights without the express consent of the third party where the third party has communicated acceptance and and/or relied on the term which the promisor knew or ought reasonably to have known of. However, s 2(3) goes on to state that contracting parties may opt out of this clause by stipulating a particular type of acceptance or act from the third party, or indeed by reserving the right to vary or cancel the right.

10.5 Statutory Intervention in Ireland

While it took some time for the English Authorities to act on the recommendations of the Law Commission's report, it served as an impetus for some legislative changes in Ireland. One of the first changes shows the extension of provisions contained in the Married Women's Property Act 1882 (which allowed widows and children of the deceased to sue upon a life insurance policy) to include an action on endowment policies in the Married Women's Status Act 1957. In addition, the 1957 Act gives a right to a wife, husband or child of a contracting party to enforce a contract where it can be shown that the contract purports to confer a benefit on them.

Further, the Road Traffic Act 1961 provides that a person claiming against an insured motorist the right to pursue a claim against the insurers or guarantors of the insured where the insured is outside of

---

29 Paul S Davies, 'Excluding the Contracts (Third Parties Rights) Act 1999' (2021) 137 Law Quarterly Review 101.

the state, cannot be found, is immune to the process or in any other circumstances where it is just and equitable to do so.[30]

The Consumer Insurance Contracts Act 2019 increases protection and provides that a third party may proceed directly against an insurer when the insured party has incurred a liability to the third party and that insured person has died, cannot be found, is insolvent or in other circumstances where the court regards it just and equitable to allow such a claim to proceed.[31] Section 21 (2) explicitly states that

> 'a third party… has a right to recover from the insurer in accordance with the contract of insurance, the amount of loss suffered by the third party even though the third party is not a party to the contract'.

In relation to hire purchase agreements, the contract technically is with the hire purchase company and not with the seller of the goods, meaning that if the doctrine of privity applied the customer could not sue the seller for any breach of contract. Section 80 of the Consumer Credit Act 1995 allows for the consumer to have a remedy against both the seller and the hire purchase company for breach of the hire purchase agreement or any misrepresentation.

The Package Holidays and Travel Trade Act 1995 extends protection not only to the person who booked the holiday, but also to any other third party who benefits from the contract.

10.6 Proposals for Reform

In light of the somewhat piecemeal approach taken to third party rights in Ireland, the Law Reform Commission issued a consultation paper in 2006 entitled 'Privity of Contract: Third Party Rights'.[32] The paper noted that the area needed considerable reform due to the potential of injustice as the use of the privity doctrine can be used to thwart the intentions of the contracting parties[33] and followed this up with a report 'Privity of Contract and Third Party Rights' in 2008.[34] The report notes that the area of law is unclear given that there are some exceptions to the rule, it is not clear whether the court will impose the

---

30 s 76(1). See *Herlihy v Curley* [1950] IR 15; *Norton v General Accident* (1941) 74 ILTR 123; *Sinnott v Quinnsworth* [1984] ILRM 523.

31 ss 21 and 22.

32 LRC CP 40-2006.

33 See Cliona Kelly, 'Privity of Contract – The Benefits of Reform' (2008) 1 Judicial Studies Institute Journal 145

34 LRC 88-2008.

privity rule or one of the exceptions.[35] This report contained a draft bill which it recommended be enacted to reform the area.

Section 3 of the proposed bill provides that a third party may enforce a contract where either the contract expressly confers upon them the right to do so, or where the contract expressly confers a benefit on them. To enforce this right, the section further requires that the third party be expressly identified within the contract by reference to their name, membership of a particular class, or answering to a particular description, but does not require them to be in existence at the time that the contract. In other words, this means that in a contract which is made for the benefit of grandchildren could be enforced by subsequent grandchildren even if they were not born at the time the contract was entered into.

To-date, these reforms have not been acted upon and the law of privity and third party rights remains haphazard at best in Ireland.

Test Your Knowledge

Bernadette's youngest son, Joe, is about to start university away from home, and she decides that she wants to buy a car for him so that he can come home at weekends and make his classes in the event of train strikes. She uses her business, Bernie's Bakes, to contract with a local car dealer, New Wheels. During the discussion, she says that the contract she is entering into is for her son, and the salesman Dave is aware that she is purchasing the car for the benefit of another person. The contract that is entered into explicitly states, 'This car is purchased for the benefit of my son.' Two weeks after the car is purchased, the engine explodes and Joe tries to return the car. The garage refuses to deal with him, saying that he is not party to the contract. Bernadette is now out of the country on a retreat where she cannot be contacted by phone or email.

Can Joe:

A enforce the benefit of the contract as the contract specifically identified him?

B enforce the benefit of the contract as the contract stated that he could enforce it?

C not enforce the benefit of the contract as he was not privy to it?

---

[35] For example, see *Glow Heating Ltd v Eastern Health Board* [1988] IR 110. See also Roe 'Contractual Intention under Section 1(1)(b) and 1(2) of the Contracts (Rights of Third Parties) Act 1999' (2000) 65 Modern Law Review 887.

The correct answer here is C. This matter does not fall within any of the existing statutory exceptions in Ireland. His only option is to wait until his mother returns home where she, as privy to the contract, can deal with the garage.

Stretch and Challenge Question

Analyse whether it is appropriate to allow a third party attain a benefit under a contract while not imposing any burdens.

PART THREE

AVOIDING CONTRACTUAL LIABILITY

CHAPTER 11

MISTAKE

11.1 Introduction

This chapter examines the circumstances when contractual liability can be discharged and the contract avoided where one or more of the parties have entered into the contract on a mistaken belief. Where the misunderstanding arises out of the words or conduct of the other party, a claim will usually arise to have the contract set aside on the grounds of misrepresentation (considered in Chapter 12) as the grounds for mistake are narrow. Parties are not easily discharged from their obligations merely because they were operating under some mistaken belief.

The doctrine of mistake is a difficult one to grasp as the principles have not been precisely settled and the key cases may be open to a number of interpretations. It was first recognised in English law in the 19th century, and early cases appeared to favour a wider interpretation of the doctrine. This was based on the consensus theory of contract in that if there had not been 'true, full and free consent' then there could be no contract. Today, the doctrine is interpreted in a much narrower manner. Anson speculates that this may be due to the fact that when a contract is entered into under mistake, it is void *ab initio* – it has no legal effect and this has further implications for third party rights.[1]

As we will see in this chapter, the doctrine of mistake has provoked a significant amount of judicial opinion as to how and when it ought to operate. In the case of common mistake, the tests in England have gone from an initial wide approach, to a narrow one, to being widened

1 *Anson's Law of Contract*, (31st edn, OUP 2020).

again by the introduction of 'equitable mistake' by Lord Denning in *Solle v Butcher*,[2] only to have this approach rejected and the narrow approach reaffirmed by the House of Lords in *Great Peace Shipping Ltd v Tsavliris Salvage (International) Ltd*.[3] However, the courts in Ireland have not followed the narrowing approach of the English judiciary.

11.2 Categorisation

There are two types of mistake that can operate in contract law: unilateral mistake and common or mutual mistake. A unilateral mistake is where one of the parties is operating under a mistaken belief, whereas a common or mutual mistake sees both parties mistaken. It is important to differentiate between the two as we will see that the court imposes different rules depending on which type of mistake is operating.

11.3 Mistake as to the Terms of the Contract

This section examines circumstances where it appears that, to all intents and purposes, the parties have come to an agreement, but in fact they have not. This needs to be distinguished from the issues of offer and acceptance (although the two look very closely linked). In terms of coming to the agreement, where the offer and acceptance are clearly not in sync no contract will come into play. The circumstances here are where it looks like there has been an agreement, but that agreement has come about as a result of a mistaken belief on the part of one or both or the parties. For example, if an offeree accepts an offer believing the terms to be other than they are, there can be no real agreement as the offer being accepted is not the offer being made. Therefore, there has been no meeting of the minds, no real agreement and as such a contract cannot come into existence.

In general, a party will not be discharged from its contractual liability on the basis that it entered into a contract under some basic misunderstanding or made a bad bargain. The law takes an objective approach to the contractual agreement and, in the interest of market certainty, parties will primarily be held to their bargains. For example, in *Stapleton v Prudential Insurance* the plaintiff entered into a life insurance policy believing that by paying two shillings per month for 11 years she would receive the sum of £25 at the end of the period.[4] The

---

2 [1950] 1 KB 671. See John Cartwright, 'Solle v Butcher and the Doctrine of Mistake in Contract Law' (1987) 103 Law Quarterly Review 594.

3 [2002] EWCA Civ 1407.

4 (1928) 62 ILTR 56.

contract in fact provided that the sum would only be payable on her death. When Stapleton learned of this mistake, she sought to rescind the contract and have her contributions returned. However, the court held that despite the fact that she was operating under a mistake, this would not be sufficient to rescind the contract.[5] The intention of the parties in entering into a contract can be found not only in their subjective intentions, but also inferred objectively from their conduct. The 'objective test' for establishing the intention of the parties was set forth by Blackburn J in *Smith v Hughes* as follows:

> If one of the parties intends to make a contract on one set of terms, and the other intends to make a contract on another set of terms, or, as is sometimes expressed, if the parties are not ad idem, there is no contract, unless the circumstances are such as to preclude one of the parties from denying that he has agreed to the terms of the other .... If, whatever a man's real intention may be, he so conducts himself that a reasonable man would believe that he was assenting to the terms proposed by the other party, and that other party upon that belief enters into the contract with him, the man thus conducting himself would be equally bound as if he had intended to agree to the other party's terms.[6]

There are circumstances where the contract may seem to be valid but when viewed under this objective test is held to be void.[7] There are four areas in which this may arise, which are considered in turn.

11.3.1 Where There is No Coherence Between the Offer and Acceptance Despite an Outward Appearance

This arises typically in circumstances where a term or word in the offer could potentially mean two things. The offeree accepts on the basis of one meaning whereas the offeror in fact meant the other. Here there is no meeting of the minds, and despite an outward display of offer and acceptance being valid, applying the objective test as set out above it is clear that the intentions of the parties are not the same. This is an example of a mutual or common mistake as both parties meant something different. This is illustrated in the case of *Raffles v Wichelhaus* where the defendant agreed to buy bales of cotton which were 'to arrive ex peerless from Bombay'.[8] There were two ships called Peerless and they both sailed from Bombay. The defendant meant the ship that sailed in October while the claimant meant the ship that sailed in December. It was held that there was no contract as it could

---

5 See also *James v National Benefit Trust Ltd* (1902) 2 NIJR 19.

6 (1871) LR 6 QB 597, 607.

7 Daniel Freidman, 'The Objective Principle and Mistake and Involuntariness in Contract and Restitution' (2002) 119 Law Quarterly Review 69.

8 (1864) 2 H&C 906.

not be identified as to which ship was the subject matter and therefore the offer and acceptance were not coherent. Similar results have occurred in Irish case law. In *Megaw v Molloy* the plaintiff employed a broker to sell maize.[9] The maize he intended to sell via this broker was imported on the ship 'Emma Peasant'. He had also purchased a cargo of superior maize which was imported on the ship 'Jessie Parker'. On the morning of the sale a sample purporting to be from the 'Emma Peasant' was displayed but this was actually taken from the 'Jessie Parker'. The defendant had purchased the maize following the inspection but when the mistake was identified would not accept delivery of the goods. Here the defendant successfully argued that there was no contract at all as the vendor intended to sell the cargo of one ship, which the purchaser intended to buy the cargo of another.

In addition, where the terms of the contract are ambiguous, or the circumstances around the contract are ambiguous, there may be no legally binding contract. For example, in *Scriven Bros & Co v Hindley & Co* the claimant instructed an auctioneer to sell bales of hemp and tow.[10] These bales had the same shipping marks and were described in the auction catalogue with no indication of the difference of their contents. The defendant examined some samples of the hemp and intended to bid on the bales of hemp alone. At the auction, the bales of tow were put up for sale, and the defendant, believing them to be the bales of hemp, made a bid which was excessive for tow, but reasonable for hemp. This offer was accepted, with the auctioneer not realising the mistake that the defendant had been operating under. The claimant sought to enforce the contract.

It was clear in this case that the claimant sought to sell two products, while the defendant, misled by the auction catalogue, intended to buy hemp. The court, relying on the test established in *Smith*, found that the defendant had not acted in a manner such that a reasonable person would think that the defendant was assenting to the claimant's terms. There was therefore no contract, and the defendant was not liable.

However, if the agreement is clear in its terms mistake cannot be pleaded where the other party believes that a different outcome would be achieved. This is well illustrated in the Supreme Court case of *Mespil Ltd v Capaldi*.[11] Here an action was commenced for possession of rented premises for breaches of the lease. Prior to the commencement of these specific proceedings, a settlement had been reached in relation to different litigation between the parties with referred to 'full and final

9 (1878) 2 LR (IR) 530.
10 [1913] 3 KB 564.
11 [1986] ILRM 373.

settlement of all matters'. The defendant argued that when they signed this agreement, they intended it to cover all disputes, even those which were not the subject of the litigation to which the settlement related. Initially it was held that the agreement could not be extended in this manner. The Supreme Court however found that the contract was void as not only were the parties at cross purposes when negotiating the agreement, but that the wording of the agreement was capable of being interpreted either way.

This objective test can also work the other way – if the agreement appears to give the plaintiff a benefit which was not intended by the other party, the defendant will not be able to claim that the contract should be enforced in the manner in which it was intended by them. Two Irish cases provide good examples of this principle. In *Clayton Love v B&I Transport* the contract involved the transportation of frozen scampi.[12] The plaintiff intended the scampi to be loaded at sub-atmospheric temperatures while the defendant intended it to be at atmospheric temperatures. In applying the objective test set down in *Smith*, the Supreme Court held that as a result of the manner in which the defendants had conducted themselves during the negotiation process, they were bound to load the cargo as anticipated by the plaintiff therefore making them liable for the destruction of the scampi. Again in *Lucey v Laurel Construction*, the plaintiff agreed to buy a property which on the site plan showed the plot at 170 feet long.[13] However, the plan was in error and the defendant only intended the plan to show 120 feet. When the mistake was discovered, the builders sought to have the plan altered. Here, the court refused to rectify the contract as the plan was the only outward manifestation of the intentions and the plaintiff had done nothing irregular or dishonest.

Thus generally, the court will hold a party to the bargain that it has struck. The one exception to this is considered in the next section, which is where the mistake was known, or ought to have been known by the other party.

11.3.2 Where there is a Mistake that is Known to the Other Party

Generally speaking, there is no rule in law which obliges a party to disclose all material facts. The doctrine of *caveat emptor* ('let the buyer beware') applies, meaning that it is for the buyer to ask the material questions and to do their own research before entering into a contract. Even where it is known that one party is operating under a mistaken belief, there is no outright rule which says that all facts must be

---

[12] (1970) 104 ILTR 157.

[13] Unrep, High Court, 18 December 1970.

disclosed. There are certain exceptions to this, for example a contract *uberrimae fidei* (a contract of the utmost good faith). Insurance contracts are a good example where there is an obligation to disclose all facts.

While there is no duty to actively disclose material, concealing information or deliberately or recklessly giving wrong information may constitute fraudulent misrepresentation.

However, a mistake as to a term of the contract is different from a mistake as to the terms or surrounding circumstances. As we have previously seen the law in relation to terms is mainly concerned with whether a term has been incorporated into the contract or not. In such cases both parties are aware of the term itself and the crux of the matter hinges on whether it was incorporated and if so, how that term is classified. This section differs in that here there is a fundamental mistake as to the core term of the contract. For example, let's say that I want to buy a purebred Jack Russel dog and I respond to an advertisement from a breeder selling puppies. There is generally no obligation on the breeder to tell me that the dogs are purebred, however, if through my discussions with them they know that I want a purebred dog and that I believe that the dogs they are selling are indeed purebred, the law will then require them to clarify my mistake and tell me that they are not. If I buy the dog and then discover that he is not pure Jack Russell but say a Jack Russel / Parson Russel mix, the law will allow the mistake that I was operating under to be sufficient to void the contract as the seller was aware of my mistaken belief and will not be able to enforce the contract. In other words, the law will not allow one party to enforce a term when they were aware that this was not the term that the other was agreeing to.

In *Smith v Hughes*, Smith sued Hughes for the price of oats plus damages for failing to accept the oats when delivered.[14] The reason for this refusal was that Hughes argued that Smith had offered to sell a parcel of oats described as 'good old oats'. When the oats were delivered, they were found to be new oats which were not suitable for the purpose for which they were required. Smith denied that the word 'old' had been used. The trial judge directed the jury to consider:

(a) whether the word 'old' had been used, and if so they were to find in favour of Hughes;
(b) if the word 'old' had not been used, whether they believed that Smith believed that Hughes thought he had contracted for old oats.

The jury found in favour of Hughes but did not say on which ground.

[14] (1871) LR 6 QB 597.

A retrial was ordered on the basis that the direction given by the judge was insufficient. It was stated that 'in order to relieve Hughes, it was necessary that the jury should find not merely that Smith believed Hughes to believe that he was buying old oats, but that he believed Hughes to believe that he, Smith was contracting to sell old oats.

11.3.3 Res Extincta

Res extincta ('the matter has ceased to exist') relates to a mistake as to the existence of the subject matter of a contract. Where the subject matter was not in existence at the time the contract was made, there can be no contract. In *Couturier v Hastie* there was a contract between the parties for a cargo of corn.[15] Unbeknownst to the parties, the captain had already sold the corn as it had begun to ferment. It was held that there was no contract as the subject matter did not exist at the time that the contract was entered into. However, to achieve this outcome, it must be clear that neither of the parties were aware that the subject matter was not in existence. If one party is aware, then there could be issues of fraudulent misrepresentation which we will consider in the next chapter.

11.3.4 Where there is a Mistake as to the Written Document

Where a contract has been reduced to writing and signed by both parties, it is a difficult task to persuade the courts that what is written in the document is not what was agreed by the parties. There are two ways in which the court may intervene. The first is where the doctrine of *non est factum* may apply (see below). The second is the equitable remedy of rectification where there is an error in the contract which the court rectifies so that the contract reflects the true intentions of the parties. We consider rectification separately in Chapter 20.

11.3.4.1 Non Est Factum

This is a defence that may allow a person to escape the effect of a document they have signed. This plea was initially confined to circumstances where a blind or illiterate person signed a contract where the terms had been misrepresented. The effect of successfully pleading *non est factum* is that the contract is void *ab initio* (this Latin phrase translates to 'from the beginning'). It is, however, interpreted narrowly, and a party who has not read the document or did not understand its contents will not be able to rely on it. This was explained by Donovan LJ in *Muskham Finance Ltd v Howard* where he stated that 'much confusion and uncertainty would result in the field of contract

[15] (1856) 5 HL Cas 673.

and elsewhere if a man were permitted to try to disown his signature simply by asserting that he did not understand that which he had signed'.[16]

In order to successfully plead this defence, the party must show that the contract they signed was substantially different to the transaction intended although it is not a requirement that fraud be shown.[17] The test was established by the House of Lords in *Saunders v Anglia Building Society*.[18] In this case, an elderly widow gave her nephew the title deeds to her property in order that he could use it as security to borrow money. She intended this to be a gift to her nephew, with the condition that she reside in the property for the rest of her life. She was asked to sign a document by a friend of the nephew who told her that it was to do with the gift of the house to her nephew. She had broken her glasses and could not read the document but signed it regardless. It transpired that the document was in fact a sale to the friend, who subsequently mortgaged the property to Anglia Building Society. In applying the test that there must be a radical or essential or fundamental or serious or very substantial difference between the document signed and that which the person signing believed it to be, the claim of *non est factum* failed in this case. While the court was sympathetic to the claimant, it found that it was not fundamentally different to the document that she thought she was signing and therefore Anglia Building Society could enforce the mortgage.[19]

A further aspect to this case is that even where the document signed is held to be substantially different, a party will not be able to rely on the doctrine unless they can show that they have exercised reasonable care in the circumstances. This will be very fact specific in each case.

The judgement of Morris J in *Ted Castle McCormack and Co v McCrystal* suggests that for this defence to succeed, a temporary disability may be sufficient.[20] The defendant signed a personal guarantee in respect of oil and petrol supplied to his business believing that he was signing an exclusive supply agreement. Evidence was adduced that at the time of signing he was suffering from anxiety and depression. In allowing

---

16 [1963] 1 QB 904, 912.

17 *Bank of Ireland v McManamy* [1916] 2 IR 161.

18 [1971] AC 1004.

19 This case has been applied in Ireland in *Bank of Ireland v McCabe and McCabe*, Unrep, High Court, 23 March 1993 and *ADM Londis Plc v Arman Retail Ltd* [2006] IEHC 306.

20 Unrep, High Court, 15 March 1999. See also Mark J Heslin, 'Non Est Factum – when the Contract I Signed is "not my deed"' (2013) 20(6) Commercial Law Practitioner 119.

the defence to succeed, Morris J summarised the core requirements from *Saunders* as:

> I am satisfied that a person seeking to raise the defence of non est factum must prove:
>
> a. That there was a radical or fundamental difference between what he signed and what he thought he was signing;
>
> b. That the mistake was as to the general character of the document as opposed to the legal effect and
>
> c. That there was a lack of negligence, i.e that he took all reasonable precautions in the circumstances to find out what the document was.

11.4 Mistake as to Identity

This type of mistake has posed significant difficulties because such cases often involve the court trying to decide which of two innocent parties ought to bear the loss.[21] In a typical scenario, A agrees to sell goods to B, but B is actually C who then sells the goods on to D. In this case, both A and D are innocent parties and C is generally a fraudster who cannot be traced. The court has to decide whether the goods should remain with D, leaving A out of pocket, or should be returned to A, leaving D out of pocket. The Irish Courts have not had to consider this issue to large degree. There are a number of elements to this, and each is considered in turn.

11.4.1 An Offer Can Only be Accepted by the Person to Whom it is Made

In *Boulton v Jones* Boulton had taken over Brocklehurst's business.[22] Brocklehurst dealt previously with Jones who was entitled to a set off in respect of sums owed to him by Brocklehurst. Jones sent an order for goods which was accepted and supplied by Boulton without telling Jones that the business had changed hands. When Jones became aware of this he refused to pay for the goods. The court found that Jones was not liable to pay for the goods. As Pollock CB stated, 'it is a rule of law, that if a person intends to contract with A, B cannot give himself any right under it.'

However, it must be remembered from Chapter 2 that offer and acceptance are judged objectively, so that if A makes an offer to B

[21] See Catharine MacMillan, 'Rogues, Swindlers and Cheats: The Development of Mistake of Identity in English Contract Law' (2005) 64(3) Cambridge Law Journal 711.

[22] (1857) 2 H&N 564.

mistaking him for C, and B accepts that offer reasonably believing that A intended to make this offer to him and not C, then A will be bound. An extreme example of this can be found in the case of *Upton-on-Severn RDC v Powell* where Powell called the Upton Fire Brigade by mistake. He should have called the Pershore Fire Brigade, which covered his area, but the call was accepted by Upton.[23] It was held that the defendant was liable to pay for the services despite the mistake made by both parties – Powell thought he was calling for a service within his area which would be free, and Upton thought that they were responding to call within their area for which there would be no charge.

However, where an offer is accepted on the grounds that the offeree believes the offeror to be someone else, and the offeror is aware of that mistaken belief, there can be no contract.

In *Cundy v Lindsay* a rogue set up a business 'Blenkarn' at 37 Wood Street.[24] He ordered goods from Lindsay, imitating the signature of a firm (Blenkiron & Co) which also had an address on Wood Street and which Lindsay was aware of by reputation. Lindsay sold the goods to Blenkarn, believing it to the firm Blenkiron & Co, which then sold the goods on to Cundy. The court had to decide here where the liability would fall – if the initial contract was voidable for fraudulent misrepresentation, then Cundy would be entitled to retain the goods as it purchased them in good faith; but if the contract was void for mistake, Blenkarn could pass no title as there was no contract and Lindsay would be entitled to the return of the goods. The House of Lords held:

> Of him [Blenkarn] they knew nothing, and of him they never thought. With him they never intended to deal. Their minds never, even for an instant rested upon him and as between him and them there was no consensus of mind which could lead to any agreement or contract whatever.

As such, the court found in favour of Lindsay as when the offer was accepted, Blenkarn knew that it was done so under the mistaken belief that Lindsay was entering into a contract with Blenkiron & Co.

The House of Lords again considered this point in *Shogun Finance Ltd v Hudson*.[25] In this case a finance company agreed to sell a car on hire purchase to a fraudster who then sold the car onto Hudson. Under the Hire Purchase Act 1964 (s 27) the purchaser under a hire

---

23 [1942] 1 All ER 220.
24 (1878) 3 App Cas 459.
25 [2003] UKHL 64.

purchase agreement can acquire good title provided that the purchase has been made in good faith. The defendant's case therefore turned on the validity of the hire purchase agreement. If it was voidable for fraud then Hudson would be able to claim ownership in the vehicle; however, if it was void for mistake then the fraudster would not be classed as a 'debtor' under the legislation and Hudson would therefore have no protection. In examining the facts of the case, the fraudster had provided a genuine driving licence belonging to a Mr Patel and the finance company had checked Mr Patel's credit rating. It was held by the majority of the House of Lords that the contract was void as it could only have been made by the finance company and Mr Patel, which was impossible as Mr Patel was entirely unaware of it. As such, the finance company was entitled to receive the vehicle, leaving Hudson out of pocket and the victim of the fraud.[26]

11.4.2 The Need for an Identifiable Third Party

If a mistake does not arise in relation to the identity of a person, the contract will be valid. Here the courts will need to determine whether the mistake went to the identity of a person or their attributes or qualities. It is only in the former case that the contract will be void.

In *Kings Norton Metal Co Ltd v Edridge, Merrett & Co Ltd* the plaintiff received a letter from 'Hallam & Co' asking for a quotation for metal wire.[27] The plaintiff sent a quote and 'Hallam & Co' placed the order. However, this company was a fraud and consisted of one person named Wallis, who subsequently sold the wire to the defendant. The plaintiff argued that the contract was void and sought the return of the wire. It was held that the plaintiff intended to contract with the writer of the letter. It was acknowledged that they would not have done so had they known the true identity of the writer, but in this instance the contract was only voidable for fraud. As such, title had passed to Wallis, and the defendant as a bona fide purchaser was entitled to the goods.

Where a contract is wholly in writing, it is assumed that the parties identified in the contract are those who are contracting. In *Shogun Finance Ltd v Hudson*, the majority decision of the House of Lords was based on the fact that the contract was in writing, and therefore the only person who could have been party to the agreement was Mr

---

26 Oliver Brooks and Andrew Dodd, 'Shogun: A Principled Decision' (2003) 153 (7109) New Law Journal 1898; Christopher Hare, 'Identity Mistakes: A Missed Opportunity' (2004) 67(6) Modern Law Review 993; Keith Spencer, 'A Case of Mistaken Identity' (2003)10(11) Commercial Law Practitioner 320.

27 (1897) 14 TLR 98.

Patel, whose driving licence was used for the credit check. As it was not Mr Patel who signed the agreement, the contract could not be valid.

11.4.3 Contracts Concluded Personally

Where contracts are concluded face to face and not in writing or by distance, there is an assumption that the parties intend to deal with the person in front of them. In *Phillips v Brooks* a man called North entered Phillips' jewellery shop and selected some pearls and a ring.[28] He wrote a cheque for £3,000 saying 'I am Sir George Bullough' and giving Sir George Bullough's address. Sir George was someone who was known to Phillips as being credit worthy, and Phillips checked the directory to confirm that the address given was correct. Phillips allowed North to take away the jewellery, who then sold the ring to Brooks who had no knowledge of the fraud. It was held in this case that while Phillips believed that the person in the shop was Sir George, he contracted with the person who came into his shop and that his intention was to sell 'to the person present and identified by sight and sound'. As such, the contract was only voidable on the ground of fraud, and title in the ring passed to Brooks.

It is not a foregone conclusion from this case that in all circumstances where a contract is concluded personally that it will automatically be excluded from being void on the grounds of mistake. It is, however, more difficult to overcome the assumption that the parties meant to deal with those in front of them.

In *Ingram v Little*, three plaintiffs advertised their car for sale, and a man identifying himself as Hutchinson offered to purchase it.[29] He offered to make a payment by cheque which they refused, insisting on cash. He then gave his address and described himself as a successful businessman. One of the plaintiffs went to the post office, and from the telephone directory ascertained that there was a man of that name living at the address given. As a result, they allowed him to pay by cheque which turned out to be fraudulent. Hutchinson then sold the car on to Little who had no knowledge of the fraud. In this case, the Court of Appeal found in favour of the plaintiffs. The decision was based on the circumstances of the particular case, specifically that the telephone directory was checked which shows that the plaintiffs intended to deal with 'Hutchinson' and not the man before them. The presumption was therefore rebutted in this case.

However, in *Lewis v Averay*, Lewis advertised his car for sale, and

---

28 [1919] 2 KB 243.
29 [1961] 1 QB 31.

a man posing as the actor Richard Greene called by and offered to buy the car.[30] Lewis accepted, and payment was offered by way of a cheque signed by 'R.A. Greene'. Lewis was reluctant to let the car leave until the cheque had cleared and, to overcome this, the man provided evidence in the form of a studio pass with a photo and an official stamp. Satisfied that he was dealing with the real Richard Greene, Lewis let the car go. The cheque bounced and the car was sold on to Averay who bought it in good faith. Here, the court held that the contract was only voidable as Lewis intended to deal with the person in front of him.

It is difficult to reconcile the cases of *Ingram* and *Lewis* as they seem factually similar. It could be that the court had more sympathy for the plaintiffs in *Ingram*, being three elderly ladies, or more likely that there was some positive step taken by the plaintiffs in *Ingram* to ascertain the identity of the man, rather than accepting any information and documents produced.

11.5 Mistake as to the Subject Matter or Surrounding Circumstances

In this section we are concerned with circumstances where the parties to the contract are mistaken as to some matter which goes to the heart of the contract, either in terms of the subject matter of the contract or the surrounding circumstances. It is difficult for a party to successfully claim mistake in these circumstances because, as we have seen above, when a party has signed a contract, they are taken to have accepted the terms, and failure to carry out due diligence and take reasonable care will not be sufficient. There are different types of mistake that can be made in this regard: one of fact, which relates to the factual contents of the contract; and one of law, which relates to the legal framework governing such contracts. There is a close link here between such mistakes and the doctrine of frustration which we consider in Chapter 17. In addition, the courts will approach the matter differently depending on whether the mistake is unilateral or mutual.

11.5.1 Unilateral Mistake

A unilateral mistake, that is a mistake by one of the parties to the contract, will not be sufficient to void the contract in these circumstances. In *Smith v Hughes* it was established that where one party enters into a contract under a unilateral mistake, they will only have a remedy where either a warranty has been given or they have

---

[30] [1972] 1 QB 198.

been induced to enter the contract under a misrepresentation.[31] Either way, this will not be sufficient to render the contract void, merely voidable.

There is one exception to this rule where the disposition is a voluntary one. This was considered by the Supreme Court in *Pitt v Holt*.[32] In this case a settlor was awarded damages in a personal injury claim and created a discretionary trust under which he would be the primary beneficiary. His advisers did not appreciate that inheritance tax would be payable under this type of trust, and an application was brought to set the trust aside on the grounds of mistake. Here the Supreme Court adopted it a broad approach, holding that the focus should be on both the gravity of the mistake and the unconscionability of the situation. It stated:

> The court cannot decide the issue of what is unconscionable by an elaborate set of rules. It must consider in the round the existence of a distinct mistake ... its degree of centrality to the transaction in question and the seriousness of the consequences, and make an evaluative judgment whether it would be unconscionable or unjust to leave the mistake uncorrected.

In this case it was held that the transaction should be set aside due to the gravity of the mistake and the consequences thereof. Again, in *Wright & Anor v National Westminster Bank* the approach was affirmed and a trust document set aside on the grounds that a grave mistake would cause an unconscionable outcome if the trust was enforced.[33]

11.5.2 Common Mistake

This area has drawn considerable attention of the courts and resulted in a rather convoluted system for many years.[34] Essentially, two approaches were taken to determining whether a contract could be set aside for common mistake. The common law had one line of reasoning, and equity another. We discuss equitable jurisdiction in more detail in Chapter 20 but for the purposes of a brief explanation at this juncture, equity is a system of law which arose in the 14th century and created the Courts of Chancery. Its purpose was to mitigate the harshness of the common law and to provide remedies where the common law did not. At this stage, damages (money) were the only remedy available under the common law system, and therefore equity

---

31 (1871) LR 6 QB 597.

32 [2013] UKSC 26.

33 [2014] EWHC 3158 (Ch). See also *Longley v PBB* [2020] EWHC 977.

34 Jonathan Morgan, 'Common Mistake in Contract: Rare Success and Common Misapprehensions' (2018) 77(3) Cambridge Law Journal 559.

created a raft of remedies which would provide a more just outcome in the circumstances of the case. Equity was not restrained by the same parameters and strict rules as the common law, and it sought to find the just outcome. This meant that where the common law rules created an unjust result, equity could intervene and still provide a remedy. This was exactly the situation that arose in relation to a common mistake in contract. Where the test set down by the common law could not be met by the parties, equity retained a further jurisdiction to rescind the contract (the same effect as finding the contract void) where it was just and equitable to do so in the circumstances of the particular case.

While the two approaches have been approximated since 2002 in England, Ireland retains a separate equitable jurisdiction and it is worth examining the different approaches that the common law and equity take.

Common Mistake at Common Law

The leading English case on common mistake at common law is *Bell v Lever Brothers Ltd*.[35] The determinations of the House of Lords were somewhat difficult to interpret, which led to a fertile ground of confusion as to the application of the doctrine. The facts of the case were that Lever Brothers entered into agreements with Bell and another. The first of these agreements appointed Bell and another to the board of a subsidiary company; the second was a compensation contract in which they were both promised a considerable sum of money upon their retirement from their positions on the board. During their time on the board, both parties entered into further transactions on their own behalf, a course of conduct which would have allowed Lever Brothers to dismiss them summarily without compensation. However, as they were unaware of this and had entered into the compensation contracts, Lever Brothers paid the sums promised. They then sought to have the compensation returned to them and the contract rescinded on the grounds that they entered into it under a mistake of fact (in other words they did not know that they could have summarily dismissed Bell). By a bare majority, the House of Lords held that the contract was binding. The judgment gave rise to a number of theories and seriously complicated the law in relation to mistake in the cases that subsequently arose.

The first of those theories is that this case in fact determined that there was no doctrine of mistake operable in these circumstances. For example, Denning MR in *Solle v Butcher* stated:

[35] [1932] AC 161, HL.

> the correct interpretation of [*Bell v Lever Brothers Ltd*], to my mind, is that once a contract has been made, that is to say, once the parties, whatever their inmost states of mind, have to all outward appearances agreed with sufficient certainty in the same terms on the same subject matter, then the contract is good unless it is set aside for failure of some condition on which the existence of the contract depends, or for fraud, or on some equitable ground.[36]

It can be argued that Denning MR's interpretation takes the House of Lords' decision to a level which was not intended. It is very clear that they did narrow the doctrine considerably, allowing only the most exceptional cases to succeed, but did not outwardly dismiss the doctrine in its entirety. However, another interpretation is that Denning MR preferred to allow equity to take the lead in cases such as this and, rather than applying a fixed set of rules, use equitable principles to determine matters on a case-by-case basis.

The second theory arising from this judgment in *Bell* is that it establishes that a contract will only be void at common law if a term can be implied into both offer and acceptance which would prevent the contract from coming into operation. Lord Atkin himself in *Bell* pointed out that while this is a core principle, it is difficult to discover whether or not such a term was indeed implied.

Thirdly, it is suggested that the application of the doctrine depends on the proper construction of the contract as a whole. This is where the terms of a contract are construed in light of the circumstances which existed or were believed to exist at the time of the contract to show that it was not intended to apply.

The rationale of Bell has been accepted in Irish courts with the leading case being *Fitzsimons v O'Hanlon*.[37] This case arose over the settlement of a deceased's estate. It had been agreed between the parties that the plaintiff would be paid the sum of £60,500 with the balance (approx. £150,000) going to the defendant. Prior to the settlement efforts had been made to trace all of the assets of the deceased, but subsequently another £58,000 was discovered. The plaintiff sought to have the agreement set aside on the grounds of common mistake but Budd J disagreed. It was acknowledged that the deceased, during his lifetime was 'discreet, perhaps even secretive' about his assets and therefore it ought to have been in the minds of the parties that further assets may come to light. The court further opined that for the sake of commercial certainty, contracts should, in general, be enforced where the mistake

---

36 [1950] 1 KB 671, 691.
37 [1999] 2 ILRM 551.

does not relate to an essential or integral element of the subject matter of the contract.

Common Mistake in Equity

Given that the common law system was in such disarray in relation to the doctrine of mistake, equity filled the gap. It was unclear as to when common mistake could arise, and as the test was not clear, judges were equally unclear as to how to apply it. The easy way around this was to say that the contract was valid at common law, but could be rescinded in equity. This allowed the courts to refrain from directly challenging the House of Lords' decision and use the wider equitable jurisdiction to come to the same outcome. The key case in relation to this is *Solle v Butcher*.[38] Here, the lessee entered into a lease of a flat on the basis of a mistaken assumption by both parties that it had been reconstructed to the extent that it was no longer subject to the Rent Restrictions Acts. When it later transpired that the property was still subject to rent controls and that the amount paid was substantially higher than that permissible under the legislation, the lessee sought to recover the overpayment. This action failed, and instead the contract was set aside, with Denning MR stating:

> A contract is also liable in equity to be set aside if the parties were under a common misapprehension either as to facts or as to their relative and respective rights provided that the misapprehension was fundamental and that the party seeking to set it aside was not himself at fault.

The decision in Solle effectively extended the doctrine of equity and set the precedent that while a contract may be valid in law, it can be set aside in equity. This was adopted in several further decisions in England including *Grist v Bailey*[39] and reiterated by Denning MR in *Magee v Pennine Insurance Co Ltd*: 'A common mistake, even on a most fundamental matter, does not make a contract void at law; but it makes it voidable in equity'.[40] It was further explicitly approved of in the Irish cases of *O'Neill v Ryan*,[41] and again in *Fitzsimons v O'Hanlon*.[42]

Thus, for over 50 years, there were effectively two separate systems operating within the English court system relating to the doctrine of mistake.

---

38 [1950] 1 KB 671.
39 [1967] Ch 532.
40 [1969] 2 QB 507, 514.
41 [1991] ILRM 672.
42 [1999] 2 ILRM 551.

The case of *Great Peace Shipping Ltd v Tsavliris Salvage (International) Ltd* sought to reconcile the confusion in the area and bring certainty back to the doctrine.[43] Here, the defendant urgently needed the use of a vessel in order to carry out a salvage of another ship that was in distress. It was told by another that the claimant's vessel, the Great Peace, was in the area. The claimant was contacted by the defendant, and a contract was entered into for a period of five days, both parties believing that the ships were 35 miles away from each other. However, the Great Peace was actually 410 miles away from the distressed ship, and upon discovering this the defendant cancelled the contract and argued that it did not have to pay for the hire as the contract was entered into under the mistaken belief as to the location of the Great Peace.

In holding that the contract was valid, and the charges were payable, the court established that the following elements must be present for a contract to be set aside for mistake:

> (i) there must be a common assumption as to the existence of a state of affairs; (ii) there must be no warranty by either party that that state of affairs exists; (iii) the non-existence of the state of affairs must not be attributable to the fault of either party; (iv) the non-existence of the state of affairs must render performance of the contract impossible; (v) the state of affairs may be the existence, or a vital attribute, of the consideration to be provided or circumstances which must subsist if performance of the contractual adventure is to be possible.

The court found that, as the defendant had waited two hours following the discovery of the true location of the ship, there was evidence that the ship could still have been of use, albeit that it would have taken considerably longer to reach the distressed ship.

This case solidifies the test in relation to when a contract may be held to be void and clears up much of the uncertainty that was created after the *Bell* case. While the conditions are not easily met, they are clear.

The Court of Appeal in this case also roundly rejected Lord Denning's equitable jurisdiction, holding that *Solle v Butcher* was not good law and contrary to principle. It determined that the test in *Solle* created uncertainty and placed too much power into the hands of the court to exercise its discretion. However, this rejection of the equitable doctrine was not met with universal praise. While *Solle* was initially criticised, by the time the *Great Peace* was decided, it had been adopted into many Commonwealth countries and seen as the more favourable approach.

---

43 [2002] EWCA Civ 1407.

The discretion, as argued by Andrew Phang allows for a more flexible approach which in turn ensures that justice can be achieved.[44]

Despite this, subsequent cases in England have embraced the decision in Great Peace with enthusiasm.[45] However the Irish judiciary have been less eager to adopt this approach. It is clear from the case of *Intrum Justitia BV v Legal and Trade Financial Services* that a more flexible approach still holds.[46] In this case, the plaintiff had purchased a company and when it was discovered that there had been a large amount of embezzlement, they sought rescission of the contract. The court in finding that the remedy was unavailable in this case referenced both *Bell v Lever Brothers* and *Solle v Butcher* and applied *O'Neill v Ryan*.

Test Your Knowledge

Paul has recently entered into two contracts which he is seeking advice about. While working in his jewellery shop last week, a beautiful woman entered the shop and begun looking around. He thought that he recognised her from somewhere but couldn't quite place her. She began looking at some very expensive emeralds, and Paul thought that maybe she was too young to be able to afford them. She then produced a cheque book in the name of 'Britnay Piers'. Paul immediately thought she was the very famous international popstar! She buys £150,000 worth of jewellery and pays for this with a cheque. On the same day, Paul receives an online order for an engagement ring worth £25,000. His company offers a payment plan, and as per his company policy, he asks to see identification, proof of address and current bank details. These are sent through in the name of Mr Ted Bosworth. Paul undertakes some checks, and the bank confirms that Mr Ted Bosworth does have an account with them, and further checks on the electoral role confirm that it is the correct address.

Two weeks after these purchases, Paul is contacted by his bank. They tell him that the cheque has bounced and that the direct debit from Mr Ted Bosworth has been cancelled by his bank as the purchase was made as a result of identity theft. Advise Paul.

---

44 'Controversy in Common Mistake' [2003] Conveyancer and Property Lawyer 247. See also Simon Baughan, 'The Great Peace and the Demise of Equitable Mistake' (2003) 3(5) Shipping and Transport Lawyer International 6; TM Yeo, 'Great Peace: A Distant Disturbance' (2005) 121 Law Quarterly Review 39; James Edelman, 'An Uncommon Mistake' (2005) 15 Kings College Law Review 127.

45 See for example, *Kyle Bay Ltd v Underwriters* [2004] EWHC 607.

46 [2005] IEHC 190. See Joe Jeffers, 'Rescission in Equity on the Grounds of Mistake – A Jurisdiction on its Last Legs or Fighting Fit?' (2007) 2(3) Irish Business Law Quarterly 1 who argues that this is the correct approach and that the Irish courts ought to continue to adopt this flexible approach.

A Is Paul bound by both contracts and will have to suffer the loss?

B Can Paul claim that there was a mistake as to the identify of both parties and have both contracts set aside?

C Can Paul claim that that there was a mistake as to the identity of one of the parties?

The correct answer here is C. Paul would not be able to have the contract against Britnay Piers set aside as the courts would find that he intended to contract with the person in front of him. She did not misrepresent herself as to her identity, and Paul jumped to the wrong conclusion that she was someone that she was not. On the other hand, he did try to satisfy himself as to the identity of Mr Ted Bosworth and would be able to have the contract set aside (as per *Shogun Ltd*).

Stretch and Challenge Question

Do you agree that the common law and equity ought to take the same approach to contracts involving mistake, or should equity have retained a wider discretion to set contracts aside where it was just to do so?

Chapter 12

MISREPRESENTATION

12.1 Introduction

In the previous chapter we examined how contracts may be avoided or set aside on the grounds of mistake, either where the mistake occurs on the part of one or both of the parties to the contract. Where there has been no mistake, a party may argue that the contract was entered into on the grounds of a misrepresentation.

Essentially, this occurs where one party makes a statement to the other regarding an element of the contract. Ideally, the claimant will seek to argue that this statement formed a term of the contract (see Chapter 7), and where the statement is deemed a term, the claimant will have a remedy for breach of contract. However, in circumstances where the statement is not a term, the claimant may argue that they entered into the contract on the basis of a statement which turned out to be false, and thus they will have a remedy.

12.2 Defining Misrepresentation

At its most basic, a misrepresentation is an untrue statement which has been made by one party which induces another to enter into a contract. In order for a claim of misrepresentation to be actionable, it must fulfil three requirements: it must be a statement of fact and not one of opinion; it must be untrue; and it must induce the other party to enter into the contract.

12.2.1 Statement of Fact which is False

The statement must be more than a mere opinion and must be a statement of fact. In *Edgington v Fitzmaurice* it was held that 'the state of a man's mind is as much a fact as the state of his digestion'.[1] Therefore, a statement about what a person is thinking or believing will form a statement of fact. In this case a prospectus inviting loans from the public said that the money would be used to extend the business. It was held that this was a fraudulent misrepresentation as there was no intention to use the money in this way.

There are cases in which what may look like a statement of fact is held to be an opinion. In *Bisset v Wilkinson* a farmer told a prospective purchaser that the farm could hold 2,000 sheep despite the fact that it had never been used as a sheep farm. This was held to be an opinion rather than a statement of fact as both parties were aware that it had never been used as a sheep farm. However, where one party is in a position to know the truth, the statement may be deemed to be a misrepresentation.[2] In *Smith v Land and House Property Corp* the description of Mr Fleck as a 'most desirable tenant' was held to be a misrepresentation when it transpired that he was in significant arrears, and those employed to sell the hotel were in a position to know his record as a tenant with them.[3] A similar outcome was arrived at in *Doheny v Bank of Ireland*.[4] Here the bank was found to be liable after it gave a reference to one of its customers referring to them as 'respectable and trustworthy'. In fact, the customer had bounced several cheques and the bank knew that they had a history of dishonesty. Further in *Esso Petroleum Co Ltd v Mardon* a statement about the sales capacity of a petrol station could be treated as one of fact since, given the expertise of Esso, Mr Mardon was justified on relying on it as such.[5]

To constitute a statement of fact, it must be a statement about a fact that exists at the time and does not relate to the future. A statement of intention is not generally treated as a statement of existing fact. In *Wales v Wadham* a husband offered his wife a financial settlement on divorce on the basis that she had stated that she had no intention of remarrying.[6] Shortly after the divorce, she did re-marry and the ex-husband sought to have the settlement set aside on the grounds of misrepresentation. The court found that this was a statement of intention and true at the time it was made; the contract therefore would not be set aside. However, if, at the time of stating the intention, the person did not have any such intention, then it would be treated as a misrepresentation. In *Crystal Palace FC v Dowie* Iain Dowie was found to have fraudulently misrepresented that he had no present

---

1 (1885) 29 Ch D 459.
2 [1927] AC 177.
3 (1884) 28 Ch D 7.
4 *The Irish Times*, 12 December 1997.
5 [1976] QB 801.
6 [1977] 1 WLR 199.

intention to join rival club Charlton Athletic, a misrepresentation of fact which induced Crystal Palace to agree to release him from his existing contract as their manager.[7] In *Mulcahy v Mulcahy* a statement by one brother to his siblings that he intended to make the family home into a home for his family and their mother was not held to be a misrepresentation but rather a selling point to secure the agreement of the family.[8]

The courts will further draw a distinction between a statement of fact and a 'sales puff'. A puff was defined in *Turner v Anquetil* as 'extravagant phrasing which would naturally be discounted by sensible persons'.[9] In *Dimmock v Hallett* land for sale was described as 'fertile and improvable' and this was held to be sales talk and not a statement of fact.[10] It will often be difficult to determine this, and cases will turn on their particular facts. If we recall the case of *Carlill v Carbolic Smoke Ball Company*, the court rejected the argument that the advertisement was a mere sales puff on the grounds that the company had taken additional steps (of placing money in a separate account) which a reasonable person would believe could be relied upon.[11]

It often occurs that a statement is made some time before the contract is actually entered into. In such circumstances, it is possible that the statement was true at the time it was made, but subsequently becomes untrue by the time the contract is entered into. It must therefore be considered whether this statement becomes a misrepresentation if the maker does not subsequently correct the statement and alert the innocent party to the fact that it is no longer true. In this situation, the court may determine that there is a 'continuous representation', meaning that if the statement has a continuing effect, it will remain valid unless it is withdrawn. This concept is illustrated in the case of *With v O'Flanagan* where the claimant wanted to buy the defendant's medical practice.[12] During negotiations, the defendant stated that the practice earned around £2,000 per year. It was a further five months before the contract was signed, and during that time the defendant had fallen ill resulting in the practice taking much less money. The claimant sought to rescind the contract on the grounds of misrepresentation, and the Court of Appeal agreed, holding that the statement was one

---

7 [2007] EWHC 1392 (QB). See Mike Morgan, 'Crystal Palace FC v Dowie – Fraudulent Misrepresentation and Rescission' (2007) Sports Law Administration and Practice 10.
8 [2011] IEHC 186.
9 [1953] NZLR 952, 953 (per Adams J).
10 (1866) LR 2 Ch App 21.
11 [1893] 1 QB 256.
12 [1936] Ch 575.

designed to induce the claimant into signing the contract and therefore operated up to the point at which the contract was signed.[13]

Generally, silence cannot constitute a representation.[14] In *Turner v Green* the defendant met with the claimant's solicitor to arrange settlement of a claim.[15] Prior to this, the claimant's solicitor had received information relating to the outcome of the proceedings which were favourable to the defendant. He chose not to disclose this information until after the agreement. The claimant sought specific performance of the agreement, while the defendant sought to have it overturned on the grounds that a material fact had not been disclosed. It was held that there was no duty to disclose the information, and the order of specific performance was granted.

There are certain exceptions to this rule. First, in relation to consumer contracts, the Consumer Rights Act 2022 makes it a criminal offence where a trader misleads a consumer by failing to give information. Secondly, contracts which require the utmost good faith (contracts *ubberimae fidei*) require full disclosure. Failure to disclose in these contracts will allow the innocent party to rescind the contract. The rationale for this is that the court places a higher burden on these contracts as it believes that it would be impossible for the other party to find these facts for themselves. A good example of this type of contract is an insurance contract where there is a positive duty of full disclosure.[16] The Marine Insurance Act 1906 (no longer in force in England following the enactment of Consumer Insurance (Disclosure and Representation) Act 2012 and the Insurance Act 2015) imposes there was a duty on a person to inform the insurance company of any fact that could impact on the company's decision to provide insurance cover. The provisions of this Act have been held to apply to both marine and non-marine insurance policies.

In life insurance policies, it is usual for a company to seek a warranty that the insured is in good health and to declare any health conditions. Failure to declare these may result in the policy being repudiated. In *Keating v New Ireland Assurance Co Plc* the defendant sought to repudiate a policy on the grounds that it included a warranty that

---

13 Rick Bigwood 'Pre-contractual misrepresentation and the limits of the principle in With v O'Flanagan' [2005] Cambridge Law Journal 94.

14 Ridoan Karim and Imtiaz Mohammed Sifat, 'Treatment of Silence as Misrepresentation in Contracts: A Critical Comparative Analysis of Common Law and Islamic Jurisprudence' (2018) 60(1) International Journal of Law and Management 69.

15 [1895] 2 Ch 205.

16 B Soyer, 'Mapping Utmost Good Faith in Insurance Law – Future Condition?' (2016) 132 Law Quarterly Review 618.

the insured was in good health.[17] It transpired that the insured was, unbeknownst to him, suffering from Angina when he signed the form which declared that the answers were 'true and complete'. The Supreme Court rejected the argument by the insurers and held that the clause was to be interpreted to mean that the insured was to disclose all facts known to him.

If there is no 'basis of contract' clause (a clause which turns a representation into a warranty) or an express warranty in the proposal form, it will be difficult to repudiate an insurance policy when it has been concluded in good faith.[18] However, where this clause does exist, the answers must be accurate, and its application can result in harsh outcomes.[19] In *Keenan v Shield Insurance Co Ltd* the proposal form for a household building and contents insurance policy asked whether there had been any previous claims.[20] The plaintiff answered 'no' to this question when in fact there had been a small claim to the value of £53 the previous year. Despite the fact that this was a trivial misstatement, the fact that the plaintiff had warranted that the answers were true and complete, the insurance company was able to repudiate the contract.[21]

There is a difference in approach depending on whether there has been a false statement or whether the matter is one of non-disclosure. In *Keenan* above, despite the fact that the misrepresentation was minor in terms of the seriousness of the insurance claim, the claimant had in fact made a false statement. Where this occurs, the insurer can seek a declaration that the contract is avoided and the Supreme Court has stated *Carey v W.H Ryan Ltd* that the insurer can further seek the repayment of any moneys paid out under the policy granted on foot of a misrepresentation.[22] However, where the matter is one of non-disclosure rather than an outright false statement, the test is whether or not the non-disclosed fact was material or not.[23] The parameters of this test were explained by the Supreme Court in *Chariot Inns Ltd v Assicurazioni Generali S.P.A & Coyle Hamilton, Hamilton Philips* as:

> It is not what the person seeking insurance regards as material, nor is it what the insurance company regards as material. It is a matter or circumstance which would reasonably influence the judgment of a prudent insurer in deciding whether he would take the risk,

---

17 [1990] ILRM 110. See also *Coleman v New Ireland Assurance Plc* [2009] IEHC 173.

18 See *Manor Park Homebuilders Ltd v AIG Europe (Ireland)* Ltd [2009] IEHC 174.

19 J.E Adams, 'Basis of the Contract Clause and the Consumer' (2000) Journal of Business Law 203.

20 [1987] IR 113. See also *Farrell v S.E Lancs. Insurance Co Ltd* [1933] IR 36.

21 This decision was also upheld on appeal to the Supreme Court [1988] IR 89.

22 [1982] IR 179.

23 Howard N Bennet, 'Utmost Good Faith, Materiality and Inducement' (1996) 112 Law Quarterly Review 405.

> and if so, in determining the premium he would demand. The standard by which materiality is to be determined is objective, not subjective. The matter has, in the last resort, to be determined by the court: the parties to the litigation may call experts in insurance matters as witnesses to give evidence of what they would have regarded as material bit the question of materiality is not to be determined between the parties.[24]

In the instant case, the court found that a fire which had occurred in a building owned by an associated company in the previous two years was a material fact which ought to have been disclosed.

In some cases, the issues of disclosure will be relatively straightforward. Where the insurance policy relates to life or health insurance, the medical history of the proposed insured will be material.[25] Ultimately however it is for the court to determine whether the facts omitted are indeed material with McCarthy J stating that it is the judge who is 'the sole and final arbiter'.[26] Therefore, while expert evidence may be adduced during the hearing, the court is not obliged to follow this and rather should make its own decision on the materiality aspect.

The obligation to disclose is therefore a relatively onerous one. The Supreme Court has modified these rules on two occasions. Firstly, in *Aro Road and Land Vehicles Ltd v Insurance Corp of Ireland Ltd* the insurance policy in question, concluded over the telephone, was to transport goods between Dublin and Antrim.[27] There was no proposal form completed and the details requested were scant. During transportation, the goods were stolen at gunpoint and the vehicle destroyed. The insurer tried to avoid the policy as it was not disclosed that the managing director of the insured's company had been convicted for the offence of receiving stolen goods some 19 years prior. The court reiterated that the general standard was that all matters material to the policy ought to be disclosed. However, they found that there are exceptions to this rule, in particular, over the counter policies where no proposal form is required. In these circumstances, the test is different:

> If the judgement of an insurer is such as to require disclosure of what he thinks is relevant but which reasonable insured if he thought of it all, would not think relevant, then, in the absence of a question directed towards the disclosure of such a fact, the insurer, albeit prudent, cannot properly be held to be acting

---

24 [1981] ILRM 173, 174.

25 *Kelleher v Irish Life Assurance Co Ltd,* Unrep, High Court, 16 December 1988.

26 *Aro Road and Land Vehicles Ltd v The Insurance Corp of Ireland Ltd* [1986] IR 403.

27 [1986] IR 403.

> reasonably. A contract of insurance is a contract of the utmost good faith on both sides.

This ruling places some of the burden back on to the insurance company in circumstances where there is no proposal form. Essentially, the court is requiring the insurer to ensure that they ask the questions relevant to the policy and will not allow non-disclosure of facts as a ground to repudiate the contract where they failed to ask the relevant questions. The court makes a significant distinction here between circumstances where a person provides false information and where a person is simply not asked for the information and does not think it relevant to disclose. The court again addressed this matter in *Keating v New Ireland Assurance Co Plc* and held that as the insured was not aware of the nature of his medical condition, the policy could not be avoided for non-disclosure.[28] In the judgment, the court emphasized that the duty to disclose was based on good faith and knowledge:

> One cannot disclose what one does not know, albeit that this puts a premium on ignorance. It may well be that wilful ignorance would raise significant other issues; such is not the case here. If the proposer for life insurance has answered all of the questions asked to the best of his ability and truthfully, his next of kin are not to be damnified because of his ignorance or obtuseness which may be sometimes due to a mental block on matters affecting ones health.

The Consumer Insurance Contracts Act 2019 which fully entered into force in 2021 has had a further and significant impact on consumer insurance contracts. Importantly, this legislation applies also to businesses who have an annual turnover of less than €3 million. Section 8 of the 2019 Act replaces the duty of good faith and removes 'basis of insurance' clauses. Instead the duty of care that is placed on the insured is to answer specific questions posed by an insurer with reasonable care. Insurers are therefore required to ask clear and unambiguous questions in plain language. The insured is not under any duty to disclose further information beyond what is asked of them. The insurer will be deemed to have waived any disclosure if it fails to follow up on any incomplete or unanswered question, although this does not apply in cases of fraud or misrepresentation.

Sections 9 and 18 of the 2019 Act examine remedies where information given has been misrepresented. Where the misrepresentation is fraudulent (defined by the Act as one in which the consumer knows to be false or misleading) the insurer can refuse to pay a claim and avoid a contract of insurance. Where the misrepresentation is negligent, the remedy depends on what the insurer would have done if it had

---

28 [1990] ILRM 110.

known of the facts. For example, would the policy premiums have been higher if the insurer had known of this particular fact? If so, then the difference between the premiums paid and any amount of a claim may be deducted by the insurer. Finally, if there has been an innocent misrepresentation on the part of an insured, the insurer cannot avoid a claim.

A further exception to the rule on silence can be found where there has been a voluntary assumption of responsibility. This was affirmed in the case of *Banque Financiere de la Cite v Westgate Insurance* where the court stated that a party may be liable for remaining silent where there was a voluntary assumption of responsibility by one party and a reliance on that voluntary assumption by the other.[29] This may be difficult to show in commercial negotiations, and the House of Lords examined the matter in the case of *Hamilton v Allied Domecq* Plc.[30] Here, the claimant owned rights to some mineral water. He had begun to sell bottled water but wanted to expand the business. He began negotiations with the defendants with a view to them investing in his company and to assist with marketing and distribution. Mr Beatty, an employee of the defendant, carried out the negotiations. The claimant wanted the product to be marketed and sold in the hospitality sector to establish the brand before being marketed and sold in shops. After the contract was signed, the water was initially sold in shops and never made it to the hospitality sector. The business failed, and the claimant argued that Mr Beatty had misrepresented where his company would sell and market the product. It was held that there was no evidence that the defendant had voluntarily assumed responsibility towards the claimant and that 'a failure on the part of Mr Beatty to speak [about the marketing strategy] might be morally questionable. But that is different from saying that he was under a legal duty to speak.'

However, the courts have in certain circumstances held conduct to amount to a representation. In the case of *Spice Girls Ltd v Aprilia World Service BV* Aprilia World, a scooter manufacturer entered into an agreement to sponsor the Spice Girls.[31] As part of this agreement, the Spice Girls took part in a promotional photoshoot at a time when they knew that 'Ginger Spice', Gerri Halliwell, was about to leave the group. The court held that taking part in the shoot was a misrepresentation by conduct and granted Aprilia's claim for damages on the grounds of misrepresentation.

---

29 [1991] 2 AC 249.
30 [2007] UKHL 33.
31 [2002] EMLR 478.

12.2.2 Induces the Innocent Party to Enter the Contract

For a misrepresentation to be operative, it must have in some way induced the innocent party into entering the contract. In other words, it must at least be one of the reasons why they entered the contract.[32] Therefore, if the innocent party was not aware of the statement, it cannot be a reason for them entering into it. In *Horsfall v Thomas* the plaintiff was commissioned by the defendant to make him a gun.[33] The plaintiff made the gun and delivered it to the defendant. The gun contained a defect, which would have been noticed by the defendant had he inspected it. However, without such an inspection, he accepted the gun. Subsequently, the plaintiff then wrote to the defendant stating that the gun was made from the best metal and was free from defects. When the gun was later tested, the fault became clear and the defendant refused to honour the payment. The plaintiff sued for the cost of the gun and the defendant argued that he had been actively encouraged into accepting a defective product and that the letter sent by the plaintiff was fraudulent. The court rejected this argument, holding that the plaintiff was unaware of the defect, and had the defendant examined the gun, it would have been discovered. That was at the time that the contract was entered into. Therefore, the plaintiff did not make any representations which induced the defendant to enter the contract. The plaintiff was therefore entitled to claim his fee. A similar line of reasoning has been followed in the Irish courts. For example, in *Intrum Justitia BV v Legal and Trade Financial Services* it was affirmed that a statement will not constitute a misrepresentation if it is not read or heard by the other side.[34] In *Grafton Court Ltd v Wadson Sales Ltd* the defendants argued misrepresentation on the part of a shopping centre.[35] The defendant had agreed to lease a shop and they argued that the shopping centre had assured them the other leaseholders in the centre would be 'high quality commercial concerns'. They argued that the other tenants did not meet this criteria. It was held that if this statement had been made by the plaintiff, it had not been relied upon. At the time the lease was signed the other units had been fully occupied and the occupants could have been easily verified.

Knowledge that a statement is untrue will only prevent a claim for misrepresentation where this is actual knowledge; a suspicion that the statement is untrue will not be sufficient.[36] This means that the

---

32 Kelry CF Loi, 'Pre- Contractual Misrepresentations: Mistaken Belief Induced by Mis-Statements' (2017) 7 Journal of Business Law 598.

33 (1862) 1 H&C 90.

34 [2005] IEHC 190.

35 Unrep, High Court, 17 February 1975.

36 Rosa Lee, 'Proof of Inducement in the Law of Misrepresentation' (2017) 1 Lloyd's Maritime and Commercial Law Quarterly 150.

person making the statement must have actually known that the statement they were making was untrue. For example, let's say that I am selling my car and I say that there are no known faults with the engine. I have a suspicion that there may be something wrong with the engine as it has started to make a funny noise when it starts and stops, but there are no engine lights appearing on the dashboard and the car has passed its MOT. In this case, while I have a suspicion that the statement I have made is possibly untrue, I do not have any actual knowledge of a fault with the engine and therefore would not be sufficient for any potential purchaser to claim misrepresentation against me. In *Redgrave v Hurd* the plaintiff solicitor was planning to retire and placed an advertisement for a partner in the practice.[37] The plaintiff told the defendant that the practice earned approximately £300 per annum and showed him some papers. Had the defendant inspected those papers, it would have been clear to him that the amount was closer to £200 per annum. The defendant claimed for misrepresentation, and the court found that he was entitled to have the contract rescinded and his deposit returned as 'if a man is induced to enter a contract by a false representation, it is not sufficient to say to him "if you had used due diligence you would have found out that the statement was untrue"'.

In the more recent decision of *Hayward v Zurich Insurance Co Plc* the defendant was injured in an accident at work and claimed very substantial damages against his employer.[38] The employer's insurer, despite suspecting that the defendant had exaggerated the extent of his injuries, was unable to find evidence sufficient to prove its suspicions in court so it reached an agreement with the defendant in full and final settlement of the claim. The insurer, having subsequently received proof that the defendant had recovered from his injuries a year before the settlement had been reached, brought an action against him claiming to be entitled to rescind the settlement agreement and to repayment of the sums paid under it.

The Supreme Court held that in a claim for deceit based upon alleged misrepresentation, it had to be shown that the defendant had made a materially false misrepresentation which had been intended to induce, and had induced, the claimant to act to their detriment – it was not necessary as a matter of law for the claimant to prove that they had believed the misrepresentation to be true. It was sufficient in this case for the insurer to establish that the fact of the misrepresentation had been a material cause of its entering into the settlement.[39]

---

37 (1881) 20 ChD 1.
38 [2017] AC 142.
39 Paul S Davies and William Day, 'A Mistaken Turn in the Law of

However, where the innocent party does not rely on the statement then they will not be able to successfully claim misrepresentation. In *Attwood v Small* the owners of a mine made claims as to the earning capacity of the mine to prospective purchasers.[40] These purchasers subsequently engaged their own surveyors who wrongly agreed with the vendors' estimates. The House of Lords found that it was not the vendors' statement that induced the purchasers to enter into the contract but rather their own surveyors' report. If they were to rely on the initial statement, they would not have engaged their own experts.

The Irish Supreme Court considered the issue of inducement in *McCaughrey v Irish Bank Resolution Corp*.[41] In this case an investor sought to have his investment set aside on the grounds of misrepresentation when it became apparent that certain material had been suppressed from the investment documentation. The court refused to set the transaction aside by holding that not only were the facts immaterial, but that if they had been disclosed, this would not have altered the investors course of action.[42] Hardiman J opined:

> When one is assessinga statement of a person as to what he would have done or not done, had matters developed differently to the way they actually developed, it is reasonable to consider, as a starting point, whether his claimed reaction would have been reasonable. It would be quite wrong of course, to proceed on the basis that the only reasonable reaction was open to him because the courts often see instances where people react to particular developments in ways which are irrational, exaggerated, unduly bellicose or unduly timid, or otherwise improbable. But the learned trial judge's findings here made every allowance for the capacity for odd reactions for subjective reasons and found that, though he did not accept Mr McCaughey's evidence that 'I would not have invested' that this reaction was subjectively genuine and the 'product of hindsight and wishful thinking', not of deliberate falsehood.

A misrepresentation does not need to be the only reason that a party enters into a contract, though it does need to be at least one reason. In *Edgington v Fitzmaurice* the plaintiff agreed to enter into a loan agreement with the company, partially due to a misrepresentation in the prospectus and partially due to his own mistaken belief that he would attain some rights in the company's property.[43] Therefore,

Misrepresentation' (2019) 3 Lloyds Maritime and Commercial Law Quarterly 390.

40 (1838) 6 CL & F 232.

41 [2013] IESC 17.

42 Mary Donnelly, 'Investment: Fraudulent and Negligent Misrepresentation – Private Banking Arrangements' (2013) 20(5) Commercial Law Practitioner 108.

43 (1885) 24 Ch D 459.

the statement in the prospectus was not the sole reason for him entering the contract, but the court held that as the prospectus was one of the reasons, it could be set aside. It has been suggested by the House of Lords in *Standard Charter Bank v Pakistan National Shipping Corp (No 2)* that this decision will only apply in cases of fraudulent misrepresentation.[44]

12.3 Types of Misrepresentation

There are three types of misrepresentation which are considered in turn in this section. It is important to distinguish between the types of misrepresentation as the remedy that is available differs.

12.3.1 Fraudulent Misrepresentation

This type of misrepresentation is also known as the tort of deceit. It was defined in the seminal case of *Derry v Peek* where the defendants planned to run horse-drawn and steam-powered tramcars.[45] The steam-powered tramcars required consent from the Board of Trade, but as the company had already succeeded in passing an Act through Parliament which allowed for the use of steam-powered tramcars, they believed this consent to be a mere formality. Their share prospectus falsely stated that they had permission to run these steam-powered tramcars, and in reliance on this statement, the claimant, amongst others, bought shares in the company. The Board of Trade subsequently refused consent and the company was wound up with a loss to the claimant. The directors were sued, and the court found that as they believed that the consent would be a formality given the Act of Parliament, the statement was inaccurate but not fraudulent.

The House of Lords stated that for a statement to be fraudulent, it must be made (a) knowingly, or (b) without belief in its truth, or (c) recklessly, careless as to whether it is true or false. This appears to be a difficult test to prove as it is subjective, ie whether the person making the statement believes it to be true or not, as distinct from being negligent as to the truth of the statement.

The test was made out in the case of *Vahey v Kenyon*.[46] Vahey was negotiating the purchase of land from Kenyon and asked him about its flooding history, because it was near a flood plain. Kenyon said that despite local flooding 30 years previously, his land had not been affected. Later, when the house was found to be damp, he admitted

44 [2003] 1 AC 959.
45 (1889) 14 App Cas 337.
46 [2013] EWCA Civ 658.

after further questioning that the stream which flowed through the grounds occasionally burst its banks but had never flooded the house. The sale went ahead subject to a £10,000 discount.

Soon after completion, the property was flooded and Vahey discovered that the garage and house had been flooded some years before during Kenyon's occupancy. The Court of Appeal held that the contract was voidable for fraudulent misrepresentation. It was clear from his enquiries that the issue of flooding concerned Vahey and that the reassurances from Kenyon had been material in Vahey entering into the contract and not seeking to negotiate a higher discount.

In *Fenton v Schofield* the vendor of a property made statements that he knew were untrue relating to the amount of money he had spent on renovating the property and the yield of salmon from a river running through the land.[47] The land was valued based on these statements and the purchaser was able to recover the difference between what he paid and what the land was actually worth.

A claim for fraudulent misrepresentation can succeed even in circumstances where the person making the statement does not necessarily know that the statement is false. In *Pearson v Dublin Corporation* an agent told the plaintiff that the foundations of a wall was on the site, when he did not know whether this was true or false.[48] This statement was held to be a fraudulent misrepresentation.

It is not required that the person making the statement intends any loss to accrue to the innocent party. In *Delaney v Keogh*, the defendant was an auctioneer employed by a third party to sell that third party's interest in a leasehold property.[49] The conditions of sale included a statement that while the rent was currently £25 on the property, that the landlord would accept £18. The landlord then informed Keogh that the full rent would be payable by the new owner. The third party, who was a solicitor stated that it was his belief that the landlord would be estopped from charging the full rent and advised the defendant not to change the particulars of sale. The original trial judge found that Keogh was not liable as he had no intention to deceive, a decision which was overturned by the Court of Appeal. It was determined that the failure to make known to a prospective purchaser that he had reason to believe that the full rent was payable was a misrepresentation and the fact that he believed what his client told him was not a defence to this.

47 (1966) 100 ILTR 69.
48 [1907] AC 351.
49 [1905] 2 IR 267.

Finally, in *Keegan Quarries Ltd v McGuinness* it was held that 'being careless as to whether the information provided was true or false' would amount to negligent misrepresentation.[50] In this case a statement made by the plaintiff that quarrying had taken place on the land since 1958 was held to be a negligent misrepresentation in circumstances where there was other evidence to suggest that this statement was false.

12.3.2 Negligent Misstatement

Negligent misstatement was developed at common law from the case of *Hedley Byrne v Heller* in tort.[51] The plaintiffs wanted to check a company's creditworthiness, so contacted the company's bankers (the defendant) which provided a credit reference. When the company defaulted on some payments, the plaintiffs sued the defendant bankers. Although the claim failed because of a disclaimer by the bankers, the House of Lords said, obiter, that the defendant did owe a duty of care to the plaintiffs because there was a special relationship between the parties and that the defendant was in breach of that duty by failing to take reasonable care that the representation was correct.

It is not completely clear what the 'special relationship' referred to by the House of Lords means, but it appears to arise in circumstances where the maker of the statement has some particular skill or relevant knowledge and is aware that the innocent party will rely on it.[52] For example, in *Esso Petroleum v Mardon*, an Esso sales representative assured the defendant about the sales capacity of a petrol station.[53] On the strength of this statement, Mardon entered into a tenancy agreement with Esso. Petrol sales turned out to be much less than this forecast (as in the meantime the local authority had stipulated changes to the plans of the site which would reduce the sales potential). Although there was no claim available in fraudulent misrepresentation as the inflated figures presented by the defendant were an estimate rather than a hard fact, the court applied the *Hedley Byrne* principle and allowed Mardon to recover damages for negligent misstatement. This was on the basis that the defendants had employed experts to provide estimates of sales and they owed a duty to the plaintiff to ensure that this was carried out correctly.

---

50 [2011] IEHC 435.

51 [1964] AC 465.

52 David Campbell and David Milman, 'The Unexplored Contract and Insolvency Law Dimensions of Hedley Byrne v Heller' (2023) 82(1) Cambridge Law Journal 58.

53 [1976] QB 801.

These cases have been applied in the Irish jurisdiction[54] and in *Stafford v Keane Mahony Smith* a case was brought against an estate agent who stated that a particular property would be a good investment.[55] When the property was later sold at a loss, the action failed as the court found that any representations made were not made to the plaintiff, but rather to his brother. Doyle J stated:

> In order to establish the liability for negligent or non-fraudulent misrepresentation giving rise to an action there must first of all be a person conveying the information or representation relied upon; secondly, there must be a person to whom that information is intended to be conveyed or to whom it might reasonably be expected that the information would be conveyed; thirdly, that person must act upon such information or representation to his detriment so as to show that he is entitled to damages.

In *Doolan v Murray* the plaintiff had embarked upon building work on a property she had purchased from the defendant believing that a right of way affecting the property was a pedestrian right of way only.[56] It later transpired that the right was more extensive and the building work had to be removed. Here the plaintiff was able to succeed in an action for negligent misstatement.

The economic and banking collapse that occurred around 2008 had a significant impact on litigation in relation to banking failures. Certain legislation had been enacted in relation to addressing mismanagement of the financial sector (Investor Compensation Act 1998 and markets in Financial Instruments and Miscellaneous Provisions Act 2007) although these did not have a particular impact upon cases brought by consumers after the crash. In cases of such a nature, it is likely that the bank will try to avoid liability on the grounds that they do not owe a duty of care to their customers. It was stated in *Delaney v Allied Irish Bank Plc* that 'It is well established law that a bank owes no general duty to advise its customers on the wisdom of their commercial projects'.[57] However, where a bank does decide to give information, they are under a duty to ensure that they do so with reasonable care.[58]

The matter was considered by the Supreme Court in *Wildgust v Bank of Ireland*.[59] In this case the plaintiff had assigned life insurance policies to the bank as security for a loan whereby he was obliged to pay the monthly instalments. The assignee contacted the insurer and was told

---

54 *Bank of Ireland v Smith* [1966] IR 646.
55 [1980] ILRM 53.
56 Unrep High Court 21 December 1993.
57 [2015] IEHC 52.
58 *Bankers Trust International Plc v PT Dharmala Sakti Sejahtera* [1996] CLC 518.
59 [2006] 2 ILRM 28.

that the policies were in order. Due to an error, the instalments were not paid and lapsed shortly before one of the insured died. Wildgust was never told of the misrepresentation and did not rely on it however the court held that it was sufficient that the insurer had induced reliance by the assignee on the basis of the negligent misstatement. Kearns J in extending the premise of Hedley Byrne stated that the test:

> Must go further..... and include persons in a limited and identifiable class when the maker of the statement can reasonably expect, in the context of a particular inquiry, that reliance will be placed thereon by such person or persons to act or not act in a particular manner in relation to that transaction.

The court further explained the extension of the law in *Darlington Properties v Meath County Council*.[60] Here the plaintiff bought a site on the strength of a statement by the defendant that it could be developed with permission to build an access road. However, the defendant had already given planning permission to an adjoining site which would make the construction of an access road to the plaintiff's site impossible. Kelly J stated:

> I am satisfied that a vendor, regardless of any other special relationship, is under a duty to take reasonable care to ensure that any representations made by him with a view to inducing contract are accurate. In the present case, of course, the County Council was not any vendor. It had a particular status and a particular means of knowledge. It was after all, the planning authority. It itself granted the planning permission which rendered the building of the distributor road impossible..... Thus even if it were necessary to show a special relationship (which it is not), I am satisfied that such a relationship existed having regard to the particular status of the County Council.

In England, the Misrepresentation Act 1967 governs the area of negligent misrepresentation. Section 2(1) of the Misrepresentation Act 1967 states:

> Where a person has entered into a contract after a misrepresentation has been made to him by another party thereto and as a result he has suffered loss, then, if the person making the misrepresentation would be liable to [pay] damages in respect thereof had the misrepresentation been made fraudulently, that person shall be so liable notwithstanding that the misrepresentation was not made fraudulently, unless he proves that he had reasonable ground to believe and did believe up to the time the contract was made that the facts represented were true.

Essentially, this section allows for an innocent party to claim for

60 [2011] IEHC 70. See also *Spencer v IBRC* [2016] IECA 346.

damages where they entered into a contract due to a misrepresentation unless it can be shown that the defendant believed the statement to be true at the time it was made and had reasonable grounds for holding that belief. Further, it does not require a 'special relationship' to be present as in negligent misstatement.

The heavy burden of proof placed on a defendant under this legislation is illustrated in the case of *Howard Marine and Dredging Co Ltd v A Ogden and Sons (Excavations) Ltd*.[61] Here the claimants were performing excavation work and needed to dispose of soil that they had dug up. They decided that this would be dumped at sea and on the basis of this hired two barges. The capacity of these barges was a crucial factor as it would determine how much each could carry and therefore how quickly the soil could be disposed of. The defendant's representative misrepresented the capacity of the barges, stating that it was much higher than it actually was. He had obtained this information from an official register of ships, usually accepted as an accurate source but on this occasion incorrect. The correct information was on file at the defendant's head office. In holding that there was liability under s 2(1), the court stated that 'the statute imposes an absolute obligation not to state facts which the representor cannot prove he had reasonable grounds to believe'.

More recently in *Myck Djurberg v Small* the buyers of two houseboats were awarded damages due to a seller's misrepresentation that the purchase prices included 125-year residential mooring licences at its marina.[62] The buyers were awarded the prices paid for the houseboats and moorings. In relation to misrepresentation, the seller had misrepresented the factual position, the buyers had relied on the seller, the seller had not believed, or had reasonable grounds for believing, that the moorings were lawful, and the buyers suffered damage as a result. The seller was held to be liable for damages for misrepresentations inducing the sales under s 2(1) of the Misrepresentation Act 1967.

It should be noted that following enactment of Consumer Rights Act 2015, the Misrepresentation Act 1967 will only apply to misrepresentations in business to business and potentially consumer to consumer contracts. In business to consumer contracts, the Consumer Rights Act 2015 will apply.

---

61 [1978] QB 574.

62 ChD, 1 September 2017.

12.3.3 Innocent Misrepresentation

Representations which are neither fraudulent nor negligent are classified as innocent or 'non-negligent'. Thus, if the maker of a statement did 'have reasonable grounds for believing the statement was true' then they can only be liable for innocent misrepresentation.[63]

12.4 Remedies for Misrepresentation

The effect of a court finding for the claimant is generally that the contract is voidable rather than void. This means that the contract will still be valid unless the innocent party chooses to set it aside.

The equitable remedy of rescission is available for all types of misrepresentation. We consider this remedy in Chapter 20 but, briefly, this remedy sets the contract aside and puts the parties back in the position they were in before the contract was entered into. As with all equitable remedies, it is discretionary, and so the courts have wide powers when deciding whether or not to grant this remedy.

Given that this is a very powerful remedy, effectively creating a situation where the contract never existed, there are some restrictions placed on when this can be utilised: first, where the innocent party affirms the contract; secondly, where there is a lapse of time; thirdly, where it is not possible to put the parties back into the position that they were in prior to entering into the contract; and finally, where to grant recission would impact on an innocent third party's rights.[64] In these circumstances, it is more appropriate for damages to be awarded. Where a party has suffered loss as a result of a misrepresentation, they are entitled to damages to cover this loss in all categories except where the misrepresentation is an innocent one, and, in those circumstances, it is at the discretion of the court. Section 45(1) of the Sale of Goods and Supply of Services Act 1980 provides:

> Where a person has entered into a contract after a misrepresentation has been made to him by another party thereto and as a result thereof he has suffered loss, then if the person making the representation would be liable to damages in respect thereof had the misrepresentation been made fraudulently, that person shall be so liable notwithstanding that the representation was not made fraudulently, unless he proves that he had reasonable ground to believe, and did believe up to the time the contract was made that the facts represented were true.

63 David Campbell, 'Oscar Chess, Dick Bentley and the Abolition of Innocent Misrepresentation' (2024) 1 Journal of Business Law 1.

64 Gearoid Carey, 'Misrepresentation and the Avoidance of Liability' (2001) 8(6) Commercial Law Practitioner 131.

This section was based on the English Misrepresentation Act 1967 in response to the restrictive nature of remedies for innocent misrepresentation in circumstances where rescission is not always possible.[65] It should also be noted that the right to damages under s 45 is limited to contracts governed by the Act and does not apply generally to all circumstances of innocent misrepresentation.

The rules governing damages are considered in depth in Chapter 19.

12.5 Excluding Liability for Misrepresentation

A party may seek to exclude liability by placing an exclusion clause in the contract. However, the court in *HIH Casualty and General Insurance Ltd v Chase Manhattan Bank* made it abundantly clear that liability cannot be excluded for fraudulent misrepresentation, stating 'it is clear that the law, on public policy grounds, does not permit a contracting party to exclude liability for his own fraud in inducing the making of the contract'.[66] This is not a new position with the House of Lords overturning an earlier decision in *Pearson v Dublin Corporation* which determined that a person cannot avoid the impact of fraudulent statements by including an exclusion clause in the contract.[67] However, where the statement is made honestly and in good faith, the clause will be enforced.[68]

In England, the law is governed by s 3 of the Misrepresentation Act 1967 which states:

> If any contract contains a term which would exclude or restrict—
> (a) any liability to which a party to the contract may be subject by reason of any misrepresentation made by him before the contract was made; or
> (b) any remedy available to another party to the contract by reason of such a misrepresentation.
>
> that term shall be of no effect except in so far as it satisfies the requirement of reasonableness as stated in s 11(1) of the Unfair Contract Terms Act 1977; and it is for those claiming that the term satisfies the requirement to show that it does.

In Ireland, misrepresentation is not specifically mentioned within the Consumer Rights Act 2022 however the legislation provides comprehensive protection for consumers where a trader is seeking to exclude liability. It is highly likely that this would fall foul of

---

65 Richard Hooley 'Damages and the Misrepresentation Act 1967' (1991) 107 Law Quarterly Review 547.
66 [2003] UKHL 6.
67 [1907] AC 351.
68 *Dublin Port and Docks Board v Brittania Dredging Co Ltd* [1968] IR 136.

the provisions relating to unfair terms (See chapter 9 for consumer contracts).

Test Your Knowledge

Georgia decided to sell 'Brighton Beautiful', her beauty salon, and met with Shelley, director of the 'Beauty4all' chain of salons which was interested in purchasing a salon in Brighton. Georgia told Shelley that 'Brighton Beautiful' had monthly profits of around £6,000, but as she wasn't sure of the exact figure Shelley could look at the accounts. Shelley intended to do that but was busy and forgot.

Georgia told Shelley that she had an agreement with 'EverYoung Beauty Supplies' that it would supply 'Brighton Beautiful' with a new tanning product. Kimberly Kardigan, the reality TV star, had promoted this and Georgia said this would definitely increase bookings. Unfortunately, 'EverYoung Beauty Supplies.' went bankrupt but Georgia forgot to tell Shelley.

Shelley told Georgia that she wanted to obtain an alcohol licence for the salon so that hen parties could have a glass of champagne. Georgia said she thought that was a great idea.

Shelley entered into a contract with Georgia in August.

A year later Shelley is furious as she feels Georgia misled her. She has discovered that the profits are £6,000 per month from April to September but are only £2,000 for the other months, that the salon is not getting the new tanning product, and that due to local licensing rules the local council will not grant 'Brighton Beautiful' an alcohol licence. Which of the statements would be classed as a misrepresentation:

A The monthly profits
B The agreement with Everyoung Beauty Supplies
C The alcohol licence
D None of the above

The correct answer here is B. A is not correct as it was not a definitive statement. Shelley had the opportunity to inspect the accounts and did not do so. She therefore cannot rely on this as a misrepresentation. C is not correct as this was a statement of intention. Georgia did not make any claims as to whether or not the licence would be granted but rather that she would like to apply for one. B is correct as it could be argued that this was one of the reasons why Shelley was interested in purchasing the salon. While the statement was true at the time of making it, it was not at the time the contract was entered into and therefore the contract may be rescinded on this ground.

Stretch and Challenge Question

Critically analyse whether the law goes far enough in protecting businesses and consumers from false statements made prior to the conclusion of the contract.

CHAPTER 13

DURESS

13.1 Introduction

The very essence of a contract is that it is entered into freely by two or more parties. The obligations that each party assumes under a contract are not imposed on them by law (for example, the duty of care in tort law is imposed by law and not freely assumed). It therefore follows that where a party is coerced or forced into entering a contract, they have not agreed to these obligations of their own free will or volition and should not be bound by those obligations.[1] There are three separate areas to consider in which it may be said that a party has not freely entered into the contract. This chapter is concerned with the common law doctrine of duress, and the next chapter will examine the equitable doctrines of undue influence and unconscionable bargain.

13.2 Common Law Doctrine of Duress

Historically, for the doctrine of duress to operate, a person would have to be induced into entering the contract either by way of violence or threats of violence. The act which is threatened must amount to an illegal act, and threats of lawful acts cannot amount to duress. For example, in *Williams v Bailey* threats of lawful imprisonment could not amount to duress.[2] In early cases it was held that, in order for duress to operate, the threat would have to be made against the person and not to goods. The doctrine has expanded considerably since then with the concept of economic duress,[3] and in *Dimskal Shipping Co SA v International Transport Workers Federation (The Evia Luck)* it was held

1 SA Smith 'Contracting under pressure: a theory of duress' (1997) Cambridge Law Journal 343.

2 (1866) LR 1 HL 200.

3 Daniel Tan, 'Constructing a Doctrine of Economic Duress' (2002) 18(2) Construction Law Journal 87.

that threats to seize or damage another's property could amount to duress. [4]

13.3 Elements of Duress

Where duress is pleaded, there are a number of elements that must be met, which we will now consider in turn. The effect of successfully pleading duress is that the contract is voidable at the behest of the wronged party, although there may also be a claim for damages in tort for, say, an assault.

13.3.1 Pressure is Exerted

As stated above, originally it was only in cases where violence or threats of violence were made to the person that the court would apply the doctrine of duress. A classic example of this can be found in the case of *Barton v Armstrong* where Armstrong threatened to kill Barton unless he purchased shares under certain conditions.[5] Despite the fact that the terms were favourable to Barton, and part of the reason he entered the contract, he was still entitled to have the contract set aside on the grounds of duress. This case further illustrates that duress need not be the only reason that a contract was entered into.

The concept of economic duress is relatively new in terms of contract law and operates where one party was forced into signing the contract because of economic pressure.[6] The doctrine began to emerge in the case of *Occidental Worldwide Investment Corporation v Skibs A/S Avanti, The Siboen and The Sibotre.*[7] In this case, charter rates had fallen substantially as a result of a recession. The charterers of two ships renegotiated their charter fees, warning the owners that they would become insolvent if they did not agree to this. The owners initially agreed but then sought to have the renegotiated contract set aside on the basis of duress. While the claim for duress failed in this case, with the court holding that commercial pressure would not suffice, Kerr J did open the door to extend the doctrine beyond that of physical harm to the person. He stated:

> For example, if I should be compelled to sign a lease or some other contract for a nominal but legally sufficient consideration under an imminent threat of having my house burned down or a valuable

---

4 [1991] 4 All ER 87.

5 [1976] AC 104.

6 PS Atiyah 'Economic duress and the overborne will' (1982) 98 Law Quarterly Review 197.

7 [1976] 1 Lloyds Rep 293.

> picture slashed, though without any threat of physical violence to anyone, I do not think that the law would uphold the agreement.

This can be somewhat difficult to determine as many contracts are entered into under economic pressure. For example, would you pay an extortionate rent if you did not need somewhere to live? Would you accept a lower salary if you did not need the job? It is clear from the case law that the pressure exerted here must go beyond what is termed 'ordinary market pressure', and the courts have attempted to outline what that is.

A leading Irish case in this area is *Smelter Corporation of Ireland v Driscoll.*[8] In this case the plaintiff sought a remedy of specific performance on the defendant's land on the basis of an option agreement giving them the right to purchase. The option had been given by the defendant as he had been advised that if he did not sell to the plaintiff, that the county council would make a compulsory purchase order. This information was untrue. The court found that as the defendant could not be said to have freely agreed to the sale, the order was refused.

The doctrine of economic duress was formally recognised in *Pao On v Lau Yiu Long*[9] which affirmed a High Court decision in *North Ocean Shipping Co Ltd v Hyundai Construction Co Ltd.*[10] In *Pao On*, the claimants threatened to breach a contract unless the defendant shareholders agreed to guarantee them against losses which may occur if the share price fluctuated. The defendants gave the guarantee because they were concerned what may happen to the reputation of the company if the contract did not go ahead. Lord Scarman confirmed that a contract could be set aside on the grounds of economic duress, but that pressure needed to be more that would be found ordinarily in the commercial world. In this case, the court found that it did not meet the standard of economic duress but rather economic pressure which fell within the normal bounds of commercial negotiation.

Where a case involves the amendment of a contract under alleged duress, there are additional factors that must be taken into account, such as consideration.

Where there has been a threat to damage or seize goods, as opposed to physical violence or economic duress, the case law is somewhat mixed. In *Skeate v Beale* a landlord took a tenant's possessions and threatened to sell them if the tenant did not pay an amount in excess

---

8 [1977] IR 305.
9 [1980] AC 614.
10 [1979] QB 705.

of the arrears that he owed.[11] The tenant paid part of the new amount agreed and stated that he only agreed to this new amount due to the threats that the landlord made to sell his property. The court refused to accept this defence and stated that the tenant should have used the legal remedies available to him to ensure the return of his property, rather than entering into a contract which he had no intention of keeping. In contrast, in *Maskell v Horner*, the defendant threatened to close down the claimant's market stall and take his goods if he refused to pay a toll.[12] There was no lawful obligation to pay this toll, and the claimant was entitled to recover the money paid as the court accepted that it was only paid as a result of the threats to his goods.

The cases are somewhat inconsistent, and it appears that it will depend on the facts of each particular case as to whether the threat to goods is sufficient to amount to duress.

13.3.2 The Pressure was Illegitimate

In the early days of the doctrine, the pressure exerted, ie the act threatened, must have been unlawful. More recent iteration of the doctrine has preferred to look at this as illegitimate pressure which extends the act beyond one which is unlawful. The threat to do an act which is unlawful will always amount to illegitimate pressure; however, where the act threatened is lawful, it may still be classed as illegitimate where it is unreasonable, and this will depend on the circumstances of each individual case.[13]

Determining illegitimate pressure is often a difficult task for the courts where threats to do what you are lawfully allowed to do (such as refusing to enter into a contract) are made. This type of pressure is what would be expected in general commercial negotiations. The court in *Lloyds Bank v Bundy* said that 'no bargain will be upset which is the result of the ordinary interplay of market forces',[14] and further in *Eric Gnapp Ltd v Petroleum Board* it was held that a party will not be able to escape its contractual obligations because it was coerced by fear of financial consequences if it refused to do so.[15]

In *CNT Cash & Carry v Gallaher Ltd* it was held that a lawful act coupled with an illegitimate demand could amount to duress.[16] However, in

---

11 (1840) 11 Ad & El 983.
12 [1915] 3 KB 106.
13 Iona Branford and Jodi Gardner, 'Reconceiving Wrongdoing in Lawful Act Duress' (2023) 139 Law Quarterly Review 629.
14 [1975] QB 326.
15 [1949] 1 All ER 980.
16 [1994] 4 All ER 714.

this case the claim was unsuccessful as a high standard is imposed on two commercial entities.[17] Further in *R v HM Attorney General for England and Wales* a former member of the SAS alleged that he had been subjected to duress in signing confidentiality agreements which prohibited him from disclosing information relating to the SAS after he left the forces.[18] He claimed he was told that if he did not sign the documents, he would be returned to his old regiment. It was held that the Crown was lawfully entitled to return him to his old regiment and therefore this was not an unlawful act. The court then had to decide whether the pressure was unreasonable or illegitimate and found that the Crown had acted legitimately in requiring confidentiality agreements to be signed, which was justified given the role of the SAS.

In *DSND Subsea Ltd v Petroleum Geo Services Asa* Dyson J gave a useful outline of what may constitute illegitimate pressure:

> In determining whether there has been illegitimate pressure, the court takes into account a range of factors. These include whether there has been an actual or threatened breach of contract, whether the person allegedly exerting the pressure has acted in good or bad faith, whether the victim had any realistic alternative but to submit to the pressure, whether the victim protested at the time, and whether he affirmed and sought to rely on the contract [....] Illegitimate pressure must be distinguished from the rough and tumble of the pressures of normal commercial bargaining.[19]

Dyson J's guidance was applied in the case of *Kolmar Group AG v Traxpo Enterprises PVT Ltd.*[20] In this case Traxpo had contracted to supply Kolmar with a quantity of a chemical called methanol which would then be sent to an important client of Kolmar in America. It transpired that Traxpo did not have the required amount of methanol, and its price had significantly increased since entering into the contract. Traxpo told Kolmar that it would back out of the agreement unless Kolmar agreed to a modified agreement which would allow them to charge more and provide less. Kolmar protested but ultimately agreed to the new terms in order to fulfil its obligations to their client. It then sued and its claim on the basis of duress was upheld as it only entered into the new agreement due to coercive and illegitimate threats.

The matter was recently considered by the Supreme Court in *Pakistan International Airline Corporation v Times Travel (UK) Ltd.*[21] The claimant's business at the time comprised almost exclusively of selling airline

---

17 Paul S Davies, 'Lawful Act Duress' (2018) 134 Law Quarterly Review 5.
18 [2003] UKPC 22.
19 [2000] BLR 530.
20 [2010] EWHC 113 (Comm).
21 [2021] UKSC 40.

tickets to Pakistan on planes owned by the defendant. Disputes arose in relation to commission that the claimant said it was owed by the defendant. The defendant threatened to repudiate the contract unless the claimant agreed to enter into a new contract which would, among other things, release the defendant from any claims that the claimant may have in relation to previously owed commission. The claimant subsequently sought to rescind the contract allowing it to claim for the unpaid commission. The court took the view that is the better option to be clear that lawful act duress does exist in English law, and that there are three things the court ought to consider when deciding when the pressure for a lawful act is illegitimate. First, the law here needed to be stated with precision and clarity; secondly, the court should focus on the nature of the demand rather than the nature of the threat; thirdly, where the demand is motivated by commercial self-interest, it will be justified; fourthly, whether the demand is made in bad faith. In applying these to the case at hand, the court found that there was indeed duress and allowed the claimant to set the contract aside.[22]

One must be careful to distinguish between what is economic duress and what is normal commercial pressure.[23] In *Walmsley v Christchurch City Council* the plaintiff had secured a contract to produce souvenir programmes for an event organised by the defendant. The product when delivered was substandard and rejected by the defendant. The defendant then pressed the plaintiff to pay for reprinting of the programmes and that the plaintiff would be entitled to any profits over and above an agreed minimum amount to the defendant. Several weeks after, the plaintiff sought to argue that this new arrangement was procured by duress. The court rejected this argument and held that the defendant was entitled to reject the product and the plaintiff had consulted with both his business partner and legal advisors prior to agreeing to the new terms.

There have been no Irish cases which engage with the issue of lawful act duress.

13.3.3 The Pressure Induced the Party to Enter the Contract

Once it has been established that pressure was applied to the party,

---

22 Timothy Pilkington and David Winterton, 'The Possibility of Lawful Act Economic Duress: Pakistan International Airlines Corp v Times Travel (UK) Ltd' (2023) 86(1) Modern Law Review 238; Jonathan Morgan. 'The Thin Edge of the Wedge: Morality, Contract Law and Lawful Act Duress' (2022) 81(1) Cambridge Law Review 17.

23 Pinar Akman, 'The Relationship between Economic Duress and Abuse of Dominant Position' (2014) 1 Lloyd's Maritime and Commercial Law Quarterly 99.

and that the pressure was illegitimate, the next step that must be established is that the pressure actually induced the party to enter into the contract. So, if Amy threatens that she will kill Paul unless he buys her car, and he wants to buy her car anyway, despite there being illegitimate pressure, it did not induce Paul into buying the car and so he will not be able to rely on the doctrine of duress.

However, as we have seen in *Barton v Armstrong*, for duress to succeed, it does not have to be the only reason that a person enters into the contract, but it does have to be one of the reasons.

13.3.4 The Claimant had No Real Choice But to Enter the Contract

The courts have spoken about how the duress must amount to a circumstance where the claimant had no real practical alternative but to enter into the contract. In the case of *Universe Tankships v International Transport Workers Federation (The Universe Sentinel)* the court considered this aspect of the test.[24] This case involved industrial action where a trade union insisted that a contribution was made to its welfare fund before it called off strike action. The payment was made, and once the strike action was stopped, the shipowners sought to reclaim the money claiming that the payment was made under duress. Having decided that the payment was made under duress, Lord Diplock stated that the real test here ought to be not whether there was a choice (as there will always be a choice even though either outcome may be unpleasant) but rather whether there was any real practical alternative. In this case, he concluded that there was no real practical alternative as the only way to end the strike action was to pay the money.

In *Atlas Express Ltd v Kafco (Importers and Distributors) Ltd* the court again had occasion to examine this matter.[25] In this case the defendant contracted with the plaintiff to deliver certain goods to Woolworths. Due to a miscalculation on the part of the plaintiff's depot manager the contract was uneconomical and as a result obtained a higher price from the defendant. The defendant agreed to this new rate as it feared that it would not find another carrier on time and would therefore be sued for breach of contract by Woolworths. It was held in this case the consent to the higher price was given under pressure which was illegitimate. In addition, it found that the agreement was unenforceable as it lacked sufficient consideration.

The case of *Carillion Construction Ltd v Felix UK Ltd* engages with the

---

[24] [1983] 1 AC 366.
[25] [1989] 1 All ER 641.

issues of duress in relation to construction contracts.[26] The defendant was contracted by the plaintiff to provide cladding. They fell behind on the work breaching the timetable agreed in the contract. Disputes arose between the parties in relation, inter alia, to pricing and the defendant stated that further deliveries of the cladding would be dependent on the settlement of the dispute. They were eventually settled on terms that were favourable to the defendant. The defendant however was aware that the plaintiff would face penalty clauses for the late completion of the work. On the day that the settlement was reached, the plaintiff wrote a letter of complaint and when the work was completed argued that the settlement had been garnered through economic duress. Reiterating the principles espoused in *DSND Subsea Ltd* the court affirmed that what the plaintiff needed to show was the presence of pressure or threats, that such was illegitimate, the practical effect of this being that there was no practical alternative but to enter the contract and that the pressure was a significant cause in entering the contract. It was held that this contract had been obtained by duress as the defendant knew that it had no rights to make the threats that it did, and in indeed ought to have used the arbitration clause in the contract for the settlement of any disputes. A further key point in this case was that once the pressure was removed (the dispute settled) the plaintiff immediately protested.[27]

13.3.5 The Claimant Protested at the Time or Shortly After the Contract was Concluded

Where it is alleged that a contract was entered into under duress, the party claiming this must show that they protested either at the time of the pressure or shortly after. The courts are aware that it may not always be possible to protest at the time the contract was entered into, and what amounts to a reasonable time for protesting will depend on the case. If the innocent party waits too long, they may be seen as affirming the contract. In *North Ocean Shipping v Hyundai Construction*, a delay of eight months in protesting the alleged duress was held to be too long and a constructive affirmation of the contract whereas a letter of protest on the day in *Carillion Construction Ltd* was instrumental in the court's decision.

Test Your Knowledge

Jamie is looking for a new flat. He talks to his former college friend

---

[26] [2001] BLR 1.

[27] Hamish Lal, 'Commercial Exploitation in Construction Contracts: The Role of Economic Duress and Unjust Enrichment' (2005) 21(8) Construction Law Journal 590.

Sally who happens to be renting out her studio flat. She tells Jamie all about it and how much the rent is. Jamie seems keen but he really thinks that the rent is too high for what the accommodation is. He tells Sally that he will 'get back to her'. Three weeks later Sally contacts him asking where his deposit is. Jamie says that he never agreed to rent the flat and is not going to be moving in, so will not be paying any deposit. Sally flies into a rage and drives straight around to Jamie's house. She barges in through his door and begins shouting at him. Jamie admits that he has not yet found another flat, but says that he does not want to move into Sally's and he is quite afraid of her. She then produces a rental agreement and a large sword. She places the sword on Jamie's neck and tells him that she has lost enough money because he had 'backed out' of their initial agreement. She tells him to sign the contract immediately and to transfer her the deposit and three months' rent, which he does with the sword to his neck. Jamie then moves into Sally's flat and finds that he actually quite likes it. He stays there for nine months, at which point he decides to move into a new flat with his girlfriend. Sally says that he cannot do this without paying the termination fee of six months' rent in the contract that he signed (which was for two years). Jamie argues that he is not bound by this as the contract was entered into under duress. Is the contract:

A void for duress?
B valid as Jamie was going to take the apartment anyway?
C valid as Jamie has affirmed the contract?

The correct answer here is C. Although there was clear duress in how the contract was entered into, Jamie never protested this, and by staying in the flat for nine months he has affirmed the contract and cannot now rely on the duress. His obligation would be to protest this at the earliest possible opportunity.

Stretch and Challenge Question

Critically analyse whether the current law on economic duress gives adequate protection to those in a weaker bargaining position.

CHAPTER 14

UNDUE INFLUENCE AND UNCONSCIONABLE TRANSACTIONS

14.1 Introduction to Undue Influence

As we have seen in the previous chapter, the common law doctrine of duress, which is somewhat expanded now, was historically rather difficult to establish, requiring either violence or the threat of violence to the person or property. This resulted in somewhat harsh outcomes: where a person could not meet this high threshold, they would be held, under common law, to the contract. Equity, however, intervened in such cases and created the doctrine of undue influence. This doctrine understands that there are some circumstances in which pressure may be applied, or a party may be coerced into entering a contract that does not meet the standard of duress, but nonetheless the party did not enter into the contract of their own free will. In these circumstances, where undue influence is shown to be present, the court may set the contract aside. Equity therefore intervenes to prevent weaker parties being victimised, manipulated or coerced by the dominant party to enter into a contract which is to their manifest disadvantage. Lindley LJ in *Allcard v Skinner* summarised equity's role thus:

> It would obviously be to encourage folly, recklessness, extravagance and vice if persons could get back property which they foolishly made away with, whether by giving it to charitable institutions or by bestowing it on less worthy objects. On the other hand, to protect people from being forced, tricked or misled in any way by others into parting with their property is one of the most legitimate objects of all laws; and the equitable doctrine of undue influence has grown out of and been developed by the

> necessity of grappling with insidious forms of spiritual tyranny and with infinite varieties of fraud.[1]

It is difficult to define precisely what undue influence is and the courts have not attempted to do so, perhaps due to the wide range of situations that it could be employed in. They have, however, endeavoured to elucidate the types of behaviour that may amount to undue influence, the most comprehensive being in *R (Proctor) v Hutton*[2] that 'that plaintiff must prove that an unfair advantage has been gained by an unconscientious use of power in the form of some unfair and improper conduct, some coercion from the outside, some over-reaching, some form of cheating'.

14.2 Classifying Undue Influence

Undue influence generally is categorised into two main areas: actual undue influence and presumed undue influence. The classifications were further explained and delineated in *Bank of Credit and Commerce International v Aboody* as:

- Class 1: actual undue influence – which requires proof of the influence;
- Class 2a: presumed undue influence – where the relationship is such that as a matter of law the presumption arises that influence was exerted;
- Class 2b: presumed undue influence – where the relationship itself does not give rise to the presumption, but evidence may be adduced that it was a relationship of trust and confidence in which there was an imbalance of power which in turn gives rise to the presumption.[3]

14.2.1 Actual Undue Influence: Class 1

Class 1 does not depend on the relationship between the parties but rather on the factual application of undue influence. In *Smith v Kay* a man who had just reached the age of majority was left in significant debt to the appellant as a result of coercion by an older man who had gained significant control over him.[4] The court found that while this was not a fiduciary relationship, the influence exerted over the young man entitled him to the protection of the court. Further, in *Morley v Loughnan* the executors of the deceased's estate sued to recover the sum of £140,000 paid by him to a member of the 'exclusive brethren'.[5]

---

1 (1887) 36 Ch D 145, 182.
2 [1978] NI 139, 146.
3 [1990] 1 QB 923.
4 (1859) 7 HLC 750.
5 [1893] Ch 736.

The deceased had lived in this man's house for several years and was under his religious influence. In finding for the executors, the court said that in cases such as this, there was no need to find a special relationship between the parties as the defendant 'took possession, so to speak, of the whole life of the deceased, and the gifts were not the result of the deceased's own free will but the effect of that influence and domination'.

In *O'Flanagan v Ray-Ger Ltd* an agreement was set aside on the grounds of undue influence.[6] This case related to an agreement between two shareholders where property was transferred to the defendant. The court noted that there was a significant difference in terms of the business acumen of the parties and negotiations took place in an environment where the dominant and persuasive powers of the defendant could operate freely. Further, the transferor was terminally ill, a fact known to the defendant.

14.2.2 Presumed Undue Influence: Class 2a

Class 2a gives rise to a presumption in law based on an inherent inequality or imbalance of power between the parties. The relationships which give rise to this presumption are neither closed nor rigid; however, the courts have been clear on certain relationships that give rise to it, which include parent and child (*Bainbrigge v Browne;*[7] *Archer v Hudson;*[8] *Wallace v Wallace,*[9] *McMackin v Hibernian Bank*[10]and *Croker v Croker;*[11] *Barry v Ennis*[12]); guardian and ward (*Mulhallen v Marum*[13]) – both of these may continue after the age of majority or marriage in certain circumstances per *Lancashire Loans Ltd v Black*[14]; those in loco parentis *(O'Connor v Foley*[15]) doctor and patient (*Re CMG*[16] and *Aherne v Hogan*[17]); trustee and beneficiary (*Beningfield v Baxter*[18]); solicitor and

6 Unrep, High Court, 28 April 1983.
7 (1881) 18 Ch D 188.
8 (1844) 7 Beav 551.
9 (1842) 2 Dr and War 452.
10 [1905] 1 IR 296.
11 (1870) 4 ILTR 181.
12 [2018] IEHC 766.
13 (1843) 3 DR & War 31.
14 [1934] 1 KB 380.
15 [1905] 1 IR 1. See also *Hebden v Domino Record Co Ltd* [2022] EWHC 74.
16 [1970] Ch 574.
17 Dru Temp Sug 310.
18 (1886) 12 App Cas 167.

client (*Wright v Carter*[19] and *Lawless v Mansfield*[20]); and religious advisor and devotee (*Allcard v Skinner*[21] and *Murphy v O'Neill*[22]).

In these circumstances, where the party in the weaker position enters into an agreement which may be to their financial detriment such as giving large gifts, providing guarantees or indemnities, or leaving large bequests in their wills, the law will assume that this weaker party, known as the donor, has agreed to these as a result of undue influence.

Once it is established that the relationship is one that gives rise to the presumption, the focus then shifts to the defendant to rebut that presumption. There are two main ways in which this can occur: first, if it is shown that independent legal advice was received by the donor,[23] and, secondly, that the donor acted of their own free will.

14.2.3 Presumed Undue Influence: Class 2B

Class 2b comprises relationships where there is not an obvious and inherent imbalance of power on the face of the relationship, but where in fact one person relies on the other. So, for example, if a brother enters into an agreement to guarantee his brother's debts, this relationship would not fall within class 2a as it would appear, to all intents and purposes, that the relationship is one of equality.[24] If, however, we then discover that the brother who has guaranteed the loan suffers from a severe physical disability and is entirely reliant on his brother, there is now an imbalance of power in the relationship. Therefore, there will not automatically be a presumption of undue influence in such a case (whereas there will be for doctor/patient; solicitor/client); but where it can be shown that there is an imbalance of power in that particular relationship, the presumption will arise.

The presumption arose under this category in the case of *Tate v Williamson* where Tate needed to pay off his student debt of £1,000.[25] He was estranged from his father and turned to his great uncle for advice. His great uncle was very ill and requested that his nephew, Williamson, assist. During discussions between Tate and Williamson, Tate expressed a desire to sell part of his estate and Williamson offered

---

19 [1903] 1 Ch 27.

20 (1841) 1 Dr & War 557.

21 (1887) 36 Ch D 145.

22 [1936] NI 16. See also *Patrick McCormack v Our Lady Queen of Peace* [2018] IEHC 26.

23 Mary Donnelly, 'Vitiating Factors – Undue Influence – Unconscionability – Independent Legal Advice' (2017). 24(3) Commercial Law Practitioner 65.

24 *Armstrong v Armstrong* (1873) IR 8 Eq 1; *ACC Loan Management v Sheehan* [2015] IEHC 818.

25 (1886) LR 2 Ch App 55.

to buy it for £7,000. Before the sale went through, Williamson had obtained a report valuing the property at £20,000 but did not disclose this fact. Tate died one year later, and it was held that this transaction should be set aside as Williamson, having placed himself in the position of adviser, was in a position of trust and confidence and this required him to disclose all material facts.

In *Carroll v Carroll* the court overturned a transaction in which an elderly father transferred a public house to his son.[26] This case shows the importance of the shift in burden of proof as, despite the fact that the court could find no undue influence, the presumption had been made out and the defendant could not rebut this, resulting in the transaction being set aside.

14.2.4 The Special Case of Husband and Wife in Commercial Transactions

Notably, the relationship of husband and wife is not one that automatically gives rise to the presumption of undue influence under class 2a; rather this falls under class 2b. There has been much debate on whether this is the correct classification, but interestingly the focus of the courts has not been on whether or not undue influence has actually been exerted but whether (as these cases inevitably involve a bank enforcing a guarantee) the bank was fixed with notice of the undue influence, and if so, what steps did it take.[27]

These types of cases tend to require the court to make determinations on competing interests. On the one hand, the bank is attempting to enforce the terms of its mortgage or loan, usually as against the family home, and on the other hand the wife is attempting to keep her family home, alleging that the mortgage or loan was entered into on the basis of undue influence on the part of her husband. The applicable principles in cases such as these were first considered by the House of Lords in *Barclays Bank Plc v O'Brien*.[28] Here the wife executed a charge securing an unlimited guarantee for her husband's company liabilities over the family home, under the mistaken belief that it was temporary security for a fixed sum of £60,000 as a result of her husband's misrepresentation to her. She did not read the documents before signing, and it was held that the bank could not enforce its security as it had constructive notice of her right to set aside the transaction. The court determined that in cases such as these, there are

---

26 [2000] 1 ILRM 210.

27 See Barry Allan, 'Trust Me, I'm Your Husband: Undue Influence and Royal Bank of Scotland v Etridge' (2006) 11(2) Otago Law Review 247.

28 [1994] 1 AC 180.

two paramount considerations. First, was the bank on notice as to the existence of misrepresentation or undue influence and, if so, did it take reasonable steps to ensure that the third party understood the terms of the transaction. It determined that in every case where a wife acted as a surety for her husband's debt, the creditor was automatically put on notice of the substantial risk that she entered into the transaction under undue influence. This was not confined to wives but also extended to cohabiting couples and longstanding relationships provided that the bank was aware of the relationship.[29]

Of particular importance to the court's decision in *O'Brien* was that the transaction was not to the wife's advantage as she had no interest in the company. This was considered in *CIBC Mortgages v Pitt* where the wife was unduly influenced into entering a joint loan, the purpose of which was to pay off an existing mortgage and to finance a holiday home.[30] Despite the wife not obtaining independent advice, this case was contrasted with the surety case above in that the loan was for the benefit of both parties and the bank could enforce the terms. Here, the court was attempting to try to strike a balance between the potential vulnerable wife and the lender and determined that if it came to the opposite conclusion, it would have presented significant practical difficulties in relation to joint loans. However, the mere fact that the loan is a joint loan will not automatically mean that the *O'Brien* principles are inapplicable. So, where the loan, while officially joint, is in fact for the husband's sole benefit, is substantively a surety, or where the advantage to the wife is significantly smaller to that of the husband, the bank will be fixed with notice. Therefore, not only did the wife need to show that she was unduly influenced; she also needed to satisfy the court that the transaction was to her manifest disadvantage in order to succeed. This is at distinct odds with the general principles of equity and places a high burden on the wife.

The phrase 'manifest disadvantage'[31] was coined by Lord Scarman in *National Westminster Bank Plc v Morgan*,[32] where he determined that there was no authority to set aside a transaction which was manifestly disadvantageous to the person influenced, purely on the basis that the transaction was manifestly disadvantageous. Previous cases such as *Lloyds Bank Ltd v Bundy*[33] where there was no discussion of this requirement at all and *Wright v Carter*[34] where the disadvantage of the

---

29 *Massey v Midland Bank Plc* [1995] 1 All ER 929.
30 [1994] AC 200.
31 Mindy Chen-Wishart, 'Loss Sharing, Undue Influence and Manifest Disadvantage' (1994) 110 Law Quarterly Review 173.
32 [1985] 1 All ER 821.
33 [1975] QB 326.
34 [1903] 1 Ch 27.

transaction was not held to be a relevant consideration in determining whether the presumption arose, but rather in establishing whether the presumption was rebutted are evidence of the changing perceptions of this element. The case of *Bank of Credit and Commerce International v Aboody* took the *Morgan* requirements even further in refusing the allow the appeal of Mrs Aboody as, notwithstanding that the court accepted that actual undue influence existed, she could not show that the transaction was to her manifest disadvantage.[35]

This requirement to show a 'manifest disadvantage' was the subject of heavy criticism, inter alia, because of the lack of a precise definition, leaving Nourse LJ in *Barclays Bank Plc v Coleman* to conclude that the authorities on the matter 'have now got into a very unsatisfactory state'.[36]

The principles surrounding these types of cases were considered at length by the House of Lords in *Royal Bank of Scotland v Etridge (No 2)*.[37] This case consisted of eight separate appeals joined for the purpose of this hearing. Of the eight cases, seven concerned wives who had signed loans securing the business debts of their husbands under alleged undue influence, while one concerned a wife suing the solicitor who advised her prior to entering the guarantee. In discussing the concept of manifest disadvantage, Lord Nicholls found it a label difficult to apply and that in cases such as this it was not an easy consideration meaning that it was difficult to determine whether or not such transactions were in fact detrimental to the wife. On a narrow interpretation, he felt that a wife securing her husband's business debt was to her disadvantage; she undertakes a serious financial responsibility and receives no personal advantage. However, in a wider sense, he found that the wife would benefit as 'the fortunes of the husband and the wife are bound up together'. As a result of the analysis by Lord Nicholls, the label of 'manifest disadvantage' was abandoned, and in its place the question would be whether it was a 'transaction which called for an explanation' – a test more in line with that set down in *Allcard* rather than *Morgan*. Lord Clyde acknowledged the difficulty in defining precisely what undue influence is and was critical of the classifications employed, finding that they 'add mystery rather than illumination'. Lord Scott in particular expressed consternation with class 2b and questioned whether it should have ever existed. Lord Hobhouse in agreement stated:

> It is a fallacy to argue from the terminology normally used,

---

35 [1990] 1 QB 923.
36 [2000] 1 All ER 385.
37 [2001] 4 All ER 449.

> 'presumed undue influence', to the position, not of presuming that one party reposed trust and confidence in the other, but of *presuming* that an abuse of that relationship has occurred; factual interference, yes, one the issue has properly raised but not a *presumption*.

Lord Brown-Wilkinson in *O'Brien* considered that the effect of the doctrine was that the bank was on notice every time the wife acted as surety for her husband. In exploring the extent of this obligation, Lord Nicholls in *Etridge* found that the bank was on notice in every case where the relationship between the surety and the debtor was non-commercial. He then turned to setting out the steps that the bank should take once put on notice and concluded that 'the furthest that a bank can be expected to go is to take reasonable steps to satisfy itself that the wife has had brought home to her in a meaningful way, the practical implications of the proposed transaction'. This does not necessarily mean that the wife must have independent legal advice; however, where this is provided, Lord Nicholls noted that, as a minimum, the solicitor should explain the nature of the documents and the practical consequences, expose the serious nature of the risks involved, clearly state that the client has a choice in whether or not to sign the documents, and finally, should the client wish to proceed, the solicitor should write to the bank outlining their consultation with the client.[38]

The House of Lords in *Etridge* also confirmed that the bank could rely on a certificate provided by a solicitor even where they are not acting exclusively for the wife, and the fact that the solicitor is also acting for the bank does not in itself give rise to prejudice. Where the solicitor also acts for the husband, the court found that it should be able to rely on the professional competence of the solicitor to advise the wife properly. The court here makes the presumption that the solicitor will act in a professional and impartial manner. While the solicitor may in fact do this, it does not take into account the realities for those in a situation of coercive control or domestic abuse.[39] A wife may feel she has no option but to sign the documents in circumstances where her controlling husband is sitting beside her.[40]

---

38 Edwin C Mujih, 'The Role of the Solicitor in Guarantee Cases 10 years after Royal Bank of Scotland Plc v Etridge (No.2)' (2012) 27(12) Journal of International Banking Law and Regulation 520.

39 Eleanor Rowan, 'Independent Legal Advice in (re)Mortgage Transactions 20 years on from RBS v Etridge (No.2)' (2023) 2 Conveyancer and Property Lawyer 166.

40 David Capper, 'Banks, Borrowers, Sureties and Undue Influence: a half baked solution to a thoroughly cooked problem' (2002) 10 Restitution Law Review 100.

Of the eight cases that were joined in *Etridge*, the appeals were allowed in five and dismissed in three, primarily on the basis of whether the bank could rely on the fact that the wife had been independently advised, and thus shifting the focus from whether there was in fact undue influence.

The decision in *Etridge* has been strongly criticised[41] for placing an unduly harsh burden on those who guarantee the debts of their spouse. Intimate partner relationships cannot be placed into class 2a where there is always an imbalance of power within such relationships. Therefore, it is proper that they are placed in class 2b. On the face of the relationship, it ought to be that intimate partners are equal. However, this is not always the case. In circumstances where undue influence can be shown by proper construction, the transaction ought to be set aside. Rather, the courts have focused on whether or not the wife or partner has received independent advice and understood the nature of the document that they were signing. This shows a fundamental misunderstanding by the courts of the nature of domestic abuse and coercive control. *Etridge* remains good law, but since then the offence of coercive control has been created by s 76 of the Serious Crime Act 2015 in England and s 39 of the Domestic Violence Act 2018 in Ireland. It would be interesting to see whether the current Supreme Court would follow *Etridge* in light of this legislation as it would be a serious flaw in the law if there was a finding of coercive control, but the bank was still able to enforce its security. While it may be understandable from a commercial perspective to focus on whether the bank fulfilled its obligations, the disproportionate impact that such a transaction may have on the wife due to the husband's behaviour ought to be the paramount concern.[42]

In Ireland the matter has received no less attention and the decisions of *O'Brien* and *Etridge* have come under scrutiny in the Irish courts. In *Bank of Nova Scotia v Hogan* the court adopted the O'Brien principles and stated:

> A wife who has been induced to stand as a surety for her husband's debts by his undue influence, misrepresentation or some other legal wrong has an equity against him to set aside that transaction, under the ordinary principles of equity her right to set aside that transaction will be enforceable against third parties

---

41 Not least by Rosemary Auchmuty 'Judgement: Royal Bank of Scotland Plc v Etridge (No 2)' in Rosemary Hunter, Clare McGlynn and Erika Radley (eds) *Feminist Judgments: From Theory to Practice* (Hart 2010).

42 Orit Gan, 'Spousal Agreements and Patriarchal Bargains: A Wife's Guarantee of her husband's Business Debts' (2022) 18(2) European Review of Contract Law 175.

> if.... The third party had actual or constructive notice of the facts giving rise to her equity.[43]

In *Ulster Bank Ltd v Fitzgerald* the court considered what circumstances would constitute the third party being fixed with notice.[44] Here the wife claimed that the bank should not be able to enforce guarantees against her on the grounds that she had no financial interest in it and which she entered into under pressure from her husband. The court found that while it may be prepared to accept that the husband unduly influenced his wife to sign the documents, but was not persuaded that the bank had any notice that she was not acting of her own free will. Further, the court did not accept that she had no financial interest as the family benefitted from the business income. In the absence of notice, the bank was not obliged to take any further steps to ensure that she obtained independent advice. Again, in *Danske Bank AS trading as National Irish Bank Plc v Madden* it was stressed that it is necessary for the bank to have notice and further that the onus is on the defendant to show that the bank had notice of the fraud or undue influence, a much stricter approach than that taken in either *O'Brien* or *Etridge (No 2)*.[45]

Detailed consideration was given to the matter by Clarke J in *Ulster Bank Ltd v Roche and Buttimer*.[46] Here the bank sought to enforce the terms of a guarantee against the second named defendant who had secured the business liabilities of the first named defendant with whom she was in a relationship. She had a very minor role in the business and it was accepted that she signed the guarantee under the influence of her partner. Clarke J found that the test set down in *Fitzgerald* was too strict in that:

> A regime which places no obligation on a bank to take any steps to ascertain whether, in the presence of circumstances suggesting a non-commercial aspect to a guarantee, the party offering the guarantee many not be fully and freely entering into same, gives insufficient protection to potentially vulnerable sureties.[47]

Clarke J determined that the general principle of *Etridge* was that that the bank is placed on notice where there is a non-commercial element to the guarantee and adopted this into Irish law. In this case, the bank were aware that the parties were in a relationship and that while Ms Buttimer was a director of the company she was in name only and had no shareholdings therein. He concluded that the bank

---

43 [1996] 2 IR 239, 248.
44 [2001] IEHC 159.
45 [2009] IEHC 319.
46 [2012] 1 IR 765.
47 ibid, 780.

should take some steps, but unlike the judgment in *Etridge* did not set out precisely what steps the bank should take. It is interesting that in his judgment Clarke J commented that the couple were unmarried Ms Buttimer and therefore was in a less secure position than that of a spouse of civil partner who would have an interest in the business by virtue of marriage.

In *Ulster Bank (Ireland) Ltd v De Kretser & Anor* the Court of Appeal considered a case relatively similar to that in *Roche*.[48] Here, the second named defendant Ms Fox guaranteed the business loans of her husband, the first named defendant for a company in which she had a 1% shareholding. Her claim failed as the although she did not have independent legal advice, nor did she read the guarantee in advance, she was a businesswoman in her own right and therefore the court was of the opinion that she knew of the effects of a personal guarantee (and indeed had executed previous guarantees for her husband's business). However, in his dissenting judgment Hogan J found that Ms Fox had raised an arguable case that the bank was under an affirmative duty to ensure that she received independent advice prior to executing the guarantee.

The matter was again considered in *Ross v Harper* where the wife signed documents that had been represented to her as necessary to amend some discrepancies in the land registry title.[49] The documents were in fact charging debts against the family home in respect of loan defaults made by her husband in relation to holiday cottages. Some years later the bank sought to enforce security against the family home. While in this case the wife sought an interlocutory injunction, the court found that the principles of *Ulster Bank v Roche* were applicable and that the bank had not acted in line with necessary professional standards:

> In my view, the plaintiff has raised a fair question to be tried that the Bank and its successors Link, should be fixed with constructive knowledge. The correspondence between the Bank's Solicitor and the Solicitor demonstrates that the Bank had material concerns about the enforceability of its security and had requested the Solicitor to address this issue urgently. Against this backdrop, it is arguable that the Bank's knowledge of the circumstances under which the mortgage was concluded was sufficient to place upon it an obligation to ensure if the plaintiff had entered into the mortgage openly and freely. Yet, no documentation has been put before the court suggesting that the bank undertook any such enquiries.

48 [2016] IECA 371.
49 [2022] IEHC 255.

14.3 Rescission in Undue Influence

The right to rescind a contract applies where it has been entered into under undue influence.[50] This means that the parties are put back into the position that they were in prior to the contract being entered into. However, even where it is not possible to put the parties back into their precise position, the flexibility that equity retains means that the court can fashion a remedy depending on the justice of the case. An example of this flexibility can be seen in the case of *O'Sullivan v Management Agency and Music Ltd*.[51] Here, a musician sought to set aside a contract with an internationally renowned management company on the grounds of undue influence. The parties were not able to be restored to their original position, mainly as the musician had now attained considerable fame. The management company was therefore ordered to account for the profit they had received from the agreement, while also receiving a reasonable remuneration for the work that they had undertaken in promoting the musician.

The right to rescind may be lost where the party who has been influenced has affirmed the contract. For example, in *Mitchell v Homefray* a patient gave a gift to her doctor[52]. This is the type of relationship that would fall into class 2a and a presumption of undue influence would arise. However, it was shown that the patient was determined to continue with the gift once the relationship ended and therefore was deemed to have affirmed the transaction. The same finding was made in *Allcard v Skinner* where it was shown that Allcard had made no attempt to retrieve any of the property in the six years since she had left the religious order thereby affirming the gift. The affirmation will only be held to be valid where there has been a complete cessation of the undue influence.

14.4 Unconscionable Bargain

Unlike under the common law, equity can intervene to set aside contracts on the basis that one party has been taken advantage of by reason of ignorance, poverty or some other factor.[53] Unconscionable transactions differ from undue influence as they are concerned with the nature and circumstances of the bargain, whereas undue influence is

---

50 Paul Morris, 'Remedies and Rescission on the Grounds of Undue Influence' (1999) 1(2) Finance and Credit Law 5.

51 [1985] 1 QB 428.

52 (1881) 8 QBD 587.

53 David Capper, 'The Unconscionable Bargain in the Common Law World' (2010) 126 Law Quarterly Review 403.

concerned with the relationship between the parties and the motivation behind entering into the agreement.[54]

14.5 Elements of an Unconscionable Bargain

It is not enough to show that the contract was unreasonable or that the defendant drove a hard bargain.

Early case law such *Slator v Nolan* show how the doctrine operates with Sullivan MR stating:

> I take the law of the court to be that if two persons – no matter whether a confidential relationship exists between them or not – stand in such a relation to each other that one can take undue advantage of the other, whether by reason of distress or recklessness or wildness or want of care and where the facts show that no party has taken undue advantage of the other, by reason of the circumstances I have mentioned – a transaction resting upon such unconscionable dealing will not be allowed to stand.[55]

So, in *Rae v Joyce* a transaction to mortgage a reversionary interest in property was set aside on the rounds of unconscionable bargain in circumstances where the plaintiff was pregnant, the mortgagee a moneylender who was far more astute, and the plaintiff being in a particularly needy situation culminated in an agreement which included a 60% interest rate.[56]

In modern law, three distinct elements must be shown, as set down in *Alec Lobb (Garages) Ltd v Total Oil (Great Britain) Ltd*:

> First, one party must be at a serious disadvantage to the other, whether through poverty, or ignorance, or lack of advice, or otherwise, so that circumstances existed of which unfair advantage could be taken. Second, this weakness of the one party has been exploited by the other in some morally culpable manner … and third, the resulting transaction has been not merely hard or improvident but overreaching and oppressive.[57]

Jamie Glister and James Lee more accurately state that the three requirements are: that one party is at a significant disadvantage by reason of poverty, ignorance or otherwise, leading to circumstances existing in which unfair advantage could be taken; the transaction was

---

54 Clare Stanley, 'Vulnerable Gifts made by Vulnerable People' (2017) 23(5) Trusts and Trustees 542.

55 (1876) IR 11 EQ 367, 409.

56 (1892) 29 LR (IR) 500.

57 [1983] 1 WLR 87.

at an undervalue; and there was a lack of independent legal advice.[58] A more modern definition of 'poor and ignorant' was established in *Cresswell v Potter* as members of a lower socio-economic group.[59]

For the contract to be set aside on the grounds that the transaction was at an undervalue, this must reach the standard of being at such a gross undervalue that it shocks the conscience of the court. Further, the conduct must be what the court deems as morally reprehensible. In *Portman Building Society v Dusangh* the 72-year-old defendant, who was of low income, could not read or write, and had very little understanding of the English language, obtained a mortgage to assist his son's business.[60] This was not set aside on the grounds of unconscionable transaction, as although it was an ill-advised transaction, it was not morally reprehensible. This does appear to be a harsh ruling given the circumstances of the defendant, and the court's reluctance to set contracts aside where there is a commercial aspect (ie a bank enforcing security) appears to be more to do with the fear of opening floodgates rather than focusing on whether in fact there was either undue influence or an unconscionable transaction.

The concept of moral turpitude is an absolute requirement in the law of England and Wales in order to establish a case of an unconscionable transaction. However, this is not the case in all jurisdictions. In Ireland there is no need to establish this element. In the case of *Prendergast v Joyce*. an elderly vulnerable lady in a confused state of mind transferred monies into the joint names of both herself and the defendant.[61] The court was satisfied that she was at a disadvantage owing to her mental state, the transaction was at an undervalue and she did not have any independent advice. In the circumstances, the transaction should be set aside on the basis that it was improvident.

An unconscionable transaction is voidable at the behest of the weaker party. The same rules apply as in relation to undue influence, and the right to rescind may be lost where the party has later affirmed the contract or has inordinately delayed in asserting their right.

Test Your Knowledge

Gloria and Jean have been married for 15 years. They have three adopted children and Gloria has stayed at home to raise them, while Jean has excelled in her career as a consultant. Jean has also made some

---

58 *Hanbury & Martin Modern Equity*, 22nd ed (Sweet and Maxwell 2015).

59 [1978] 1 WLR 255.

60 [2000] All ER 221.

61 [2009] IEHC 199.

investments in various other businesses, shares and property. Gloria has generally been unaware of the precise nature of the investments that Jean has entered into as she leaves all of the financial decisions to Jean. Unbeknownst to Gloria, Jean has made some bad decisions and she needs to find money quickly. She decides that the best way to do this is to remortgage the family home. She brings the paperwork home to Gloria who, although usually happy to leave financial matters to Jean, is concerned as this could impact on the home of their children. Gloria keeps questioning Jean who eventually loses her cool. She tells Gloria that either she signs the documents or she is leaving, there will be no more money for her and she will have to find work. The children will need to change schools and it will have a devastating impact on them. Reluctantly Gloria agrees. They go to the bank the following day, and as they are about to enter, Jean pinches Gloria roughly and says 'remember what I told you'. The bank does not mention a requirement to seek independent legal advice, and Gloria signs the documents.

Several months later, Jean has defaulted on the loan and the bank is trying to repossess the family home. Is the loan:

A capable of being rescinded on the grounds of undue influence?
B valid as the bank can rely on the documents that Gloria has signed?
C capable of being rescinded as the bank did not offer independent legal advice?

The answer here is likely to be C. Despite the fact that Gloria has clearly been influenced by Jean into singing the documents, from *Etridge* the court will look at what steps the bank took to ensure that Gloria was aware of the terms of the loan. The fact that they did not require her to seek independent legal advice is likely to be key in a finding in her favour. Had they taken all reasonable steps, they would have been able to rely on the documents that she signed.

Stretch and Challenge Questions

Consider whether the *Etridge (No 2)* decision would stand up today in light of the subsequent introduction of laws criminalising coercive control.

Should the courts require 'morally reprehensible' conduct in order to have a transaction set aside for unconscionability, or should it be enough that a weaker party was exploited?

CHAPTER 15

ILLEGALITY AND PUBLIC POLICY

15.1 Introduction

There are certain circumstances where the law will impose restrictions on an individual's freedom to contract. A contract which would otherwise, to all intents and purposes, seem valid may be tainted by illegality. Either the contract will be invalid because there is a piece of legislation which makes the subject matter or the type of contract illegal, or there will be circumstances where the court finds that the law ought to, as a matter of public policy, make certain contracts illegal. The result, regardless of whether it is viewed through statutory intervention or public policy, is that the contract is deemed illegal.

The law surrounding illegality in relation to contracts is rather complex and there are no uniform rules. This is because the nature of the illegality may vary from something that is very serious (for example, murder) to something that is relatively minor (for example, breach of licensing requirements). Therefore, the way that the courts have treated the subject of illegality has varied widely.

15.2 Defining Illegality

In some circumstances, the court will take a strict view, while in others a more flexible approach will be taken. The first case that properly considered the appropriate role of the courts in determining illegality was *Tinsley v Milligan*.[1] Here, the parties both contributed to

[1] [1994] 1 AC 340, HL.

the purchase of a home which was registered in the name of Tinsley only. The reason for this was to enable Milligan to make fraudulent welfare claims. Milligan claimed her interest in the property, and Tinsley argued that she could not succeed in this claim as the purpose of the contract was illegal (defrauding the social welfare system). The House of Lords found that what the courts need to consider here is whether the claimant had to rely on their illegal act in order to establish a claim and that there was no room for the weighing of public policy considerations. The court allowed the claim to succeed as Milligan did not have to establish why she conveyed the property to Tinsley; the fact that she contributed to the property and there was an understanding that the property would be shared was sufficient. There was no need to resort to the illegality.

While it is acknowledged that the House of Lords was in a rather difficult position in this case in determining where the interest should lie, the result is somewhat unsatisfactory. Should the court have found in favour of Tinsley, it would have given her the entire legal and equitable interest in the property in circumstances where she was also aware of, and therefore was in some moral sense involved in, the illegality which would equally not be a palatable result.

Following this judgment, the Law Commission published a consultation paper entitled 'Illegal Transactions: The Effect of Illegality on Contracts and Trusts' where it defined illegal contracts as including 'any contract which involves (in its formation, purpose or performance) a legal wrong (other than the mere breach of the contract in question) or conduct otherwise contrary to public policy'.[2] This clearly brings the element of public policy back to the fore and argues that the law ought to, in certain circumstances, intervene on public policy grounds even if it is a contract that both parties have freely entered into.

In 2009, in a further report entitled 'The Illegality Defence' the Law Commission stated:

> The illegality defence should be allowed where its application can be firmly justified by the policies that underlie its existence. These include: (a) furthering the purpose of the rule which the illegal conduct has infringed; (b) consistency; (c) that the claimant should not profit from their own wrong; (d) deterrence; and (e) maintaining the integrity of the legal system.[3]

---

2 LCCP No 154, 1999.

3 Law Com No 189. See Paul S Davies, 'The Illegality Defence – Two Steps Forward, One Step Back?' (2009) 3 Conveyancer and Property Lawyer 182.

The Supreme Court in *Hounga v Allen*[4] accepted this definition but rejected it in *Les Laboratoires Servier v Apotex*, where it held that the illegality defence was a rule of law based on public policy and not the exercise of discretionary power.[5] In this case it resoundingly rejected the definition of the Law Commission.

The matter came before the Supreme Court again in *Patel v Mirza*.[6] This case involved a claim by Patel to recover the sum of £620,000 that he had paid to Mirza to bet on the price of shares using insider information. The bet did not take place and Patel wanted his money back. This contract was illegal as it involved the offence of insider dealing, and Mirza argued that Patel could not recover on this ground. In holding that Patel could recover, Lord Toulson set out a three-stage test to determine whether or not the contract would be enforceable:

> The essential rationale of the illegality doctrine is that it would be contrary to the public interest to enforce a claim if to do so would be harmful to the integrity of the legal system .... In assessing whether the public interest would be harmed in that way, it is necessary a) to consider the underlying purpose of the prohibition which has been transgressed and whether that purpose will be enhanced by denial of the claim, b) to consider any other relevant public policy on which the denial of the claim may have an impact and c) to consider whether denial of the claim would be a proportionate response to the illegality, bearing in mind that punishment is a matter for the criminal courts. Within that framework, various factors may be relevant, but it would be a mistake to suggest that the court is free to decide a case in an undisciplined way. The public interest is best served by a principled and transparent assessment of the considerations identified, rather [than by] the application of a formal approach capable of producing results which may appear arbitrary, unjust or disproportionate.

This is the leading authority on the issue of illegality and appears to be a rational test which allows the court to take in a multitude of factors. This is an acknowledgement that in many cases that come before the court, it is not always a clear-cut matter where only one party has engaged in illegal activity, with the other being completely innocent.[7] In cases such as *Patel v Mirza* and *Tinsley v Milligan*, none of the parties could be said to be completely innocent, and the courts need an appropriate and proportionate test to deal with such cases, which is set down in *Patel*.

---

4 [2014] UKSC 47.

5 [2014] UKSC 55.

6 [2016] UKSC 42.

7 Nelson Enonchong, 'Supervening Illegality: Effect on the enforcement of an illegal agreement' (2000) 116 Law Quarterly Review 377.

The Irish Supreme Court case of *Quinn v Irish Bank Resolution Corporation (In Liquidation)* considered the parameters of the illegality issue in this jurisdiction.[8] Clarke J drew attention to the fact that since the inception of this area of law the statutory regime has expanded considerably and therefore the approach that the courts should take in determining the matter 'is statute specific, not case specific'. This was in response to concerns of the court that illegality was coming into play in circumstances where no rule of the criminal law or principle of morality were being infringed.[9]

15.3 Statutory Illegality

15.3.1 Express Prohibition

There are occasions where the legislation will expressly prohibit the type of contract entered into. In such cases, the contract cannot be enforced by either party even in circumstances where one of them is innocent. For example, The Family Home Protection Act 1976 states under s 3 that a spouse is required to give written consent to any transfer of interest in the family home, without which any such transfer will be void; The Consumer Credit Act 1995 requires that all hire purchase agreements will be unenforceable unless they are evidenced in writing;[10] the Holidays (Employees) Act 1973 provides that contracts which relinquish rights to holiday pay are void; as are contracts which subvert the requirements of minimum notice rights under the Minimum Notice and Terms of Employment Act 1973.[11] The Land and Conveyancing Reform Act 2009 provides that any transfer of land made with the intention of defrauding a creditor or any other person is voidable by any person prejudiced by the transfer.[12]

15.3.2 Implied Prohibition

The position is the same where there is an implied prohibition in the statute. The role of the court is to determine whether the legislation, interpreted in light of the purpose of said legislation, would not only prohibit the express conduct, but whether it ought to be extended to cover the contract in the instant case. For example, if the purpose of a piece of legislation is to protect consumers from fraud, it is likely

---

8 [2015] IESC 29.

9 John Breslin and Elizabeth Corcoran, 'Ex Turpi Causa and Statutory Illegality Part Two: Quinn v IBRC' (2016) 23(5) Commercial Law Practitioner 130.

10 See *Henry Forde & Son Finance Ltd v John Forde & General Accident Fire and Life Assurance Co*, Unrep, High Court, 13 June 1986.

11 See *Foley v Labtech Ltd* EAT M259/1978.

12 See *Keegan Quarries Ltd v McGuinness* [2011] IEHC 453.

that all contracts made in contravention of this legislation, whether the contract itself is expressly prohibited or not, will be prohibited.

So, in *Smith v Mawhood* the court considered a contract made relating to the sale of tobacco which had been prohibited by statute to restrict unlicenced dealers.[13] The plaintiff, an unlicenced dealer, brought an action against the defendant in relation to tobacco sold to him, and the defendant argued that the contract was unenforceable due to illegality. In this case the court had to determine whether the legislature meant to imply that such contracts were illegal. It was found that this was not the intention, rather that the intention was to raise revenue from taxes on tobacco sales and therefore the contract was enforceable.

The leading English case in this area is *St. John Shipping Corp v Joseph Rank*.[14] The case involved a contract between the parties to transport cargo. The master of the vessel had, in contravention of a statute, overloaded the cargo on the basis that if it was caught, the profit would still far exceed the maximum fine that could be imposed upon him. The court in this case held that the contract could be upheld. It was lawful when the contract was entered into and the breach occurred during performance. The court stated that the test to be imposed was not whether there was an illegal performance, but whether that illegal performance turns the contract into one which is prohibited by statute.

In *Hortensius Ltd and Durack v Bishop*, the defendant Trustees had used trust funds to purchase investment opportunities from the plaintiff in contravention of the Trustees Acts 1893-1979.[15] It was then argued that certain contracts and mortgages were void as being illegal contracts. The court however noted that the purpose of the legislation was to make trustees liable for breach of trust, and not to make contracts unlawful where they were entered into on foot of a breach of trust.[16]

15.3.4 Illegal Performance

This operates in circumstances where the contract itself is not illegal, but where one party commits an illegal act in the performance of their duties under the contract.[17] This does not automatically turn the contract into an illegal one (except where both parties have expressly agreed to the carrying out of an illegal act); instead, the innocent party will still have full rights under the contract. In *Marles v Philip*

---

13 (1845) 14 M &W 452.

14 [1957] 1 QB 267.

15 [1989] ILRM 294.

16 See also *Gavin Lowe Ltd v Field* [1942] IR 86.

17 Anthony Pugh Thomas, 'The Enforcement of Illegally Formed Contracts' (1996) 7(2) International Commercial and Company Law Review 61.

Trant & Sons Ltd Trant bought wheat from a third party described as 'spring wheat'.[18] Trant then sold the wheat to various farmers, including Marles. The wheat turned out not to be spring wheat and the crops failed. Marles brought an action against Trant, who then brought the third party into the action to indemnify him. The third party argued that Trant had not delivered particulars in writing to Marle as required under s 1 of the Seeds Act 1920, and therefore he did not have to indemnify Trant as the contract was illegal. The Court of Appeal held that the contract was not illegal from the beginning, but only by the method of performance which did not comply with the legislative requirements. The third party's argument therefore failed.

However, where the other party is aware of or participates in the illegal conduct, they will not be able to enforce the contract. In *Ashmore Benson Pease & Co Ltd v Dawson Ltd* the defendants carried tube banks in contravention of legislation which specified the maximum weight load of lorries.[19] The claimant's tube bank was damaged as a result of carrying loads that were too heavy but was unable to claim damages as its representative was present at the loading and did not raise any objection.

It is clear that where the purpose of the statute is undermined, the guilty party cannot enforce the contract. However, there is more flexibility where that purpose is not undermined. For example, in *Shaw v Groom* a landlord failed to give a tenant a rent book which he was required by law to do.[20] However, the landlord was still able to recover the rent as the legislation provided a penalty and did not impact the tenancy agreement itself; it was not an avenue to allow tenants avoid paying their rent.

The Court of Appeal in *ParkingEye Ltd v Somerfield Stores* adopted a flexible approach to dealing with illegality of performance.[21] In this case, the parties had contracted for ParkingEye to install a monitoring system in supermarket car parks which were run by Somerfield. The contract was to last for 15 months. ParkingEye monitored usage and then sent demands for payment to overstayers; it then collected and retained the payments. Somerfield cancelled the contract after six months, and ParkingEye claimed damages for loss of revenue for the remaining 11 months of the contract. Somerfield argued that, contrary to public policy, ParkingEye's letters to customers used deceptive and illegal language to induce payment.

---

18 [1954] 1 QB 29.
19 [1973] 1 WLR 828.
20 [1970] 2 QB 504.
21 [2013] QB 840.

The court found that the law in such cases is not static and that once illegality was shown, unenforceability would necessarily follow. Rather, the court ought to consider three things: (a) the object and intent of the party seeking to enforce the contract, (b) the centrality and gravity of the illegality, and (c) the nature of the illegality. Weighing the balance of these considerations, the court here found that repudiation of the contract was an overreaction, and the claimant was allowed to succeed.[22]

15.4 Contracts Contrary to Public Policy

Judges tend not to like the idea of resorting to public policy to rule contracts unenforceable, with Burrough J in *Richardson v Mellish* referring to it as an 'unruly horse'.[23] This is because it allows judges to use individual moral guidelines to determine whether a contract ought to be unenforceable for the protection of society in general.[24] For example, where a contract offends public morality, even though it is not expressly illegal, should the court hold that this type of contract is unenforceable? Despite judicial reluctance in this area, the courts have over time carved out several areas in which a contract will be unenforceable on these grounds.

15.4.1 Contracts to Commit Crimes

An agreement which has as its object a deliberate commission of a crime, whether this is a criminal offence under statute or common law, will be unenforceable. Further, it is contrary to public policy to allow a criminal or their estate to benefit from the commission of a crime. In *Gray v Thames Trains Ltd* a passenger suffered psychological injuries as a result of a train crash caused by the negligence of the defendant.[25] The injuries resulted in the passenger committing manslaughter by reason of diminished responsibility. The passenger was unable to recover damages resulting from his conviction from the train company as they flowed from a criminal act. The matter was considered again by the UK Supreme Court in *Henderson v Dorset Healthcare University NHS Foundation Trust*.[26] The plaintiff, a psychiatric patient, was under the care of the local authority when she killed her mother. She pleaded guilty to manslaughter and subsequently claimed damages from the defendant arising out of deficiencies in her supervision at the time

---

22 Robin M White, 'Parking's not fine' (2017) 28 Scots Law Times 151.

23 (1824) 2 Bing 229.

24 Warren Swain, 'Contracts "not for the public good" and the classical law of contract' (2022) 43(1) Journal of Legal History 1.

25 [2009] UKHL 33.

26 [2020] UKSC 43.

of the killing. The Supreme Court upheld a long standing principle that one cannot benefit from a criminal offence and that given the seriousness of the crime it was one in which this policy ought to prevail. In addition, there was the consideration that any damages she would receive would come from the NHS budget and this again was a valid public policy argument in rejecting her claim.

Contracts which seek to subvert the cause of justice, while not in themselves a criminal offence, are illegal and cannot be enforced. In *Brady v Flood* the defendant paid money to try and have a criminal charge of conspiracy dropped.[27] The court refused to entertain litigation pertaining to this as it was clearly illegal. Where criminal proceedings have commenced, public interest requires that the trial conclude and the courts take a dim view on contracts which seek to undermine this.[28] However, where the trial has not commenced, an action to enforce a contract may succeed. In *Rourke v Nolan* the plaintiff held a negotiable instrument which he suspected had been forged by a relative of the defendant.[29] When confronted, the defendant undertook personal liability for the document in return for a promise not to charge the relative with forgery. It was held that this agreement could be enforced as it was not an agreement to subvert proceedings already in train.

15.4.2 Contracts to Commit Civil Wrongs

The law is more contentious where the case involves a civil rather than a criminal wrong. The Supreme Court in *Les Laboratoires Servier v Apotex Inc* drew a distinction between cases of civil liability which raised private rather than public interests and criminal liability which did engage the public interest. [30]

15.4.3 Contracts to Defraud the Revenue

One of the most common types of illegal contracts are those designed to defraud the Revenue. In *Alexander v Rayson* Alexander entered into a rental contract to lease a flat for a rent of £1,200 per annum[31]. The transaction comprised of two documents: one was a lease for rent at £450 per annum and covering certain services to be provided by the landlord, and a second agreement to render substantially the same services for a fee of £750 per annum. A dispute arose between the parties, and Rayson refused to pay an instalment under the second

---

27 (1841) 6 Circuit Cases 309.
28 See *Keir v Leeman* (1846) 9 QB 371; *Nolan v Sheils* (1926) 60 ILTR 143.
29 (1879) 4 LR (Ir) 166.
30 [2014] UKSC 55.
31 [1936] 1 KB 169.

agreement. When Alexander sued for this amount, Rayson argued that the purpose of having the two documents was that only the first document would be disclosed to the Revenue in order to deceive them as to the true rateable value of the property. The Court of Appeal held that if the documents were to be used for this fraudulent purpose then Alexander would not be entitled to the assistance of the law in enforcing either of the agreements. In *Starling Securities v Woods* the plaintiff purchased lands under a contract which would have been enforceable had it not become known that the plaintiff had deliberately misstated the consideration in order to reduce his tax liability on the transaction.[32]

The fraud does have to relate to the case at hand. In *K/S Lincoln v CB Richard Ellis Hotels Ltd* a defence to a professional negligence claim raised allegations of tax evasion.[33] The court noted that the fraud in this case did not taint the underlying contract which formed the basis of the claim, and so allegations of illegality were likely to fail.

Collusive agreements between an employer and employee where an employee is given certain 'tax free' benefits are also illegal and may result in the employee being unable to assert statutory rights. In *Lewis v Squash Ireland Ltd*, the plaintiff was employed as a managing director in the defendant company.[34] He received a salary of £14,000 plus an addition £2000 as expenses. The plaintiff claimed unfair dismissal against the defendant and in the Employment Appeals Tribunal, it was found that the additional £2000 was in fact salary being described as expenses in order to minimise the tax liability on the plaintiff. The plaintiff was therefore aware that his salary was misdescribed and the agreement was illegal. The plaintiff was unable to sustain his claim for unfair dismissal. This decision has since been reversed by s 7 of the Unfair Dismissals (Amendment) Act 1993.

15.4.4 Contracts Prejudicial to Morality

In reality, this section deals more with morality as it relates to sexual morality. A traditional approach saw a promise to pay to induce a woman into becoming a man's mistress as unenforceable[35] and a contract to hire a carriage known to be for the purpose of prostitution was also unenforceable.[36]

---

32 Unrep, High Court, 24 May 1977.

33 [2009] EWHC 2344 (TCC).

34 [1983] ILRM 363. See also *Hayden v Sean Quinn Properties Ltd*, Unrep, High Court, 6 December 1993.

35 *Benyon v Nettlefold* (1850) 3 Mac &G 94.

36 *Pearce v Brooks* (1866) LR 1 Ex 213.

As attitudes of society generally towards sexual morality have changed, this has also become evident in the court's decisions of rejecting the public policy argument in these cases. For example, in *Armhouse Lee Ltd v Chappell* a contract for advertising the use of telephone sex lines was not unenforceable on the grounds of public policy, leaving the operator having to pay for the advertising.[37] Further in *Sutton v Mischon de Reya* a cohabitation agreement between two parties to live in a master/slave sexual relationship was not contrary to public policy.[38]

15.4.5 Public Corruption

Contracts which further corruption in public office are illegal and unenforceable. In *Parkinson v College of Ambulance Ltd* Parkinson was led to believe that if he made a large donation to a particular charity, the officers of that charity would be able to procure him a knighthood.[39] The claimant paid, and when no knighthood was forthcoming, he sought to recover his donation. The court found that he was unable to recover this money as the contract was illegal under the Honours (Prevention of Abuses) Act 1925.

In *Lord Mayor of Dublin v Hayes* the defendant was appointed to the position of Marshall of the City of Dublin. As part of this role, he was the Registrar of Pawnbrokers which entitled him to collect fees from the city's pawnbrokers which he agreed would be transferred to the City Treasurer. It was found that the appointment of the defendant was made in exchange for his promise (to transfer the fees to the City Treasurer), and such was unenforceable as it may encourage corrupt practices.

15.5 Effect of Illegality

The general principle to be applied is that when a contract is found to be illegal, it is unenforceable. The case of *Patel v Mirza* established the test which will be applied to determine whether or not the contract can be enforced.[40]

In some cases, the entire contract will not be held to be unenforceable, in circumstances where the illegal part can be severed. However, if the entire contract is tainted by illegality, it cannot be saved by severance. This was considered by the Supreme Court in *Tillman v*

37 [1996] EWCA Civ J0723.
38 [2003] EWHC 3166 (Ch).
39 [1925] 2 KB 1.
40 James Goudkamp, 'The End of an Era? Illegality in Private Law in the Supreme Court' (2017) 133 Law Quarterly Review 14.

Egon Zehnder Ltd.[41] This case contained a restraint of trade clause in which the employee, who was engaged by the defendant's recruitment company, agreed that she would not 'directly or indirectly engage or be concerned or interested in any business carried on in competition with any of the businesses' of the employer. The employment ceased in January 2017, and in May 2017 the employee made her intention known that she would be joining a rival firm. She argued that this clause was void and the Supreme Court agreed. In reviewing the law on severance, the Court stated that this could occur if two things were present: that the offending clause or element of the clause could be removed without altering what remained; and the removal of the unenforceable provision would not have any major change in the overall effect of the post-employment restraints. In applying this to the facts, the words 'or interested' could be removed (as it was argued that this could extend, for example, to owning shares in a competitor's business). This removal would not affect the remainder of the clause and would not have any major impact on the overall restraint.[42]

Where a party seeks to recover money or property under an illegal contract, the law prior to *Patel v Mirza* was complex, with various exceptions being established by the court as to when this could occur. *Patel* now simplifies the matter significantly and overcomes the possibility of outcomes which are unfair or disproportionate.

15.6 Void Contracts at Common law

There are certain circumstances in which a contract will become completely void and where there can be no severance of the illegal term. The distinction was described by Somervell LJ in *Goodinson v Goodinson* as:

> There are two kinds of illegality with differing effect. The first is where the illegality is criminal, or contra bonos mores, and in these cases which I will not attempt to enumerate or further classify, such a provision, if an ingredient in the contract, will invalidate the whole, although there may be many other provisions in it. There is a second kind of illegality which has no such taint. The other terms in the contract stand if the illegal portion can be severed, the illegal portion being a provision which the court, on ground of public policy, will not enforce.[43]

---

41 [2019] UKSC 32.

42 Andrew Bowen, 'Post Employment Covenants, The Doctrine Against Restraint of Trade and Severability' (2019) 163 Business Law Bulletin 1.

43 [1954] 2 QB 118 [21].

It is generally agreed that there are three types of contracts which fall within this second description and are considered hereunder.

15.6.1 Contracts to Oust the Jurisdiction of the Court

Any contract which ousts the jurisdiction of the court will be illegal. However, arbitration clauses are lawful (Arbitration Act 2010).[44]

Contracts between spouses in which one agrees not to apply to the court for maintenance have been held to be contrary to public policy. This is supplemented by the Matrimonial Causes Act 1973 which states that it is only the provision that restricts the right to apply to court that is void, and not the entire agreement. As such, all other promises in the contract will be enforceable. *McLeod v McLeod* considered the 1973 Act in light of agreements made after marriage which dealt with provisions for future separation.[45] The court held that these would be valid, save for any provision which restricted or prohibited application to the court.

In Ireland the nature of similar provisions under the Family Law (Maintenance of Spouses and Children) Act 1976 was considered in *HD v PD* where Walsh J stated 'it is not possible to contract out of the Act by an agreement made after the Act came into force or by an agreement entered into before the legislation was enacted'.[46] This decision was followed in the case of *JH v RH* where the court allowed a wife to make an application for revised maintenance.[47] The court found that the test to be applied, notwithstanding a full and final settlement under the Judicial Separation and Family Law Reform Act 1989, was whether or not the husband has failed to provide proper maintenance having regard to all of the circumstances.

15.6.2 Contracts which Subvert the Sanctity of Marriage

Contracts in which a fee is paid to a marriage broker to find a husband or wife are void.[48] In *Williamson v Gihan* the plaintiff obtained the assistance of the defendant in whisking away a young heiress to Scotland, whereupon he married her.[49] The plaintiff promised to pay

---

[44] However, the court does retain the jurisdiction to determine that an arbitration clause in a contract is not fair and reasonable. See *McCarthy v Joe Walsh Tours Ltd* [1991] ILRM 813. Adam Johnson, 'Illegal Contracts and Arbitration Clauses' (1999) 2(1) International Arbitration Law Review 35.

[45] [2008] UKPC 64.

[46] Unrep, Supreme Court, 8 May 1978.

[47] Irish Times Law Report, 30 October 1995.

[48] *Hermann v Charlesworth* [1905] 2 KB 123.

[49] (1805) 2 Sch & Lef 357.

the sum of £500 from his wife's estate to the defendant for his help. It was held that the defendant could not enforce this promise to pay with the court frowning on marriages arising from elopement in the fear that it would lead to 'fortune hunting'.

Contracts which provide for payment should the marriage break down have historically been held as void for weakening the marriage bond. In *H v H* the court dealt with an agreement entered into by two married couples.[50] It was agreed that each would divorce their current partners and then marry their respectives. It was agreed prior to the second marriage that each man would provide financial support for his new wife. The court refused to uphold this agreement as it involved the breaking up of two marriages.

Pre-nuptial agreements, those made in advance of marriage, were the subject of the UK Supreme Court's decision in *Granatino v Radmacher*.[51] Here the Court held (with Baroness Hale dissenting) that effect should be given to such agreements where they have been freely entered into with a full appreciation of what the implications would be, unless there were circumstances arising in which it would not be fair to hold the parties to their agreement.

The Irish courts have yet to follow this decision however there have been calls for such agreements to be enforceable in Irish law with the caveat that the courts will be free to depart from them where the circumstances so require it.[52]

Cohabitation agreements, whether entered into in contemplation of marriage or not are void as contrary to public policy. In *Ennis v Butterly* the parties were married to other people but in a relationship together.[53] It was agreed that she would move into a property bought by them and would give up her employment to take on the role of homemaker. She also alleged an agreement to marry on the completion of respective divorces. The court found that the contract in which the consideration of 'wifely services' was provided were not recognised by law. Kelly J stated:

> Given the special place of marriage and the family under the Irish Constitution, it appears to me that the public policy of this state ordains that non-marital cohabitation does not and cannot have the same constitutional status as marriage. Moreover, the state has pledged to guard with special care the institution of marriage.

---

50 (1983) 127 SJ 578.
51 [2010] UKSC 42.
52 See for example 184 Seanad Debates Cols 1751-1770.
53 [1997]1 ILRM 28.

> But does this mean that agreements, the consideration for which is cohabitation, are incapable of being enforced? In my view it does since otherwise the pledge on the part of the state, of which this court is one organ, to guard with special care the institution of marriage would be much diluted. To permit an express cohabitation agreement (such as is pleaded here) to be enforced would give it a similar status in law as a marriage contract.

While the Law Reform Commission suggests that this case does not invalidate all cohabitation agreements, the case does still present a significant obstacle where the agreement covers anything more that property and financial regulation of a cohabiting couple making legislation in this area imperative.[54] In 2010 the Civil Partnership and Certain Rights and Obligations of Cohabitants Act was enacted which goes some way in bridging the gap. The Marriage Act 2015 further enhances the protection for same sex spouses.

15.6.3 Contracts in Restraint of Trade

A contract which restrains trade has been defined in *Petrofina (Great Britain) Ltd v Martin* as 'one in which a party agrees with any other party to restrict his liberty in the future to carry on trade with other persons not party to the contract in such a manner as he chooses'.[55] The Irish Court has followed this definition in *John Orr Ltd and Vescom BV v John Orr* with the court summarising the doctrine as:

> All restraint of trade in the absence of special justifying circumstances are contrary to public policy and therefore void. A restraint may be justified if it is reasonable in the interest of the contract parties and in the interest of the pubic. The onus of showing that a restraint is reasonable between the parties rests on the person alleging that it is so...... the court may in some circumstances enforce a covenant in restraint of trade even though taken as a while the covenant exceeds what is reasonable by the severance of the void parts from the valid parts.[56]

Two categories of contract have long been recognised by the courts as including legitimate restraint of trade contracts: employment contracts (where an employee agrees not to set up a business to rival the employer or to join a rival firm) and agreements between a buyer and seller of a business (where the seller agrees not to compete with that of the buyer). However, these are not an exhaustive list, and in *Esso Petroleum Co Ltd v Harpers Garage (Stourport) Ltd* it was cautioned

---

54 Rights and Duties of Cohabitees, LRC Consultation Paper 32-2004.

55 [1996] Ch 146.

56 [1987] ILRM 702, 704.

that 'the classification must remain fluid and the categories can never be closed'. [57]

15.6.3.1 Origins of the Modern Doctrine

The foundation of the modern doctrine of restraint of trade comes from the case of *Nordenfelt v Maxim Nordenfelt Guns and Ammunition Co Ltd*.[58] In this case Nordenfelt was the maker of guns and ammunition who sold his business to Maxim Nordenfelt and agreed that he would not, for a period of 25 years, engage 'either directly or indirectly in the trade or business of a manufacturer of guns, gun mountings or carriages, gunpowder explosives or ammunition, or in any business competing or liable to compete in any way with that for the time being carried on by the company'. However, Nordenfelt expressly retained the right to deal in explosives other than gunpowder, in torpedoes or submarine boats and in metal castings or forgings. Some years post agreement, Nordenfelt entered into business with a rival company of Maxim Nordenfelt dealing with guns and ammunition, and Maxim Nordenfelt sought an injunction preventing Nordenfelt from doing this.

The House of Lords held that the restraint of trade covenant not to compete 'in *any* business' was unreasonable as it attempted to protect the company not only from the business that it was carrying out at the time the contract was entered into, but also future activities of the company. The clause was therefore void, but as it was distinct from the rest of the covenant, the rest remained enforceable. In other words, the part of the clause which protected the business as sold was enforceable.

As a result of this case, and later decisions which applied it, there are a number of key points in relation to restraint of trade clauses:

(1) All restraint of trade clauses, in the absence of justifying circumstances, are contrary to public policy. However, that does not mean that the entire agreement will be unenforceable.
(2) It is a question of law for the court to decide whether or not the circumstances justify the restraint.
(3) A restraint can only be justified if it is reasonable in the interest of the parties and in the interest of the public.
(4) The onus of showing that the restraint is reasonable rests with the person alleging that it is reasonable.
(5) Restraint of trade covenants are interpreted in light of the objective of the clause (ie to protect one of the parties) and

---

57 [1968] AC 269.
58 [1894] AC 535.

> in the light of the factual circumstances that existed at the time the clause was entered into.

In *Esso Petroleum Co Ltd v Harpers Garage (Stourport) Ltd* the House of Lords clearly established that the following questions ought to be asked when determining whether a clause is valid:

1. Does the restraint go further than to afford adequate protection to the party in whose favour it is granted? If so, the covenant is prima facie void.
2. Can it be justified as being in the interests of the party thus restrained?
3. Is the covenant contrary to public policy?

The doctrine is required to be flexible as there are often two competing considerations at play. The first is that the court ought to enforce a contract that a person has freely entered into[59] and the second that this freedom to contract should not be used in a manner which prevents him from earning a living.[60] This balance is achieved by way of utilising the reasonableness test.[61] What is reasonable between the parties will vary on a case-by-case basis. However, in *Herbert Morris Ltd v Saxelby* the court provided some guidance as to how it would approach the issue.[62] In this case, the defendant's contract of employment contained a clause which prevented him from engaging in a wide range of trades for a seven-year period covering the whole of the United Kingdom. The employer sought to enforce this clause and failed. The House of Lords identified two different approaches that it ought to take when dealing with these types of clauses:

(1) In contracts of employment, it would not normally be reasonable to prevent a former employee from working in any capacity for a competitor; but restraints to prevent the loss of trade secrets or poaching customers are permitted.
(2) In the sale of a business, restraints are permitted that seek to preserve the value of the goodwill of the business by preventing the vendor from setting up in competition with the purchaser.

Therefore, the first stage of the process is that it must be established that there is a legitimate interest to protect. Then, it must be shown that the clause goes no further than what is reasonable in both duration and geographical extent than is necessary to protect that legitimate interest. In *Mason v Provident Clothing Supply Co Ltd* the restraint of trade clause

---

59 *Murphy v O'Donovan* [1939] IR 457.
60 *Langan v Cork Operative Bakers TU* [1938] Ir Jur Rep 65. William Day, 'Freedom to Contract and Restraint of Trade' (2020) 79(1) Cambridge Law Journal 11.
61 *TFS Derivatives Ltd v Morgan* [2004] EWHC 3181.
62 [1916] AC 688.

prevented an employee from entering into a similar business within 25 miles of London.[63] The clause was held to be wider than reasonably required for the protection of the employer and was therefore void.

The reasonableness of the clause will normally be determined by reference to the time at which the clause was entered into, and not the time at which a party is seeking to enforce it. However, in *Shell UK Ltd v Lostock Garage Ltd* Lord Denning stated that there may be circumstances in which a clause would be reasonable at the time it was entered into, but could later become unenforceable due to circumstances which were not envisaged at the time.[64]

15.6.3.2 Contracts Traditionally within the Doctrine

As explained at the outset, traditionally there are two types of contracts in which this doctrine operates which are considered in this section.

Employment Contract

In addition to the restraint of trade clause that may be incorporated into a contract, the common law may offer further protection.[65] This can be derived from the imposition of an implied term in the contract that there is a duty to serve the employer faithfully;[66] or that there was a confidential relationship which creates a situation in whereby an obligation arises not to abuse that trust or confidence.[67] However, the incorporation of a specific clause within the contract does have some advantages over relying on the common law doctrines. There is a great degree of certainty in that each party knows precisely what the restraint covers and what remedies may be available. It is essential for an employer seeking to uphold such a clause to show that he has a legitimate interest and that the restraint goes no further than necessary to protect such an interest.

Numerous Irish cases have examined the applicability of the doctrine in relation to employment contracts. In *Murgitroyd & Company Ltd v Purdy* the court found that a clause which restricted the defendant from 'carrying on any business which competes with the business of the company' for a period of 12 months and covered the entire republic of Ireland was too broad and therefore void.[68] In *O'Gara v Teva*

---

63 [1913] AC 724.
64 [1976] 1 WLR 1187.
65 Frank Carrigan and Peter Radan, 'The Post Employment Restraint of Trade Doctrine – A Critical History' (2020) 31(1) Kings Law Journal 121.
66 *Arclex Optical Corp v McMurray* [1958] Ir Jur Rep 65.
67 *House of Spring Gardens Ltd v Point Blank Ltd* [1985] FSR 327.
68 [2005] IEHC 153.

Pharmaceuticals the court found that a broad indefinite restriction was unenforceable and cautioned that these clauses needed to be tailored to the specific role and circumstances of the employee.[69] However in *AIB v Diamond* a clause which restricted a senior employee from working for competitors in a specific area for a period of six months was upheld as being reasonable and necessary to protect the bank's confidential information and customer relationship.[70]

The issue of drafting the clause sufficiently was again highlighted in the case of *Ryanair DAC v Peter Bellew*.[71] The clause in question in this case read: "For a period of 12 months after the termination of your employment you shall not, without the prior written consent of the Company, directly or indirectly in any capacity either on your own behalf or in conjunction with or on behalf of any other Person; a. *be employed, engaged, concerned or interested in any capacity in any business wholly or partly in competition with the Company for air passenger services in any market...*". The defendant had tendered his resignation and intended to take up a new post with another airline, Easyjet. The High Court held that while Ryanair had established that it had a legitimate interest that it sought to protect, a restriction that sought to prevent Mr Bellew from taking up any position with any airline in any capacity that is wholly or partly in competition with Ryanair was too wide and was therefore void and unenforceable as an unjustified restraint of trade.[72]

Contracts for the Sale of Businesses

In the context of the sale of a business, restraint of trade clauses are designed to ensure that the seller does not engage in actions that would undermine the value of the business sold to the buyer. For these clauses to be enforceable, they must be reasonable concerning their duration, geographic scope, and the interests they seek to protect. In *Nordenfelt v Maxim Nordenfelt Guns and Ammunition Co Ltd* this landmark case involved a clause preventing the seller from engaging in the manufacture of guns and ammunition for 25 years.[73] The House of Lords upheld the clause, finding it reasonable given the specific nature of the business and the legitimate interest in protecting the goodwill and competitive position of the buyer.

---

69 [2019] IEHC30.
70 [2011] IEHC 505.
71 [2019] IEHC 907.
72 Breda O'Malley and Niamh Cassidy, 'Ryanair DAC v Bellew – What does the decision mean for restrictive covenants?' (2020) 4 Industrial Relations News 24; Claire Bruton, 'Ryanair v Bellew- What does the decision mean for restrictive covenants in Ireland' (2020) 17(2) Irish Employment Law Journal 36.
73 [1894] AC 535.

The matter was considered at length in the UK Supreme Court in the Northern Ireland case of *Peninsula Securities Ltd v Dunnes Stores (Bangor) Ltd*.[74] The facts of the case were that Mr Shortall bought, in his own name, land in 1979 which was designated for retail use. In 1980 he obtained planning permission and sought an 'anchor tenant' who would be a prestigious retailer which would attract other retailers and customers alike. In that regard he approached Mr Ben Dunne, the founder of Dunnes Stores. Terms were agreed between them and it was promised by Mr Shortall that he would not cause or permit the establishment on any other part of the site of a unit measuring more than about 3,000 square feet for the sale of food or textiles. In 1981 the lease for a term of 999 years was signed. The restrictive agreement was further incorporated into the lease and read:

> 'That any development on the Lessor's lands comprised in the Lessor's folio and on his other lands adjoining the premises shall not contain a unit in size measuring three thousand square feet or more for the ... purpose of trading in textiles Provisions or groceries in one or more units'.

In 1983 Mr Shortall transferred his freehold interest in the land to Peninsula Securities Ltd, a company owned by him. The success of the shopping centre has declined and it was argued in this case that the reason for such decline was the inclusion of the restrictive clause. The Supreme Court found that the fact that Peninsula is a developer rather than a trader was not determinative and that no law had been cited to the court which would point to any other conclusion. It was held that at the time the agreement was entered into, Mr Shortall had a free but limited choice – to take Dunnes Stores on the terms of the offer or potentially have no anchor tenant. In that regard the appeal by Peninsula Securities was dismissed and the clause remains valid.

Solus Agreements

A solus agreement is an exclusive dealing arrangement and most of the case law in this area comes from petroleum wholesalers are retailers. Commonly, these agreements are that the wholesaler will supply all of the petroleum that a retailer needs and in return the retailer will order all of the petroleum it needs from the supplier. The Fair Trade Commission reported in 1961 that while these agreements were generally of benefit to the public, the profitability of the retail trade led to an undesirable proliferation of outlets. A statutory instrument was therefore enacted which sought to regulate this system.[75] Under this, a solus agreement could last for no longer than five years, retailers could

---

[74] [2020] UKSC 36 on appeal from [2018] NICA 7.
[75] SI No 294 of 1961.

not obtain price advantages under such an agreement as suppliers could not discriminate between retailers who had a solus agreement and those who did not although rebates could be paid to those who had. This instrument had the effect of suppliers buying their own retail outlets and in 1972 it was amended to increase the duration of the agreement to ten years and placed a ban on wholesalers acquiring retail outlets.[76] In 1981 the instrument was again amended and while the 10 year duration was maintained, as well as the non discrimination aspect, it allowed wholesalers to provide training or give loans to build or repair stations.[77]

The leading Irish case on solus agreements is *Continental Oil Co of Ireland Ltd v Moynihan*.[78] In this case Moynihan entered into a solus agreement in 1970. The agreement was to run for 5 years and he was to buy the petrol at the plaintiff's scheduled price, giving 48 hours notice of requirements. Further, he could not order a consignment of less than 800 gallons at a time, the station was to be kept clean and in good repair, and the number of pumps could not be reduced. Moynihan further benefited from the scheme by purchasing new pumps on an interest free hire purchase arrangement. The plaintiff then operated a new pricing scheme which threatened Moynihan's already small profit margins and he refused to order any more supplies from them. In upholding the agreement and imposing a prohibitive injunction, Kenny J found that at the time the agreement was entered into, it was reasonable between the parties. However, the English decision in *Shell UK v Lostock Garage* has held that where the revised price scheme operates harshly the agreement may not be enforced.[79]

15.6.4 Expansion of the Doctrine

In recent years the doctrine of restraint of trade has had significant expansion in the area of sports stars and their contracts. In *Eastham v Newcastle United* a professional football player who, under the rules in an agreement between his club and the Football Association, could be barred from playing for any other club successfully claimed that these rules were invalid.[80] Lord Wilberforce acknowledged that some restrictions were necessary for the organisation, but that these rules were too restrictive on the players' employment rights and went further than protecting their legitimate interest. Further, in *Proactive Sports Management Ltd v Rooney* the restraint involved exclusivity of

[76] SI No 150 of 1972.
[77] SI No 70 of 1981.
[78] (1977) 111 ILTR 5.
[79] [1977] 1 All ER 481.
[80] [1964] Ch 413.

'image rights' which, at 17, the footballer Wayne Rooney had agreed to give for eight years with a commission of 20% being paid.[81] The court struck down this agreement in light of Rooney's age, the fact that he had received no legal advice, the duration of the contract and the flat rate commission. The relevance of the inequality of bargaining power was highlighted in *Dwyer (UK Franchising) Ltd v Fredbar Ltd*.[82] Although this case related to a restrictive covenant in a franchise agreement, the principles apply beyond.

Test Your Knowledge

Jake and Kevin are in a same sex relationship and they decide that they want to have a baby. They approach their friend Mary and ask her if she would be willing to act as a surrogate for them. Mary agrees and they enter into a surrogacy agreement whereby Jake and Kevin will pay for all of Mary's expenses and ancillary costs relating to the pregnancy. They spend several thousand pounds in advance to cover health checks and tests on Mary and they buy her lavish gifts and days out. After four months, Mary changes her mind and says that she does not want to be a surrogate after all. Is the contract:

A enforceable against Mary?
B invalid due to illegality?
C invalid due to public policy?

The correct answer here is C. The contract itself is not illegal but it is unenforceable on the grounds of public policy. The court could not order that Mary become pregnant and carry to term. Jake and Kevin will not be able to recover the moneys that they have spent on Mary unless they can show that there was some form of misrepresentation on her part.

Stretch and Challenge Question

Consider the role that public policy plays in determining whether contracts are enforceable. Do you think that morality has any role to play in contracts which are freely entered into between private parties?

---

81 [2011] EWCA Civ 1444.
82 [2022] EWCA Civ 889.

PART FOUR

DISCHARGING THE CONTRACT

CHAPTER 16

DISCHARGE BY PERFORMANCE AND AGREEMENT

16.1 Discharge Through Performance

The general rule is that when a party is performing an obligation under a contract, performance of that obligation must be done to the exact specification and time frame as set out. In some cases, this obligation will be construed strictly, and in others, a more relaxed approach is taken. In those cases, the court will interpret the contract to understand what the parties meant by 'performance' and then determine whether what has been done corresponds to that which was promised.

16.1.1 Performance Must be Precise

Where there is the slightest deviation from the terms of the contract, the party who has not defaulted will be able to say that the contract has not been performed and will be able to sue for damages for breach of contract, and in certain circumstances, have the contract discharged In *Re Moore & Co and Landauer & Co* the defendant agreed to buy 3,000 tins of canned fruit from Australia which were to be packed in cases of 30 tins each.[1] When the cargo arrived, it was discovered that many of these cases contained 24 and not 30 tins. Here the defendant was entitled to reject the entire cargo, as despite the fact that the consignment as a whole did not deteriorate in value, the manner of performance was not as prescribed. It is only where the deviation is microscopic will the contract be taken to have been properly and wholly performed.

Where a party is prevented from fulfilling their obligations by the other party, they will be able to claim a remedy. In *Arterial Drainage Co Ltd v Rathangan River Drainage Board*, the plaintiff agreed to drain land for the defendant.[2] The contract allowed for the defendant to terminate

[1] [1921] 2 KB 519. *Nash v Hartland* (1840) 2 Ir Lrd 190.
[2] (1880) 6 LR (Ir) 513.

the contract if the works were not being carried out diligently. The defendant attempted to execute this right however it transpired that the work was not progressing as swiftly due to the fact that the defendant had not made the land or plans available to them. As the plaintiff was prevented by the defendant from carrying out their contractual obligations, they were allowed by the court to treat the contract as rescinded and to claim for the works carried out.

16.1.2 Timing of the Performance

Under the common law, where a time frame for performance was prescribed in the contract, this was held to be sacrosanct. If the condition relating to the time frame was not adhered to, the other party could treat the contract as breached. Equity, however, did not hold such a strict view, and could order specific performance of the contract where to do so would not cause an injustice to either of the parties.[3] In *Crean v Drinan* a completion date was specified by the plaintiff in relation to the purchase of lands.[4] It was also specified that an assignment would be procured relating to interest held by third parties by that date. It was held that while the failure to complete on the prescribed date did not in itself invalidate the contract, the failure to obtain the assignment did and the plaintiff was entitled to the return of his deposit. However, each case will turn on its own particular facts.[5]

Where a contract specifically makes completion on a specific date 'of the essence' the courts will be more likely to hold that there has been a breach where that date has passed.[6] In *Ochre Ridge Ltd v Cork Bonded Warehouses and the Port of Cork Co* Smyth J stated that where time is of the essence:

> The date so fixed must be strictly adhered to, and the time allowed is not to be extended by reference to equitable principles.[7]

If the contract initially does not make timing 'of the essence' one party may serve notice to state that from that date timing will be of the essence.[8] In *Nolan v Driscoll* the plaintiff agreed to purchase

---

3 *Maye v Merriman,* Unrep, High Court, 3 February 1980.

4 [1983] ILRM 82.

5 See *Sepia Ltd and Opal Ltd v M&P Hanlon Ltd,* Unrep, High Court, 23 January 1979 where the failure to obtain planning permission was not sufficient to excuse non-performance of the contract.

6 John Stannard, 'So What if Time is of the Essence?' (2005) Singapore Journal of Legal Studies 114.

7 [2006] IEHC 107.

8 John Stannard, 'The Contractual Last Chance Saloon: Notices Making Time of the Essence' (2004) 120 Law Quarterly Review 137.

the defendant's property in December 1975.[9] Due to registration difficulties the sale had not completed two years later. In March 1977 the defendant was of the view that proper title had been shown and served notice that he wished to make time of the essence and that completion should take place by the end of the month. The court upheld the defendant's decision to treat the contract as breached when the plaintiff failed to complete within that time period and refused an order of specific performance sought by the plaintiff.

16.1.3 Place of Performance

The place of performance depends on the express or implied intentions of the parties as judged from the contract as a whole. If there is no place of performance specified either expressly or impliedly, then the general rule is that for a contract for the sale of goods, it is the buyer's responsibility to collect the goods, and in relation to the repayment of a debt, it is the debtor's responsibility to pay the creditor and the place and in the manner proscribed by the creditor.

16.1.4 Payment

There is a mistaken belief that one must produce a receipt in order to prove payment where payment of money is the obligation under the contract. Payment may be proven by other evidence adduced. Traditionally, payment was understood to mean payment of cash, but in today's world payments are now made most often by bank transfer. Issues arise, however, as to when payment is deemed to have taken place. In *Mardorf Peach & Co Ltd v Attica Sea Carriers Corporation of Liberia* there were differing opinions of the court, with Lord Salmon and Lord Russell taking the view that once the money was sent to the creditor's bank, that would be sufficient to discharge the obligation.[10] However, Lord Fraser believed that the payment could only be deemed to have taken place when the money went into the actual account of the creditor.

This matter was again considered by the House of Lords in *A/S Awilco of Oslo v Fulvia SpA di Navigazione of Cagliari, The Chikuma.*[11] This case involved the charter of the ship, The Chikuma. Payment of an instalment fell due on 22 January, and on 21 January Awilco instructed its bank in Norway to make the payment via bank transfer. This arrived into Fulvia's account on 22 January, but under Italian law, interest would not be paid until 26 January and Fulvia would have

---

9 Unrep, High Court, 25 April 1978.

10 [1977] AC 850.

11 [1981] 1 WLR 314.

incurred a penalty if it had withdrawn the money prior to this. As per the contract, Fulvia withdrew the vessel for failure to pay punctually. The House of Lords agreed and stated that the payment on 22 January was not the same as payment in cash as it could not be used to earn interest. The fact that it could be withdrawn, but at a fee, did not make it equivalent to cash.

However, where payment is made by credit or debit card, this is deemed an absolute payment unless the contract specifically provides otherwise. Therefore, if the credit/debit card company fails to pay, the cardholder is not liable for this.

16.1.5 Vicarious Performance

There are certain circumstances, where the contract permits, that a party to the contract may fulfil its obligations but have a third party carry out its duties. Where the contract does not expressly provide for vicarious performance, this may be inferred where it is of really no relevance whether the obligation was carried out personally by the contracting party or another. So, in *British Waggon Co v Lea & Co* a contract to lease railway wagons and to keep them in good repair could be vicariously performed as the repairs were those that ordinary workmen with knowledge of the business would be able to carry out.[12] However, where a party has been selected by reference to their special skill and qualification, this cannot be vicariously performed without the express permission of the other party. In these circumstances, where the promisee agrees to the contract being performed by a third party, the contract will be discharged.

16.1.6 Alternative Modes of Performance

A contract may provide for alternative modes of performance in two ways. The first is known as the contract option. *Anson's Law of Contract* gives an example of this where a shipper's obligation is to load a cargo of wheat, but the contract gives it the option to change, say, to a load of barley. Once the option to change the cargo has been exercised, the contract is effectively amended and becomes one to load barley instead of wheat.[13] The exercise of this option must be communicated at the earliest opportunity.

The second alternative mode is known as a performance option. This is where the contract gives a party a number of options, under which it could potentially perform its obligations without specifying the

---

[12] (1880) 5 QBD 149.
[13] (31st edn, OUP 2020).

preferred mode. Here the party has a true choice as to which option to take, but once it has made its decision, it must follow through with that option. Where one of several options becomes unavailable, this does not have a significant impact on the contract but rather just narrows down the choices for performance.

16.1.7 Part Performance

As the general rule is that performance must be complete and exact, where performance has only been partially completed, nothing can be recovered for partial performance. For example, if you entered into a contract with a painter to decorate your entire house, and they painted only one wall in one room, they would not be able to recover for the work done as performance was not exact and complete, ie they did not decorate the entire house. It does not matter why the performance was incomplete. So, in *Cutter v Powell* a seaman was employed as a second mate for a sailing from Jamaica to Liverpool.[14] His payment was to be made at the completion of the journey; however, he died some two weeks before the journey was complete. His widow sued to recover his payment for the journey. Her action failed as the contract was construed as an 'entire contract'; in other words, the seaman would only receive the sum when the voyage was complete. This line of reasoning was followed in Ireland in *Coughlan v Moloney*.[15] Here the plaintiff agreed to build a house for the sum of £200, to be completed by Christmas 1902. The work was left incomplete and the plaintiff builder sued for the cost of the works done. As there was no express agreement for periodic payments the court found that the action failed as the plaintiff could not show that there was an implied agreement to pay.

The strict application of the rule can, as seen in *Cutter*, produce some very unfair results. It has, however, been justified in that the contracting party has not contracted for part of the performance for a proportionate price, but rather the whole performance. As Jessel MR in *Re Hall and Barker* explained, 'if a shoemaker agrees to make a pair of shoes, he cannot offer one shoe and ask you to pay half of the price'.[16] Further, the rule is said to hold people to their promises. This is particularly useful where there is an inequality of bargaining power and in hindering opportunistic behaviour. In the example given above, let us say that the painter paints more than the one room but does not finish and moves on to the next job, leaving your house in a state of disarray. This rule allows you to withhold payment until the

14 (1795) 6 Term R 320.
15 (1905) 39 ILTR 153.
16 (1878) 9 Ch D 538.

job has been completed and so is an incentive for the painter to finish work before moving onto the next job.

The rule has, however, been criticised as its strict application is unconcerned with the reasons behind the lack of full performance and can cause significant injustice.[17] This has led the court to develop exceptions to the rule which fall mainly within three categories: (a) part performance has been accepted as performance of the whole obligation. This arises where incomplete performance has been accepted, or full performance has been waived. It will only apply in circumstances where the party not in default has the option of whether to accept or refuse the partial performance; (b) part performance has benefitted the other party. This arises where it can be shown that the party who has received the part performance has accrued a realistic benefit or (c) the obligation has been substantially performed.

16.1.8 The Doctrine of Substantial Performance

Where the contract has been substantially performed, payment may still be required, but this can be offset against any works that have not yet been completed. For this doctrine to operate, the court needs to be satisfied that the works do not fall too short of full completion and that the cost of remedying what remains is not too great.[18] In *H Dakin & Co Ltd v Lee* Dakin, a builder, agreed to repair Lee's building for a fee of £1,500.[19] The builder carried out the vast majority of the works but failed to carry out three tasks; the cost of remedying these amounted to £80. It was initially held that as Dakin had not completed the works, it was not entitled to the recovery of any payment. On appeal, this was overturned, and it was held that Dakin was entitled to recover for the works completed less a deduction for the breach. There is authority in Ireland to suggest that where a builder has abandoned works, the doctrine will not apply. In *Kincora Builders v Cronin* it was held that where the builder refused to insulate the attic, this constated abandonment, and therefore was denied any remedy claimed for substantial performance.[20] It should however be noted that the Construction Contracts Acts 2013 requires parties to a construction contract to fix a schedule for interim and final payments which ameliorates the issues that arise relating to building work.

---

17 Gerwyn Griffiths, 'Part Performance – Still Trying to Replace the Irreplaceable' (2002) Conveyancer and Property Lawyer 216.

18 Anthony Beck, 'The Doctrine of Substantial Performance: Conditions and Conditions Precedent' (1975) 38 Modern Law Review 413.

19 [1916] 1 KB 566.

20 Unrep, High Court, 5 March 1973.

16.2 Discharge By Agreement

As a contract is one that is freely entered into between the parties, there is no great difficulty in understanding that those same parties can agree to end the contract when they so choose.[21] The requirement is that the discharge is mutual, and freely given. In other words, no party has been under any duress or undue influence to end the contract. However, there may be circumstances where a party subsequently changes their mind and wants to reinforce the contract. In circumstances where this occurs, an agreement to discharge the contract will have no legal validity, unless all of the formalities have been met and in particular fresh consideration provided, and as such it is always recommended that they enter into a second discharge contract. In *The Hannah Blumenthal* it was confirmed that the requirements for entering into a discharge contract are the same as the formalities for any other contract, and consideration must be present.[22] There is one exception to this, known as the 'mutual release exception'. This in effect discharges both parties from any future obligations and will be held to be valid consideration. This is because both parties are seen as providing something; mutually releasing each other from any further obligations under the contract. As they are both providing this it can be seen as a quid pro quo and therefore valid consideration.

The mutual release exception does not apply where there is only one party who has obligations outstanding. In these circumstances, the parties must enter into a deed of release.

In some cases, where there has been a long period of delay or inactivity, the court may hold that the parties have 'abandoned' their contract and effectively agreed to discharge it.[23]

Further, there are cases where the parties want to change the terms of the contract. Rather than entering into a discharge agreement, they supplant the old contract with a new one. In *Morris v Baron & Co* a claim had begun in relation to a dispute over a contract for the sale of cloth.[24] Prior to the case coming for hearing, the parties came to an oral agreement that the action would be withdrawn, an extension of credit would be given (this was also owed under the previous contract) and providing a new arrangement for an option for the buyer to take previously contracted for, but not yet delivered, cloth. The House of

---

[21] SJ Stoljar, 'The Discharge of Contracts by Agreement' (1956) 3 Queensland Law Journal 356; Saloni Choudhary, 'Discharge of Contracts by Agreement' (2022) 5(4) International Journal of Law, Management and Humanities 274.

[22] [1983] 1 AC 854.

[23] *Phones 4 U Ltd v EE Limited* [2018] EWHC 49.

[24] [1918] AC 1.

Lords held that in these circumstances it must be concluded that the parties had discharged their previous contract and supplanted it with this new one.

Test Your Knowledge

Daisy runs a decorating company and has taken on two jobs at the same time. She has been contracted to decorate the kitchen of Jared's house and the entire upstairs of Helen's house. It has been agreed that the fee will be €500 for Jared's kitchen and €2,000 for Helen's upstairs, both of which are payable on completion. Daisy decides that she is going to try and put more hours into Jared's job first as it is smaller and will be completed quickly. As a result, she spends six hours per day at his property and three at Helen's. After one week Daisy's is involved in an accident where she is injured and can no longer work. She has completed all of Jared's kitchen, with the exception of one shelving unit, but has only partially painted one room out of four in Helen's house. Both Jared and Helen are refusing to pay Daisy. Advise Daisy:

- A She can recover all of the money from both Helen and Jared.
- B She cannot recover any of the money from both Helen and Jared.
- C She can recover some of the money from either Helen or Jared.

The correct answer here is C. Helen will be able to recover some of the money from Jared under the doctrine of substantial performance. This will not be the full amount as there is some work still outstanding, but this is relatively minor. There will be a deduction made from the €500 for the work on the shelving unit that is still outstanding. This doctrine will not apply to Helen as the work has not been substantially performed. Therefore, Daisy will not be able to recover any money from Helen.

Stretch and Challenge Question

Analyse whether the doctrine of substantial performance adequately balances the rights of both parties to the contract.

Chapter 17

DISCHARGE BY FRUSTRATION

17.1 Introduction

If a contract becomes impossible to perform for some reason outside of the control of either party after it is made, it is said to be frustrated and both parties are discharged from that moment. The doctrine is residual and will only apply if the parties have not provided for the risk in the contract.[1] As explained by Rix LJ in *Edwinton Commercial Corp v Tsavliris Russ (Worldwide Salvage & Towage) Ltd (The Sea Angel)*, the doctrine is one of very narrow application:

> Since the subject matter of the doctrine of frustration is contract, and contracts are about the allocation of risk, and since the allocation and assumption of risk is not simply a matter of express or implied provision but may also depend on less easily defined matters such as 'the contemplation of the parties', the application of the doctrine can often be a difficult one. In such circumstances, the test of 'radically different' is important: it tells us that the doctrine is not to be lightly invoked; that mere incidence of expense or delay or onerousness is not sufficient; and that there has to be as it were a break in identify between the contract as provided for and contemplated and its performance in the new circumstances.[2]

Prior to the establishment of this doctrine, it was a rule of contract law that a person was obliged to perform every duty in the contract and could not be excused by the mere fact that it was now impossible

---

1 Ryan Catterwell, 'Frustration and Assumption of Risk' (2022) 1 Journal of Business Law 76.

2 [2007] EWCA Civ 547.

to perform.[3] In *Paradine v Jane* lands leased by Paradine to Jane were occupied by the British Cavaliers during the English Civil War which they held for three years.[4] Paradine then sought the rent for this period, and Jane claimed that it should not be payable as, through events outside of his control, he did not have possession of the property. The court found that the fact that he was not in possession of the lands was not an excuse to terminate the contract and stated:

> when a party by his own contract creates a duty or charge upon himself, he is bound to make it good, if he may, notwithstanding any accident be inevitable necessity, because he might have provided against it by his contract. And therefore, if the lessee covenant to repair a house, though it be burnt by lightning or thrown down by enemies, yet he ought to repair it.

It has always been open to the parties to include in their contract a provision stating if or when liability will be discharged and, in certain circumstances, the court will imply a term (revisit Chapter 7 for more on implied terms).

It was the use of such an implied term that began the doctrine of frustration.[5] The case of *Taylor v Caldwell* involved the hire of a music hall which, the day before the performance, was destroyed by a fire.[6] Under the old rules from *Paradine*, Caldwell would be liable to pay for the hall even though he could now not use it for the performance. The court found that he was not liable as

> the contract is not to be construed as a positive contract, but as subject to an implied condition that the parties shall be excused in case, before breach, performance becomes impossible from the perishing of the thing without default of the contractor.

Taylor was concerned with a case of literal impossibility; there was no music hall and therefore there could be no performance in that music hall. It was not long, however, before the courts began to expand the doctrine beyond instances of impossibility.

A number of legal bases have been put forward for the justification of

---

3 Michael Bridge QC, 'Frustration and excused non-performance' (2021) 137 Law Quarterly Review 580.

4 [1647] EWHC KB J5.

5 Catharine MacMillan, 'English Contract Law and the Great War: The Development of a Doctrine of Frustration' (2014) 2(2) Comparative Legal History 278.

6 (1863) 3 B & S 826. See also *Kean v Hart* (1869) IR 3 CL 388.

the doctrine of frustration.[7] The only Irish case to discuss the theoretical basis for the doctrine is *Mulligan v Browne*.[8] In this case Kenny J opined:

> During the past seventy years it has been developed and refined by many decisions of the House of Lords and the Privy Council. The expression 'the contract is frustrated' so commonly used today is misleading: the doctrine relates, not to the contract but to the events and transactions which are the basis of the contract.

The justifications for the doctrine were summarised by Smith J in *Canary Wharf (BP4) T1 Ltd v European Medicines Agency*:[9]

> (1) *The implied term or implied condition theory.* By this theory, the court must consider whether a term or condition can be implied into the contract, providing for the subsequent event. The problem with such an approach is that it turns on a test of what the parties would have said in response to the interjection of the 'officious bystander' at the moment of the parties' agreement. This theory was approved in the Irish case of *Cummings v Stewart (No 2)*.[10]
>
> (2) *The total failure of consideration theory.* By this theory, a contract can only be frustrated where the subsequent event causes one party to sustain a total failure of consideration. As an explanation for the doctrine of frustration, it is inadequate on two grounds:
>
> (a) First, as Lord Hailsham noted in [*National Carriers Ltd v Panalpina (Northern) Ltd*][11], 'many, if not most, cases of frustration which have followed *Taylor v. Caldwell* have occurred during the currency of a contract executed on both sides, when no question of total failure of consideration can possibly arise'.
>
> (b) Secondly, there will be cases of total failure of consideration, where there is no subsequent 'frustrating' event. Not every total failure of consideration ends in the contract being frustrated, and the total failure of consideration theory says nothing about what constitutes a 'frustrating' event.
>
> (3) *The 'frustration of the adventure' or 'frustration of the foundation of the contract' theory.* Although attractively phrased, this theory is no more than a form of words, with no clear meaning behind it. As Lord Hailsham said in *Panalpina*: 'This, of course, leaves open the question of what is, in any given case, the foundation of the contract or what is "fundamental" to it or what is the "adventure".'
>
> (4) *Construction of the contract theory.* This involves ascertaining

---

7 Richard Posner and Andrew Rosenfield, 'Impossibility and Related Doctrines in Contract Law: An Economic Analysis' (1977) 6(1) Journal of Legal Studies 83.

8 Unrep, High Court, 9 July 1976.

9 [2019] EWHC 335 (Ch).

10 [1913] IR 95.

11 [1981] 1 AC 675.

precisely which obligations each party did, and did not, assume. Plainly – and unsurprisingly – where the contract makes sufficient provision for the subsequent 'frustrating' event, the contract will prevail, and there will be no discharge. This is, quite simply, a matter of the due and proper construction of the contract. But, just as with the implied term or implied condition theory – of which this is a more sophisticated variant – whilst the true construction of the contract may be relevant to the question of frustration, it is not *of itself* the test *for* frustration.

(5) *Performance rendered radically different by fundamental change in circumstances.* Lord Radcliffe's dictum [in *Davis Contractors v Fareham UDC*][12] is said to encapsulate this theory, which has found favour in the recent case law.

In analysing each of these justifications, the court came to the conclusion that it is the fifth one that provides the most adequate reason and that it:

> best encapsulates the essence of the doctrine of frustration. Whether a contract is frustrated depends upon a consideration of the nature of the bargain of the parties when considered in the light of the supervening event said to frustrate that bargain. Only if the supervening event renders the performance of the bargain 'radically different', when compared to the considerations in play at the conclusion of the contract, will the contract be frustrated.

17.2 Areas where Frustration Arises

Generally, the doctrine does not apply to situations which were foreseeable by the parties. The rationale here is that if the parties foresaw the possibility of a particular event occurring, they should then make provision for it in their contract. This rule was until recently strictly interpreted and applied. However, in *The Sea Angel* (approved in *Canary Wharf Ltd v European Medicines Agency*),[13] the court found that it was not an absolute exclusion and stated:

> In a sense, most events are to a greater or lesser degree foreseeable. That does not mean that they cannot lead to frustration. … However, … the less that an event, in its type and impact, is foreseeable, the more likely it is to be a factor which, depending on other factors in the case, may lead on to frustration.

17.2.1 Destruction of the Subject Matter

This is the most straightforward example of frustration and, as in

[12] [1956] AC 696.

[13] Simon Baughan, 'Until the Crack of Doom? The Sea Angel and Frustration' (2007) 6(4) Shipping and Transport International 24.

Taylor v Caldwell, relates to destruction of something integral to the performance of the contract.

17.2.2 Non-Occurrence of an Event

Examples here centre on the underlying reason for entering into a contract and whether the contract becomes frustrated if that underlying reason evaporates. In *Krell v Henry* Henry hired out a room for two days in order to watch the coronation procession of King Edward VII.[14] The coronation procession was then cancelled due to the ill health of the King, and Krell, who had received only one-third of the rent payable under the contract, sought to recover the rest. While technically the contract was still capable of being performed (the room was available and could have been used), the Court of Appeal found that it had been discharged as the entire purpose of the contract was to view the procession.

However, the same court came to a different conclusion in *Herne Bay Steam Boat Co v Hutton*.[15] Here Hutton had chartered a boat to see the coronation naval review and to tour the fleet. As with the coronation procession, the naval review was cancelled, but the fleet remained. The court did not hold this contract as discharged as only part of the purpose had been cancelled; it was still possible to sail around the fleet.[16]

17.2.3 Death or Incapacity

The contract will be frustrated where the obligation is one of personal service which can no longer be performed due to death or incapacity of that person. In *Stubbs v Holywell Railway Co* it was held that a contract for personal services was discharged due to death.[17] Further, in *Robinson v Davison* a piano player failed to perform due to ill health and was sued for breach of contract.[18] The court found that there was no breach, and the contract was frustrated due to ill health. A number of factors will be considered where the contract is one of employment and the employee is absent, even for prolonged periods of time.[19] In

---

14 [1903] 2 KB 740.

15 [1903] 2 KB 683.

16 Sergio Garcia Long, 'While English Lawyers Say No, Civil Lawyers Say Yes: The Intriguing Case of Frustration of Purpose in Comparative Law' (2023) 31(5) European Review of Private Law 979.

17 (1867) LR 2 Ex 311.

18 (1871) LR 6 Ex 269.

19 Cliona Kelly, 'Frustration and Employment Contracts' (2004) 11(11) Commercial Law Practitioner 286; Kara Turner, 'Jurisdiction of Tribunal: Frustration of Contract of Employment' (2008) 5(3) Irish Employment Law Journal 100.

Marshall v Harland & Wolff Ltd the test for frustration of a contract of employment was set down as follows:

> Was the employee's incapacity of such a nature, or did it appear likely to continue for such a period, that further performance of his obligations in the future would either be impossible or be a thing radically different from that undertaken by him and agreed to be accepted by the employer under the agreed terms of his employment?[20]

However, the application of this doctrine can give rise to some harsh results, such as in *Northcutt v Universal Equipment Co (London) Ltd*. In this case an employee suffered a heart attack, and it was clear that he would never work in the same capacity again.[21] The contract was held to be frustrated, and this absolved the employer from statutory obligations of notice periods to terminate the contract and payment during the notice period. In a more recent case, *Warner v Armfield Retail and Leisure Ltd*, the English Employment Appeal Tribunal held that the doctrine of frustration did apply to employment contracts (here, up until his stroke in 2010, the appellant had been a site manager for the respondent company, a small business specialising in shop and pub refurbishments and his duties involved high levels of mobility).[22] There was, however, an additional requirement to consider first whether the employer was in breach of its duty to make reasonable adjustments under the equalities legislation.

In Ireland, the most comprehensive analysis for incapacity was undertaken by the EAT in *Donegal County Council v Langan*.[23] Langan was employed as a general labourer since 1974. In 1985 he was incapacitated with back pain which lasted for three years. In April 1988 the council wrote to him stating that they would not reemploy him and in July 1988 he was certified as fit to return to work. In an action for unfair dismissal, the council claimed that the contract had been frustrated. The EAT set out a number of elements which ought to be considered in cases such as this, being:

- (a) the length of employment;
- (b) how long it is expected that the employment will last;
- (c) the nature of the employment;
- (d) the nature, length and effect of the illness or disabling event;
- (e) the need of the employer for the work to be done;
- (f) whether wages have continued to be paid;
- (g) the actions of the employer;

---

20 [1972] 1 WLR 899.
21 [1986] 1 WLR 641.
22 (UKEAT/0376/12).
23 UD 143/89. See also Jeffrey Greene, 'Terminating Employment on Incapacity Grounds' (2016) 13(2) Irish Employment Law Journal 43.

(h) whether consideration was given to retaining the employee on the books if not in employment;
(i) whether discussions were had with the employee and his trade union;
(j) whether adequate medical investigations were carried out;
(k) whether, in all the circumstances, a reasonable employer could be expected to wait any longer.

In this case it was held that frustration had not occurred as Langan was not a key worker, had only been paid for the first 12 weeks of his absence, there was no discussions with him or his trade union and there was no medical examination undertaken prior to dismissal.

The EAT further held in *Mooney v Rowntree Mackintosh Ltd* that the doctrine is inappropriate where an employee is intermittently absent from work due to a series of minor ailments.[24]

17.2.4 Substantial Interruption

In war time, ships were often requisitioned by governments, and if that ship was under charter at the time, the question arose as to whether the requisition frustrated the rights of the shipowner and the charterer. In *FA Tamplin Steamship Co Ltd v Anglo-Mexican Petroleum Products Co Ltd* a ship was chartered for five years to December 1917.[25] In February 1915 the government requisitioned the ship to be used as a troopship and made alterations. The charterers were willing to continue with their obligations, but the shipowners wanted to declare the contract as frustrated so as to obtain a higher level of compensation from the state. The House of Lords held that the contract continued as the interruption to the contract was not substantial enough in duration.

National Carriers Ltd v Panalpina (Northern) Ltd involved the lease of a building for a 10-year period.[26] Due to the possible collapse of a nearby building, the government closed the street for 20 months so that structural repairs could be conducted. In this case, the court did not hold the lease frustrated as again the interruption was not substantial enough.

This doctrine was considered recently in the case of *Foot Locker v Percy* by the Court of Appeal.[27] The case centred around government mandated closures as a result of Covid 19 and the plaintiff argued that it was not liable to pay rent for the period of closures as this amount

---

24 UD 473/1980.
25 [1916] 2 AC 397.
26 [1981] 1 AC 675.
27 [2024] IECA 65.

to a frustrating event. The High Court dismissed the claim stating that there was no concept of 'temporary' frustration in Irish Law. The Court of Appeal upheld this decision and dismissed the appeal. It confirmed that frustration in this jurisdiction cannot be temporary or partial and that the plaintiff was liable for the rent during that period of mandated closure.[28]

17.2.5 Extreme Impracticality

In order for a contract to be frustrated on these grounds, it must be shown that it was virtually impossible to comply with the contract.[29] Delay, inconvenience or additional expense will not be sufficient grounds. In *Tsakiroglou & Co Ltd v Noblee Thorl GmbH* the contract was to ship groundnuts from Sudan to Hamburg during November or December 1956.[30] Due to the Anglo-French invasion of Egypt in 1956, the Suez Canal closed on 2 November 1956 and remained closed for five months. The contract was priced on the basis of shipment through the canal, and it was claimed that it was frustrated due to its closure. The court found that there was no frustration as it was still possible to perform the contract through another route. While this second route (around the Cape of Good Hope) would be more expensive and take longer, this was not sufficient to have it discharged.

Again, in *Davis Contractors Ltd v Fareham UDC*, the delay of 16 months in completing the contract with an additional £20,000 expenditure was not sufficient to frustrate the contract.[31]

This approach has been followed by the Irish Courts in *McGuill v Aer Lingus and United Airlines*.[32] Here the plaintiffs booked an internal holiday flight in the USA with the second defendants. The second defendants were aware at the time that they had been served with strike notice but had neglected to either inform the plaintiff or to put an appropriate clause in the contract. As a result, the plaintiff had to travel on different flights with other airlines and their holiday was cut short. The defendant pleaded frustration. While the court did not rule

---

28 See also *Oyster Shuckers Ltd T/A Klaw v Architecture Manufacturing Support (EU) Ltd and Wooi Heong Tan* [2020] IEHC 527 where a similar outcome was determined. However, this case needs to be distinguished on the basis that it was seeking an interlocutory injunction and no decision on the facts can be made at this stage.

29 Melvin Eisenberg, 'Impossibility, Impracticality and Frustration' (2009) 1(1) Journal of Legal Analysis 207.

30 [1962] AC 93.

31 [1956] AC 696. See also *Amalgamated Investments v John Walker* [1977] 1 WLR 164.

32 Unrep, High Court, 3 October 1983.

out the possibility that industrial action could constitute frustration, it found that on the facts of this case, it did not.

17.2.6 Illegality

A contract may be frustrated here where a change in the law would make performance of the contract illegal. For example, in *Fibrosa Spolka Akcyjna v Fairbairn Lawson Combe Barbour Ltd*, where the outbreak of war would make the performance of the contract illegal by contravening laws which make it illegal to trade with an enemy or an enemy occupied state, the contract was deemed to be frustrated.[33]

17.3 Contracts Concerning Land

It has been a matter of some controversy as to whether the doctrine could apply to cases involving contracts for land. In *Cricklewood Property and Investment Trust Ltd v Leightons Investment Trust Ltd* the House of Lords considered that the doctrine could never apply in these circumstances.[34] However, in *National Carriers Ltd v Panalpina (Northern) Ltd* a 10-year lease was of a property was interrupted for 20 months by the closure of a road which was the only way in which lorries could access the premises. The House of Lords found that this was not a substantial enough interruption as there would still be three years left on the lease once the interruption had concluded. However, it was accepted that, in rare circumstances, a contract concerning land could be deemed to be frustrated.

In Ireland, Deasy's Act[35] creates contractual rights in favour of a tenant to enter onto an estate, but does not confer an estate in land upon the tenant. Thus, this Act provides a solution to some of the 'frustrating' issues that may arise in relation to land by providing that in the absence of any express covenants to repair, a tenant may surrender his tenancy if the premises are destroyed or rendered uninhabitable by fire or some other inevitable accident.[36] However, where the frustrating even falls outside of the scope of the Act, it is clear that the English decision above are being followed with O'Higgins CJ in *Irish Leisure Industries Ltd v Gaiety Theatre Enterprises Ltd* holding that in certain circumstances a lease may be frustrated.[37] In this case the defendant agreed to lease a

---

33 [1943] AC 32. See also the earlier case of *Ross v Shaw* [1917] 2 IR 367 which successfully argued that the German occupation of Belgium made lawful performance impossible.

34 [1945] AC 221.

35 The Landlord and Tenant Law Amendment (Ireland) Act 1860.

36 ibid S 40.

37 Unrep, Supreme Court, 12 February 1975.

premises for three years to the plaintiff, commencing six months from the date of execution. However during that time the existing tenants had obtained a new six year lease by making an application under the Landlord and Tenant Act 1921. On the facts of this case the court held that the lease was frustrated.

17.4 The Foreseeability Issue

The doctrine has evolved as a means for dealing with unforeseen events which render the performance of the contract impossible, illegal, or substantially different from that which was agreed upon. Where parties make provision for certain situations within their contract, they then cannot rely on the doctrine as the event would not qualify as unforeseen. The issue here comes down to risk allocation, as frustration is only available where there is an intervening act outside of the control or contemplation of the parties. In these cases, the court will determine as a matter of construction whether it was a risk borne by one of the parties or whether the contract has been frustrated. In *Canary Wharf Ltd v European Medicines Agency* (above) the court had to determine whether, in light of Brexit, a 25-year lease to the EMA would be frustrated. At the time, it was unclear how and when Brexit would actually occur, but it was known that EMA would not be able to operate in the UK after Brexit. Here, the court found that, despite considering a number of different scenarios, the lease would not be frustrated as it contained express provision for assigning or subletting of the property.[38]

Many contracts will contain what are known as *force majeure* clauses, where the parties will be discharged from their liability on the occurrence of certain events. The main consideration here is whether the event which actually occurred falls within the clause.[39] In *2 Entertain Video Ltd v Sony DADC Europe Ltd* Sony agreed to store goods belonging to 2 Entertain in its warehouse.[40] The contract contained a clause which stated, 'Neither party shall be liable for its failure or delay in performing any of its obligations hereunder if such failure or delay is caused by circumstances beyond the reasonable control of the party affected including but not limited to industrial action (at either party), fire, flood, wars, armed conflict, terrorist act, riot, civil commotion, malicious damage, explosion, unavailability of fuel, pandemic or

[38] See David Langwallner, 'Come Hell or High Water' (2023) 173 New Law Journal 22; Jamie Sutherland, 'Leases, Brexit and Frustration' (2019)23(5) Landlord and Tenant Review 191.

[39] David Thomas, 'Frustration and Force Majeure: A Hard Line in English Law' (2011) 6(2) Construction Law Review 21.

[40] [2020] EWHC 972 (TCC).

governmental or other regulatory action.' In August 2011 there were riots across London and the warehouse was broken into. Much of the stock was stolen by looters and the rest was destroyed by fires that were deliberately set. The court held that the *force majeure* clause did not apply as, while these particular riots were not foreseeable, the risk of a break-in was, as there had been previous attempts. As such, Sony was found not to have acted in compliance with its duty to take care of the goods. The court further found that Sony ought to have taken reasonable steps, such as enhanced security or sprinkler systems in the warehouse, to protect the goods, which it did not.

Therefore, as a general rule, where the parties have thought of a particular event that might occur, they ought to provide for it in the contract. In *Neville & Sons Ltd v Guardian Builders Ltd* the defendant bought a plot of land for development.[41] The land bordered two local authorities and in order to access the land to develop it, planning permission needed to be obtained from the bordering property owners. The plaintiff obtained the contractual rights to carry on the work, however difficulties arose. Both parties were aware at the time of their contract that access to the site depended on Dublin City Council selling a strip of land to the defendant, which did not occur. The Supreme Court took the view that this did not constitute a frustrating event as both parties were aware of the geographical location of the land, the need for planning permissions, and would have anticipated some issues with obtaining access, they did not make any provision for them in the contract.

However, the issue of foreseeability is not necessarily determinative in all cases, and a more liberal approach has been taken. In *Ocean Tramp Tankers Corporation v V/O Sovfracht, The Eugenia*, Lord Denning MR said:

> It has frequently been said that the doctrine of frustration only applies when the new situation is 'unforeseen' or 'unexpected' or 'uncontemplated', as if that were an essential feature. But it is not so. It is not so much that it is 'unexpected', but rather that the parties have made no provision for it in their contract. The point about it, however, is this: If the parties did not foresee anything of the kind happening, you can readily infer that they have made no provision for it. Whereas, if they did foresee it, you would expect them to make provision for it. But cases have occurred where the parties have foreseen the danger ahead, and yet made no provision for it in the contract ...[42]

Following from this case, there cannot be a hard rule that the doctrine of frustration will never apply where the risk is foreseeable. However,

---

41 [1995] 1 ILRM 1.
42 [1964] 2 QB 226.

that is not to say that the issue of foreseeability is irrelevant to such cases. Rix LJ explained in *The Sea Angel*:

> In a sense, most events are to a greater or lesser degree foreseeable. That does not mean that they cannot lead to frustration. Even events which are not merely foreseen but made the subject of express contractual provision may lead to frustration: as occurs when an event such as a strike, or a restraint of prices, lasts for so long as to go beyond the risk assumed under the contract and to render performance radically different from that contracted for. However ... the less that an event, in its type and its impact, is foreseeable, the more likely it is to be a factor which, depending on other factors in the case, may lead on to frustration.

17.5 Self Induced Frustration

It is a well established principle that the doctrine only applies in circumstances where the event was outside of the control of either of the parties to the contract. Therefore, where the event is the fault of one of the parties, they cannot rely on the doctrine as this would amount to self-induced frustration.[43] In *Maritime National Fish Ltd v Ocean Trawlers Ltd* the Privy Council confirmed that where the frustrating event was caused by the complaining party, they could not rely on frustration.[44] The same applies to breach of contract. In *The Eugenia* a clause in the contract stated that the vessel could not be taken into a war zone without prior consent. In breach of this clause, the vessel entered the Suez canal and became stuck when the canal was blocked. The court found that the charterers could not use the fact that they were trapped in the canal as a frustrating event, as it was as a result of their own breach of contract.

Where a party is alleging that the contract is not frustrated as the event was due to the fault of the party claiming it, they must prove that. In *Joseph Constantine Steamship Line Ltd v Smelting Corporation*, a ship was chartered to Smelting Corporation with the intention that it would sail to Australia to load cargo.[45] Before this could happen, a boiler on the ship exploded causing such a delay that there was no doubt the contract could not be performed. The reason for the explosion was never discovered, but the ship's owners believed that it was due to the fault of Smelting Corporation and as such argued that the doctrine should not apply, unless they could prove that it was not their fault. The court rejected this argument and held that the burden of proving

[43] P.A Chandler, 'Self Induced Frustration, Foreseeability and Risk' (1990) 41(4) Northern Ireland Legal Quarterly 362.

[44] [1935] UKPC 1.

[45] [1942] AC 154.

any negligent breach or fault lay with the person alleging that there was such a breach and, in the absence of this, the doctrine would apply.

The leading Irish case on self induced frustration is *Herman v Owners of SS Vicia*.[46] Due to the war, the owners of the vessel were to obtain 'travel warrants' which would allow it to dock. When they failed to obtain these, they claimed that this frustrated a contract entered into with the plaintiff to sail them from the US to Britain and back again. Their claim did not succeed as their failure to obtain the required documentation was entirely their own fault.

17.6 The Effect of Frustration

The effect of frustration is to discharge the contract, and both parties are absolved from their future obligations without incurring any liability for breach of contract (as it is something outside of the control of either party). It differs from where there is a breach of contract, as depending on the type of breach, the innocent party may elect to have the contract discharged. This was confirmed in *Hirji Mulji v Cheong Yue Steamship Co Ltd* where the House of Lords stated that there was no scope to elect to either affirm or discharge the contract after the frustrating event.[47] If the event was sufficiently serious to frustrate the contract, it would be automatically discharged from that date.

However, up until the frustrating act, the contract was still in force and questions arose as to the liability for obligations already performed. Initially, as a result of the judgement in *Chandler v Webster*, the position was that as the contract was not void *ab initio* (only from the frustrating event), monies already paid under a contract prior to that frustrating event could not be recovered; the loss lay where it fell.[48] This meant that where a party had already paid money, they were unable to recover it, or if a party had provided a service, they would not be able to claim for payment of this service. Such a situation clearly resulted in unjust outcomes, particularly in circumstances where the event was something unforeseen and outside of the control of either party – why should one party be enriched by this event occurring?

This position was overruled in *Fibrosa Spolka Akcyjna v Fairbairn Lawson Combe Barbour Ltd* where the House of Lords found that once it could be shown that the basis upon which money was paid had totally failed, money could be recovered.[49] However, where a party received some

---

46 [1942] IR 304. See also *Byrne v Limerick Steamship Co Ltd* [1946] IR 138.
47 [1926] AC 497.
48 [1904] 1 KB 493.
49 [1943] AC 32.

service or goods for the money paid, they would get nothing back. The party needed to show that it received absolutely nothing in return for their money and that there was a total failure of performance.

In Ireland, the courts have yet to choose between following the decisions in *Chandler* or *Fibrosa,* nor has there been any legislative intervention. In the UK following the *Fibrosa* case, the Law Reform (Frustrated Contracts) Act 1943 was enacted, which allows for recovery of moneys to be returned less any deduction for part services or goods received. This is very similar to the application of the doctrine of part performance which was considered in Chapter 16.

The application of the legislation was considered in *Gamerco SA v ICM/Fair Warning Agency Ltd*.[50] This case involved a contract to promote a concert which was frustrated when the stadium was closed due to safety issues. The defendants had been paid an advance of USD$412,000 and the claimants had incurred expenses themselves of USD$450,000. It was assumed that the defendants had expenses of approximately USD$50,000 although there was no concrete evidence as to whether this figure was higher or lower, up to the date of the frustrating event. In applying the legislation, Garland J found that it gave him a wide discretion to do justice and 'mitigate the possible harshness of allowing the loss to lie where it has fallen'. Given the loss faced by the claimants, the court ordered the full repayment of all moneys without any deductions. Arguably, the judge here was not impressed with the fact that no records had been kept, and it was not possible to say how much of the money was actually spent and on what. Further, the judge was not persuaded by the argument that the up-front payment was a sort of insurance against loss from the contract.

The legislation also applies to issues of performance. Where there has been no payment up front, but partial performance has been made to such a degree that it confers a benefit to the other party before the frustrating event occurs, the court has the power to award payment in a sum that it feels just for the performance. In doing so, the court must be cognisant of three things as set down in s 1(3) of the Act: the sum awarded may not exceed the value of the benefit, the expenses incurred by the party receiving the benefit, and the effect of the frustrating event on that benefit. The operation of this part of the legislation was considered in *BP Exploration Co (Libya) Ltd v Hunt (No 2)*.[51] This case involved a potential oil field in Libya where the oil company would carry out prospecting and development of the field. Four years after this began, there was a decision by the Libyan

---

50 [1995] 1 WLR 1226.

51 [1979] 1 WLR 783 (affirmed in the House of Lords [1983] 2 AC 352).

government to nationalise all oil fields, thereby frustrating the contract by an intervening illegality. The oil company then sought payments for benefits received as a result of its work prior to the nationalisation. Goff J, in summarising the requirements to succeed stated:

> First, it has to be shown that the defendant has, by reason of something done by the claimant in, or for the purpose of, the performance of the contract, obtained a valuable benefit (other than a payment of money [to which s 1(2) applies]) before the time of discharge. That benefit has to be identified, and valued, and such value forms the upper limit of the award. Secondly, the court may award to the claimant such sum, not greater than the value of such benefit, as it considers just having regard to all the circumstances of the case.

Goff J was of the opinion that the point of the legislation was to prevent unjust enrichment, and that the benefit of certain services was the end product of the service, not the service itself. Therefore, if the end product was not delivered, there would be no valuable benefit and as such no unjust enrichment to remedy.

Finally, it should be noted that the Act does not apply to all contracts, and there are notable exceptions:

(1) It does not apply where the parties have made express provision for the consequences of frustration (s 2(3)).
(2) Neither does it apply to wholly performed contractual obligations, which may be severed from those that are affected by the frustrating event (s 2(4)).
(3) Certain types of contracts for the carriage of goods by sea (s 2(5)(a)) and contracts of insurance (s 2(5)(b)) are excepted from the scope of the Act, since such contracts are themselves largely concerned with the allocation of risk and it was not intended that the courts should interfere with such allocations.
(4) Contracts for the sale of specific goods, which are frustrated by the goods perishing, are outside the terms of the Act (s 2(5)(c)). Section 7 of the Sale of Goods (SGA) Act 1979 is specifically mentioned and provides for an agreement to sell specific goods to be avoided where the goods perish before the risk passes to the buyer. It is difficult to see how frustration could occur in other instances involving the perishing of specific goods, and the confusing wording of this final exception appears to reflect excessive caution on the part of the draftsperson.

Test Your Knowledge

Jack has recently contracted with Wise Bros Building Co to undertake some work on his land. He lives in a beautiful rural area surrounded by woodlands and lakes. Jack has requested that a building be constructed that he can use to hire out for functions such as retreats and weddings. In addition to the building, he wants some smaller cabins that guests can stay overnight in, together with an area for carparking. Wise Bros quote Jack €560,000 for the complete job, a price which Jack agrees to. Under the terms of the contract, Jack is to pay €160,000 up front to cover material costs, and the balance will be paid on the completion of the works. Eight months into the job, when the main building is finished, there is a forest fire and the whole of Jack's land is devastated. Jack has decided to cut his losses and sell the land to a developer. He claims that he does not have to pay Wise Bros any more as the job was never completed.

Is the contract:

- A enforceable in full by Wise Bros Building Co?
- B frustrated with Wise Bros being unable to claim any further money?
- C frustrated with Jack being able to reclaim the €160,000?
- D frustrated with Wise Bros being able to claim a portion of the balance owed for works that were carried out?

The correct answer is D. A is incorrect as the fire is clearly an intervening event which was not foreseen by either party and neither party were to blame for this. Therefore, the contract is frustrated. B is incorrect as the law allows Wise Bros to make a claim for works undertaken. C is incorrect as Jack has received some services for the money paid. D is the correct answer as there was a frustrating event and the law allows for Wise Bros' to claim for works undertaken up to the point of the frustrating event.

Stretch and Challenge Question

Analyse what reforms are needed to the law of frustration in Ireland.

CHAPTER 18

DISCHARGE BY BREACH OF CONTRACT

18.1 Introduction

The vast majority of contracts will come to an end naturally where the performance of obligations has been met by each party. In the previous chapter, we examined when a contract will be discharged under the doctrine of frustration, which is an intervening event outside of the control of either party. In this chapter, we look at what happens when one party breaches their obligations under the contract. This must be distinguished from circumstances where a valid contract may be avoided due to vitiating factors that we considered in Part III.

A breach of contract occurs where one party fails to meet their obligations under the contract, whether that is a failure to pay, to perform a service or to act within a specified time period. In any circumstances where there is a breach of contract, the innocent party will be entitled to a remedy. In most cases, that remedy will be damages (see Chapter 19). However, where that breach is sufficiently serious, it will give rise to discharge of the contract. These common law rules seek to provide an innocent party with a remedy for serious breach in circumstances where monetary compensation will be insufficient.[1]

18.2 Discharge at the Option of the Innocent Party

The breach itself does not determine the contract as discharged (unlike frustration, for example, where the contract automatically becomes

1 See Neil Andrews, 'Breach of Contract: A plea for clarity and discipline' (2018) Law Quarterly Review 117.

discharged once the event occurs). The breach allows the innocent party to choose whether to treat the contract as repudiated. They have the option of affirming the contract and allowing it to continue. While they do not have to act immediately, if they delay too long in treating the contract as discharged, the courts may hold that this has effectively affirmed the contract. Further, the innocent party must communicate in clear and unambiguous terms that they hold the contract as repudiated.

For example, let us say that a company enters into a contract to buy new cars for its fleet. The contract stipulates as a condition that the cars must be automatic. When the cars are delivered, it transpires that they are in fact manual. There is clearly a breach of contract, but the company has a choice here. They can either communicate with the company that the cars are not what they contracted for and state that they hold the contract as discharged by breach. However, they can also elect to affirm the contract and keep the cars. Once the decision is made, it is irrevocable. In other words, the company cannot decide to keep the cars and use them, and then later decide that the contract has been discharged for breach.

Until such a time as the innocent party elects to treat the contract as repudiated, it remains in effect and is legally enforceable. This issue of elective rather than automatic termination was doubted by the court in *MSC Mediterranean Shipping Co SA v Cottonex Anstalt* where it was held that in particular circumstances where the contract can no longer be performed as a result of the breach, termination may be regarded as automatic rather than elective.[2]

Communication that a contract is being held as repudiated by the innocent party needs to be unequivocal. This may be determined by words or actions. In *Force India Formula One Team Ltd v Aerolab SRL* Force India stated that it would be unable to make payments of instalments owed under a contract to provide aerodynamic testing for its cars and that it would discuss the matter further after a two-week shutdown.[3] At the start of the shutdown period, Force India was disconnected from its servers. The Court of Appeal held that the action of disconnection from the servers was not sufficient to amount to an unequivocal communication that Aerolab was treating the contract as repudiated.

A question arises as to whether non-performance of obligations by the innocent party amounts to unequivocal communication. In *Vitol SA*

2 [2016] EWCA Civ 789.
3 [2013] EWCA Civ 780.

v Norelf Ltd, The Santa Clara the buyer sent a telex that amounted to a repudiatory breach, and the question before the court was whether that breach was accepted by the seller or whether it had affirmed the contract in circumstances where it simply did not comply with its obligations under the contract.[4] Lord Steyn held that whether communication was unequivocal was a matter of fact that would be different depending on the circumstances of each individual case. He found that there were cases where non-performance of obligations by the innocent party may sometimes be sufficient communication. These will be in the most exceptional of circumstances, and the general rule is that an outward display of communication is required, which was affirmed in *Vitol SA v Beta Renewal Group SA* with the court emphasising the importance of context in determining these cases.[5]

The innocent party must know of its right to accept the repudiation and treat the contract as discharged and of its right to choose to either discharge the contract, or to accept the breach. As with electing to treat the contract as repudiated, the party must also unequivocally confirm that they wish to elect to affirm the contract and that they will continue to abide by the contract. In *Yukong Line Ltd of Korea v Rendsburg Investment Corporation of Libya* the response to a repudiatory breach requested the party in breach to confirm that it would honour its contractual obligations.[6] This was held to be insufficient to deem the contract as affirmed. The innocent party must act swiftly if it wishes to have the contract treated as discharged and lengthy delays may result in the party losing this right.[7]

There are certain circumstances in which the decision to affirm the contract or not will be taken out of the hands of the innocent party. For example, where the party has delayed to such an extent that the doctrine of estoppel would apply as to allow the contract to be repudiated would cause an injustice in the circumstances. The operation of this doctrine can be seen in the case of *Peyman v Lanjani* where the defendant entered into an agreement to have a lease assigned to him which could not be assigned without the consent of the landlord.[8] It transpired that the landlord's consent had been obtained by deception. The claimant then agreed to purchase the lease, and the landlord's consent was again tainted by deception, although not on the part of the defendant. When this was discovered, the plaintiff sought the advice of a solicitor who advised him to proceed with

---

4 [1996] AC 800.
5 [2017] EWHC 1734 (Comm).
6 [1996] 2 Lloyd's Rep 604.
7 *An Bord Iascaigh Mhara v Scallan,* Unrep, High Court, 8 May 1973.
8 [1985] Ch 457.

the purchase, and the plaintiff paid the first instalment of £10,000. A month later the plaintiff sought the advice of other solicitors who advised him of his right to treat the contract as repudiated, based on the defect in the title caused by the original deception. The question before the court was whether or not the plaintiff had lost his right to rescind the contract. It was held that he had not lost the right, primarily because he was unaware of the full facts before the payment of the first instalment was made.

18.3 Circumstances which Will Result in the Right to Terminate the Contract

Generally, the right of the innocent person to terminate the contract for a breach will arise in three distinct circumstances.

18.3.1 Repudiatory Breach

There are a number of ways in which a breach of contract may be said to be repudiatory: a party may (a) renounce its obligations under the contract, or (b) by their own act make performance impossible.[9] Each of these are considered in turn.

Renunciation

This occurs where one party makes it clear that they have no intention of performing a particular term of the contract. In order for the renunciation to apply in these circumstances, the term in question must be either a condition or an innominate term as a failure to perform a term classed as a warranty will only ever result in an award of damages (recall Chapter 7 on terms).[10] Whether renunciation has occurred will be a factual matter for the courts to decide. Where this has been done in clear and unequivocal terms, evidenced in writing, the decision will be easy to make; however, there are circumstances where this can occur through conduct. As established in *Universal Cargo Carriers Corp v Citati* the test is 'whether the party renunciating has acted in such a way as to lead a reasonable person to the conclusion that he does not intend to fulfil his part of the contract'.[11]

The intention to renounce the contract is one of great importance. In *Freeth v Burr* the buyer failed to pay for one instalment of deliveries

---

9 JW Carter, 'The detrimental impact of repudiatory breach on discharge for breach of contract' (2020) 4 Journal of Business Law 287.

10 Chinyere Ezeoke, 'Assessing Seriousness in Repudiatory Breach of Innominate Terms' (2017) 3 Journal of Business Law 198.

11 [1957] 2 QB 401.

of iron.[12] He did this operating under the belief that he was entitled to do so as compensation for non-delivery of an early shipment of iron. The seller could not hold this is a repudiatory breach and was not discharged from the contract. Keating J stated: 'It is not a mere refusal or omission of one of the contracting parties to do something which he ought to do, that will justify the other in repudiating the contract; but there must be an absolute refusal to perform his part of the contract.' A similar line of reasoning was adopted by the Irish courts in *Parol Ltd v Carroll Village Retail (Management) Services Ltd* where a tenant unsuccessfully argued that a landlord's breach of a lease amounted to repudiation.[13] Clarke J made it clear in his judgment that such cases will be determined on a case by case basis and will require a high threshold for the court to hold that anything other than damages is an appropriate remedy.

Renunciation may take place either before performance is due, or during performance. Where it takes place before performance, this is known as an anticipatory breach.[14] This breach allows the party to sue for damages and to treat the contract as discharged. One of the leading cases on this point is *Hochster v De La Tour* where Hochster was contracted to provide courier services on a tour which was due to commence on 1 June.[15] On 11 May he received a letter stating that his services would no longer be required. The court upheld his right to bring an action even though the time of performance had not yet arrived. The principle was justified in *Frost v Knight*: 'The promisee has an inchoate right to the performance of the bargain, which becomes complete when the time for performance has arrived. *In the meantime he has a right to have the contract kept open as a subsisting and effective contract*. Its unimpaired and unimpeached efficacy may be essential to his interests.'[16]

The doctrine of anticipatory breach has been accepted in Ireland in the case of *Leeson v North British Oil and Candle Co*.[17] In this case the defendants contracted to supply nominees of the plaintiff with up to 300 casks of paraffin during the winter season. In January the plaintiff was informed that due to strike action there would be no supply for 2 months. The plaintiff then refused to take any orders from his own customers fearing that he would leave himself open to breach of contract claims if he could not fulfil them. The plaintiff sued

---

12 (1874) LR 9 CP.

13 [2010] IEHC 498.

14 Qiao Liu, 'Inferring Future Breach: Towards a Unifying Test of Anticipatory Breach of Contract' (2007) 66(3) Cambridge Law Journal 574.

15 [1853] EWHC QB J72.

16 (1872) LR 7 Exch 111.

17 (1874) 8 IRCL 309.

successfully and was able to recover damages for orders lost from the defendant. On appeal the defendant argued that the plaintiff should not have been able to recover damages for future orders. They stated that the plaintiff should have submitted those orders and allowed the defendant to try and obtain the paraffin elsewhere. This contention was rejected by the Court of Appeal holding that the statement made by the defendant allowed the plaintiff to treat the contract as rescinded and to recover all loss therefrom.

The application of this principle allows the innocent party to assert their rights quickly and therefore minimise the damage that may accrue. Once renunciation has been made and accepted by the other party, even prior to performance, the parties cannot then change their minds. However, if renunciation is not accepted and the innocent party insists on performance, the contract will remain in effect and the anticipatory breach cannot be relied upon. As the contract is still in effect, either party can then take advantage of subsequent breaches. In *Avery v Bowden*, Avery chartered his ship to Bowden to sail to Odessa to take a cargo from Bowden's agent which was to be loaded within a certain number of days.[18] When the vessel reached Odessa, there was no cargo there to be loaded. The master of the ship waited and demanded the cargo, but before the specified number of days had elapsed, the Crimean War broke out, making the performance of the contract illegal. Avery sued and his action failed. If Bowden's agent had stated that no cargo would be forthcoming and there was no point in staying there, the master of the ship could have treated the contract as repudiated and sailed away. Avery would then have had the right to sue.

If, during the performance of the contract, one party signifies that they are unwilling to fulfil their obligations, the innocent party is entitled to be released from any further obligations and to sue. In *Cort v Ambergate etc Railway Company* Cort contracted for 3,900 railway chairs to be delivered to the defendant in certain quantities and on certain dates.[19] After providing approximately half of the chairs, Cort was informed by the defendant that it did not want any more and to cease delivery. Cort brought an action claiming that he was willing to fulfil his obligations but had been prevented from doing so by the defendant. Cort was successful in his claim, and the court rejected the defendant's argument that Cort's assertion that he was willing to perform was not sufficient and that actual delivery would be required. It was held that as the contract had been repudiated, Cort was not

---

18 (1855) 5 E&B 714.

19 (1851) 17 QB 127.

required to undertake any additional manufacturing costs before bringing a claim.

Impossibility of Performance

If further performance of the contract is made impossible by the default of one party, the innocent party will be discharged. Renunciation is not required in these circumstances; however, it is a more difficult ground to establish. With renunciation, the innocent party needs only to show that the words or conduct amount to such that a reasonable person would believe that there was no intention to fulfil the obligations. Whereas, here, the innocent party has the more difficult task of establishing that performance of the contract became impossible as a result. Despite being a more difficult category to establish, it remains a valid option. In *Universal Cargo Carriers Corporation v Citati Universal*, Universal chartered a ship to Citati who agreed to nominate a berth, shipper and provide cargo before a certain date. Three days before the specified date, none of these things had been complied with. Universal cancelled the contract and found another charterer. The court held that while the contract had not been renounced, Citati would not have been able to perform its obligations without significant delay which would have frustrated the contract. As such, Universal could hold that the contract was discharged due to Citati's inability to perform.

As with renunciation, the impossibility can arise either before the performance is due (as in *Universal*) or during performance.

18.3.2 Where the Breach is Fundamental

Where a contract term is breached, it does not always allow the innocent party to treat the contract as repudiated. In many cases, the contract will still be valid and enforceable, with the innocent party entitled to damages for the breach. However, there are certain circumstances where the breach is so significant, that it can be termed a 'fundamental' breach which will allow the contract to be discharged.[20] In *Robb v James* the plaintiff purchased fabric at auction with the condition that the material be collected and paid for within 24 hours.[21] The plaintiff failed to comply with this term and the defendant then sold the material to a third party. The plaintiff failed in his action against the defendant with the court holding that they failed to comply with the most essential term of the contract which allowed the defendant to treat the contract

[20] Catherine Piercy, 'Breaking up is Hard to do: Termination for Repudiatory Breach' (2016) 31(8) Butterworths Journal of International Banking and Financial Law 473.

[21] (1881) 15 ILTR 59.

as discharged. This case illustrates how this doctrine operates. While the breach is not classed as a repudiation, one party has breached a term that is so integral to the contract that it allows the innocent party to deem the contract as discharged.

The modern formulation of this can be found in *Hong Kong Fir Shipping Co Ltd v Kawasaki Kisen Kaisha Ltd*.[22] Here, Hong Kong Fir chartered a ship to Kawasaki on terms that it was 'in every way fitted for ordinary cargo service' for a period of two years. The ship was old and needed to be maintained by experienced engine room staff. The chief engineer was an alcoholic and his staff inadequate, resulting in several breakdowns. In the first seven months, the ship spent only eight weeks at sea and the rest in repairs. Kawasaki refused to continue with the charterparty. It was argued that the term was a condition, and as the ship was not seaworthy, Kawasaki could treat the contract as discharged. The court did not agree and held that the delays, coupled with Hong Kong's steps to remedy the defects, when taken together were not sufficient to hold the contract as discharged. It stated that the test to be applied is as follows:

> Does the occurrence of the event deprive the party who has further undertakings still to perform of substantially the whole benefit which it was the intention of the parties as expressed in the contract that he should obtain as the consideration for performing those undertakings?

The court will therefore examine the position of the contract at the date it is argued to have been terminated, the steps that the breaching party took to remedy any defect or breach, and likely future events. [23]

This case was applied in Ireland in the case of *Uniform Construction Ltd v Cappawhite Contractors Ltd*.[24] A subcontractor here was entitled to hold that late payment of fees and attempts to impose additional obligations not contained within the original contract as a fundamental breach. Laffoy J opined that a fundamental breach was one that would 'shatter the plaintiff's confidence in the defendant's ability to pay for the goods with which the plaintiff supplied them'.

However, as the case of *Dundalk Shopping Centre Ltd v Roof Spray Ltd* shows, it is not necessary to show that the term will not be complied with – even in circumstances where the term has been complied with, but has been negligently carried out, the contract may be discharged

---

22 [1962] 2 QB 26.

23 Jordan English, 'The Nature of Promissory Conditions' (2021) 137 Law Quarterly Review 630.

24 [2007] IEHC 295.

for fundamental breach.[25] In this case the plaintiff had contracted with the defendant to carry out water proofing on the roof of their shopping centre. This water proofing did not work and water seeped into the building causing damage. It was held that the failure of the defendant to ensure that the roof was waterproof was sufficient to ensure a fundamental breach allowing the plaintiff to treat the contract as discharged and to obtain damages.

18.3.3 Where the Term Breached is a Condition

As we have already seen in Chapter 7, contract terms are divided into different categories. If the term is deemed to be a warranty, breach of the term will only entitle the innocent party to damages. Where the term is a condition, however, it will allow the innocent party to choose to deem the contract as discharged.[26] Where the term is an innominate term, it gives the court the discretion to either award damages or to hold the contract as discharged.

18.4 Consequences of Breach

Once a contract is deemed to be discharged by breach, both parties are released from all future obligations under the contract. The contract is not rescinded *ab initio*, as happens in cases of mistake or misrepresentation. If a contract is rescinded *ab initio*, the court treats the contract as if it did not happen and seeks to put the parties back into the positions that they were in prior to entering the contract. Where the contract is discharged for breach, this does not occur. It releases the parties from future obligations, but obligations which had accrued up until the date of the event remain for both parties. So, an obligation to pay instalments, for example, will remain up until the date of the breach.

The right to discharge by breach, howsoever accrued, may be lost due to acceptance, delay, waiver or affirmation.

Test Your Knowledge

Evie is a law student and she is worried about her upcoming contract law exam. She decides that she will pay for some extra tutoring. She goes online and finds a firm called 'Premier Tutors' who specifically advertise that Professor O'Donnell, a renowned contract law expert,

---

25 Unrep, High Court, 21 March 1979.

26 JW Carter, 'Breach of Condition and Express Termination Right: A Distinction with a Difference' (2017) 122 Law Quarterly Review 395.

will be giving tutorials. This firm is much more expensive than others, but Evie decides that it will be worth it if she is tutored by Professor O'Donnell. She books and pays for 10 sessions upfront. When she goes to her first tutorial, she is told that Professor O'Donnell is no longer working with the company, but that the firm has a new tutor who is just as qualified. It transpires that the new tutor is inexperienced and this is their first tutoring role. Evie is disappointed but decides that, as she needs tutorials, she will give it a try. She attends five tutorials and then contacts the company to ask for her money back, saying that this is not what she has paid for. Is the contract:

A discharged by breach allowing Evie to hold the contract repudiated?
B breached but only allowing Evie to claim damages?
C valid as Evie has affirmed the contract?

The correct answer here is C. While this is clearly a breach of contract and one that went to the root of the contract which would allow Evie to hold the contract discharged by breach, she has affirmed the contract by attending five of the sessions. It would have been up to Evie at the first session to say that this was not what she contracted for, and at that stage she would have been able to hold the contract as breached, and have her money returned.

Stretch and Challenge Question

Critically analyse the law on affirmation and determine whether the law ought to take a more flexible approach.

PART FIVE

REMEDIES

CHAPTER 19

DAMAGES

19.1 Introduction

Where one party to a contract has not performed as required, this non-performance may render that party liable for damages. The nature and extent of the detriment suffered by the other party and the culpability of the non-performing party can determine the availability of damages in the case of non-performance or defective performance. In the common law system, courts have at their disposal generally three theories under which compensatory damages can be awarded: expectation loss, reliance loss, and restitution loss. Punitive damages are also available on a limited basis. The nature of the damages will vary according to the type of contract entered. Finally, the non-performing party may have an excuse which releases or significantly reduces its liability.

19.2 The Nature of Damages

Damages for breach of contract are designed to compensate the innocent party for the loss or injury suffered as a result of the breach. In all circumstances of a breach of contract, the innocent party will be entitled to damages. However, where they have not actually suffered any loss as a result, the award will be nominal. Compensation for breach of contract is not designed as a punishment for the party who has breached the contract and so, regardless of how bad their behaviour has been, damages will be restricted to the actual loss suffered. This is in contrast to the award of damages in tort law where the role of damages is to try and put the party back to the position that they were in prior to the tort being committed. Finlay P in *Hickey & Co Ltd v Roches Stores (Dublin) Ltd* explained the rationale behind having two separate tests is that the liability in contract is strict and freely assumed meaning that the parties to the contract have the opportunity to adjust their liability during negotiations.[1]

The date at which damages are assessed is generally thought to be at the date the breach occurred.[2] However, more recently, and illustrated in the case of *Golden Strait Corporation v Nippon Yusen Kubishika kaisha, The Golden Victory*, a more flexible approach has been adopted.[3] In this case, three years into a seven-year charterparty, there was a repudiatory breach on the part of the charterers. Fifteen months after this, the Iraq war broke out, which would have entitled the charterers to terminate the contract under a war clause in the contract. The question to be answered by the court was whether damages ought to be assessed at the time of the repudiatory breach, or at the time of the trial. The House of Lords held that it ought to be the latter as the court can then more accurately determine the loss suffered.

Damages are generally not recoverable for distress caused by the breach, with two exceptions.[4] The first is where the distress is a direct consequence of the inconvenience caused by the breach; the second is where the purpose of the contract is to provide enjoyment. An example of the second exception can be seen in *Jarvis v Swan Tours Ltd*, Jarvis booked a winter sports holiday with Swan in Switzerland.[5] The holiday was advertised as a house party style with lots of entertainment being provided. During the second week at the hotel, Jarvis was the only guest and the entertainment was significantly lacking in comparison to the brochure. The Court of Appeal held that he was entitled to recover damages in the amount of the sum paid for the holiday plus £60 to compensate him for the loss of enjoyment. Originally, damages would only be available under this head where it was the sole purpose of the contract to provide enjoyment. This has now been expanded, and in *Farley v Skinner* it was held that where the provision of enjoyment,

1 Unrep, High Court, 14 July 1976.
2 Daniel Hubbard, 'Damages for Breach of Contract: The Correct Time for Assessing Loss' (2011) 26(1) Journal of International Banking and Finance Law 15.
3 [2007] UKHL 12.
4 Mysty Clapton, 'Contractual Damages for Mental Distress' (2007) 123 Law Quarterly Review 26.
5 [1973] QB 233.

peace of mind or the prevention of distress is an 'important object' of the contract, this will suffice.[6] The reasoning in Jarvis has also been followed in Ireland in *Johnson v Longleat Property* where it was held that if a builder fails to complete a house to the standards set down in the contract, damages for discomfort, loss of enjoyment and inconvenience were awarded.[7] This type of damages was examined by Hogan J in *Browne v Iarnrod Eireann (No.2).*[8] In this case the parties had an agreement to allow Mr Browne early retirement, which was then refused by the defendant. The plaintiff continued to work for a further three years and while he suffered no economic loss (indeed he increased his wealth in terms of pension entitlements) the court placed a value of his loss at €20,000 per annum, stating:

> The type of loss and inconvenience suffered by the plaintiff is undoubtedly intangible and very difficult to measure. It is nevertheless a real one. Who, for example, contemplating a difficult and taxing day at work as he or she set out for their house in teeming rain on a cold winters morning, would not long for the leisurely life of the retired? Mr Browne must surely have wistfully reflected on this from time to time as he continued in the workforce. This loss can really be regarded as a form of inconvenience and loss expectation inasmuch as Mr Browne was deprived of an important benefit – a restful and less stressful life – associated with the early retirement contract.[9]

Damages for loss of reputation can only be awarded where the damage to the reputation is such that it has had financial consequences. In *Malik v Bank of Credit and Commerce International SA* Malik, along with some other senior employees of the defendant, were made redundant due to insolvency.[10] They claimed that they were unable to obtain other employment in the financial industry because it was assumed that the defendant had been acting in a corrupt manner. It was claimed that Malik and others who were innocent of any wrongdoing were now at a disadvantage due to the stigma that attached to their former employer. The House of Lords held that the defendant was under an implied obligation not to carry out any corrupt actions that would breach the implied term of mutual trust and confidence in an employment contract. Where financial loss as a result of damage to reputation occurs as a result of a breach of this implied term, compensation is recoverable in principle.

---

6 [2001] UKHL 49.

7 Unrep, High Court, May 19 1976. See also *Leahy v Rawson;* Unrep, High Court, 14 January 2003; *Mitchell v Mulvey* [2014] IEHC 37; *Scaif v Falcon Leisure Group* [2007] IESC 57.

8 [2014] IEHC 117.

9 ibid.

10 [1998] 1 AC 20.

19.3 Classification of Damages

19.3.1 Expectation Loss

The purpose of an award of damages is to put the innocent party in the position they would have been in had the contract been properly performed. This means that the innocent party can claim for lost profits. For example, if a farmer hired machinery to harvest a crop, and due to a breach of contract that machinery never arrived rendering the crop useless as it could not be harvested, the farmer could claim not only for the hire costs, but also for the lost profits that they would have made had the harvest been successful and the crop sold.

In many cases, the assessment of damages will be made on the basis of the difference between the performance received and the performance promised by the contract – this is known as the 'difference in value'. In other cases, damages will be assessed on the basis of what it will cost the innocent party to have a third party perform the contract. This is known as the 'cost of cure'.[11]

In *Ruxley Electronics & Construction Ltd v Forsyth,* Forsyth entered into a contract with Ruxley for the construction of a swimming pool with a diving area at a depth of 7 feet 6 inches and at a cost of £17,797.[12] In breach of this contract, the depth of the diving area was only 6 feet 9 inches. This defect did not stop it from being used for diving and did not impact the market value of the pool. The cost of remedying or curing the defect was £21,560. The House of Lords here held that Forsyth was not entitled to the cost of cure in this case. He had not intended on rebuilding the pool even if awarded the money to do so, and it would have been disproportionate to award this large sum of money given that there was no real difference in market value. However, there was a breach of term, and Forsyth was awarded £2,500 for loss of amenity.

19.3.2 Reliance Loss

An award for damages may be given under reliance loss where the innocent party has expended money in preparation for performing their part of the contract. For example, say you entered into a contract with a decorator to redecorate your house. In advance of starting the work, the decorator bought new materials and you then repudiated the contract. The decorator would be entitled to recover what he had spent on preparing to fulfil his side of the bargain. This can also operate

---

11 Solene Rowan, 'Cost of Cure Damages and the Relevance of the Injured Promisees Intention to Cure' (2017) 76(3) Cambridge Law Journal 616.

12 [1996] 1 AC 344.

where expenses were incurred prior to the contract being made. In *Anglia Television Ltd v Reed* the television station was able to recover when the defendant refused, in breach of contract, to act in a play despite the fact that the expenses were incurred prior to the contract being entered into.[13]

19.3.3 Restitution Loss

Damages under this heading may arise in circumstances where one party has paid consideration under the contract and the other party refuses to comply with their obligations. For example, if I pay £700 to have a skip delivered to my house, and the company then refuses to deliver the skip, I can claim restitution loss to have my money returned to me. The purpose of this head of damages is to prevent one party becoming unjustly enriched by keeping the money that I have paid for goods or services that I have not received.[14]

19.4 Punitive Damages

As we have shown above, the general rule in relation to damages in contract law is not to punish. However, where there is an overlap in a claim between contract law and tort law, punitive damages may be awarded with the court placing an emphasis on the tortious breach.[15] In *Garvey v Ireland* the plaintiff was summarily dismissed from his position as a Garda Commissioner.[16] This action was deemed unconstitutional and as such warranted an award of exemplary damages against the state.[17] It is clear from the case law that the courts will prefer to avoid awarding exemplary damages or punitive damages in a case involving contract law. Where this occurs there is usually some additional tortious or constitutional aspect to the claim under which the court can justify their award. Indeed the Law Reform Commission has emphasised that the use of such damages in cases involving a pure breach of contract should be avoided.[18]

---

13 [1972] 1 QB 60.

14 Alan Bunbury, 'Breach of Contract and Unjust Enrichment' (2010) 13 Trinity College Law Review 94.

15 *Drame v Evangelou* [1978] 1 WLR 459.

16 Unrep, High Court, 19 December 1979.

17 See also *Irish Ferries Teoranta v Minister for Communications, Energy and Natural Resources* [2012] IEHC 256.

18 Law Reform Commission, Aggravated, Exemplary and Restitutionary Damages, LRC 60-200.

19.5 Causation

In order to succeed in a claim for damages, the claimant must establish causation – that is that the breach of contract caused the loss.[19] The 'but for' test used in tort (but for the breach of contract the loss would not have been suffered) is not sufficient in contract law. Instead, the breach must be the 'effective' cause of the loss. As illustrated in *Galoo Ltd v Bright Grahame Murray* the courts have taken a broad approach to determining this and preferred to use a common-sense approach in interpreting the facts of the case.[20]

Where there is an intervening act that was likely to occur following the breach, this will not break the chain of causation, and where the chain of causation has not been broken, all loss flowing from that breach will be recoverable. Where the intervening act was not likely to occur, the chain of causation may be held to be broken. In these circumstances, damages are only recoverable up until the event of the intervening act.

19.6 Remoteness

Where causation has been established, it does not necessarily follow that the defendant will be liable for all of the losses suffered.[21] Certain losses may be classed as being too 'remote'. The law in this area comes from the seminal case of *Hadley v Baxendale*.[22] In this case, Hadley's mill suffered a broken crankshaft, which needed to be sent to the makers of a new crankshaft as a model. The defendant delayed and the crankshaft was delivered late. The mill was non-operational during the delay because, unbeknown to the defendant, the claimant did not have a spare crankshaft, resulting in Hadley losing profits. In formulating the test, Alderson B stated that damages are recoverable due to breach of contract where (1) they are fairly and reasonable to be considered arising naturally from the breach, or (2) when they are 'such as may reasonably be supposed to have been in the contemplation of both parties at the time they made the contract, as the probably result of the breach of it'. The effect of the second part of this test will depend on the special circumstances made known to the party who has breached the contract at the time the contract was made. In *Hadley* it was held that the claimant could not recover for loss of profits when the mill

---

19 See also *Hyper Trust Ltd (T/A The Leopardstown Inn) v FBD Insurance* [2021] IEHC 279; [2022] IEHC 39.

20 [1994] 1 WLR 1360.

21 John Halladay, 'Remoteness of Contractual Damages' (2009) Denning Law Journal 173.

22 (1854) 9 Exch 341.

was idle, as it was not communicated to the defendant that a delay in delivery would so result.

Victoria Laundry (Windsor) Ltd v Newman Industries Ltd considered the rule further. In this case Victoria wanted to expand its business and agreed to buy a new boiler from the defendant.[23] It was agreed that this would be delivered on 5 June, but it transpired that it had been damaged and was not ready. It was not finally delivered until November, and as a result Victoria lost significant profits. It was initially held that Victoria could not recover the lost profits, but this was overturned on appeal. The defendant knew at the time of the contract the business that the claimant was engaged in and that the boiler was required for immediate use. From its own knowledge of the industry, the defendant was presumed to know that there would be some measure of lost profits as a result of the delay.

Combined, these cases are effectively saying that the defendant will be liable for damages that were reasonably foreseeable as a result of the breach. Therefore, it is not required that the defendant had specific knowledge, but rather what a reasonable person would conclude as being foreseeable losses. It was confirmed in *Jackson v Royal Bank of Scotland Plc* that the defendant's knowledge is to be judged at the time the contract was entered into and not at the date of the breach.[24]

More recently, the issue of remoteness of damages was considered in *Transfield Shipping Inc v Mercator Shipping Inc, The Achilleas*.[25] In this case, under a time charter, the defendant should have redelivered the ship to the claimant owner, but was over one week late in delivery in breach of contract. The owner, on the basis of the original contract, had entered into a very lucrative charter. As a result of the defendant's breach, the claimant could not honour this and ultimately agreed to a reduced rate on hire. This amounted to a net loss of $8,000 per day of the charter. The defendant accepted that it was liable for damages but argued that it should be capped at a market rate. The claimant, however, claimed for the entirety of the extra profit it would have made. The House of Lords agreed with the defendant, holding that damages for the loss of the lucrative charter were too remote. What is controversial about this judgment is that there were significant differences of opinion. Lord Rodger and Baroness Hale applied the conventional test as above – essentially asking whether it would be in the reasonable contemplation of the parties at the time the contract was entered into that there would be a follow-on contract entered

---

23 [1949] 2 KB 528.
24 [2005] UKHL 3.
25 [2008] UKHL 48.

into. (Given the nature of the parties, that answer might appear to be yes.) Lord Hoffman (with whom Lord Hope agreed) applied different reasoning to come to the same conclusion. He effectively added another element to the test that the defendant must have accepted liability for the loss, and in this case that it had not done so.

This decision has left the law on remoteness of damages in contract law in a state of confusion.[26] It is generally accepted that the rule in *Hadley v Baxendale* remains good law and that *The Achilleas* should be viewed as a 'highly exceptional case'.[27]

There are however a number of scenarios in which the rules set down in *Hadley v Baxendale* do not apply. For example, the general rule is that damages recoverable for a failure to pay a sum of money owed is limited to that sum plus interest.[28] This rule was departed from in circumstances where a banker refused to honour a cheque where the account had sufficient funds and awarded damages for reputation loss.[29]

A further exception can be seen in the case of *Mackenzie v Corballis*.[30] The plaintiff worked as a servant for the defendant in South Africa and was brought to Dublin to continue her employment. It was agreed that once her employment in Dublin finished, her employer would pay her fare back to South Africa. When her employment ceased, the defendant refused to honour this aspect of the contract and the plaintiff was required to stay in Dublin pending the outcome of the litigation. The plaintiff was entitled to damages to cover not only her fare back to South Africa, but also the cost of the lodgings during her extended stay in Dublin.

19.7 Contracts for the Sale of Land

It is worth noting that there are specific rules relating to damages for breaches of contract involving the sale of land in Ireland.

19.7.1 The Rule in *Bain v Fothergill*[31]

This rule limited damages in cases where a vendor, who without deceit

---

26 K.V Krishnaprasad, 'From the Mill Shaft to the Coal Cruiser: Contractual Damages after the Achilleas' (2011) 22(7) International Company and Commercial Law Review 218.

27 *Saipol SA v Inerco Trade SA* [2014] EWHC 2211 (Comm).

28 *Fletcher v Tayleur* (1855) 17 CB 21.

29 *Rolin v Steward* (1854) 14 CB 595. See also *Boyd v Fitt* (1863) 14 Ir CL Rep 43.

30 (1905) 39 ILTR 28.

31 (1874) LR 7 HL.

or wilful default, were unable to show good title to the property. This rule has been abolished by s 53(1) of the Land and Conveyancing Law Reform Act 2009 which states:

> The rule of law restricting damages recoverable for breaches of contract occasioned by defects in title to land (known as the Rule in *Bain v Fothergill*) is abolished.

19.7.2 Damages Following a Breach of Specific Performance

Until recently, English law held that where a party opted for a decree of specific performance (instead of damages), and that decree was subsequently unenforceable, the party would be held to his initial choice and not be able to subsequently claim damages.[32] However, the House of Lords overruled this position in *Johnson v Agnew*,[33] and this line of reasoning was following in Ireland in cases such as *Vandeleur & Moore v Dargan*.[34]

19.7.3 Deposit

Traditionally, Irish Law allowed the vendor and purchaser to bargain in relation to the deposit paid in relation to the property, and that deposit would be forfeit if the sale did not complete due to the default on the part of the purchaser. This has now been ameliorated by s 54 of the Land and Conveyancing Law Reform Act 2009 which states:

> Where the court refuses to grant specific performance of a contract for the sale or other disposition of land, or in any action for the return of the deposit, the court may, where it is just and equitable to do so, order the repayment of the whole or any part of the deposit with or without interest.

19.7.4 Purchaser Received incorrect Advice on the Value of the Property

Following from the case of *Ford v White & Co*, damages are payable in the sum of the difference between the actual value of the property and the price paid, where the purchaser has paid more for the property than it is worth following incorrect advice from a professional advisor.[35]

---

[32] See for example *Horsler v Zorro* [1975] Ch 302.

[33] [1980] AC 367.

[34] [1981] ILRM 75. See also Sorcha Lynch, 'Specific Performance: Damages in Lieu of Specific Performance' (2008) 13(3) Conveyancing and Property Law Journal 73.

[35] [1964] 1 All ER 885.

This ruling has been adopted in Ireland in *Taylor v Ryan and Jones*[36] and *Kelly v Crowley*.[37]

19.7.5 Purchaser Received Negligent Legal Advice

Where a purchaser can show that but for the breach of contract in the form of negligent advice, that they would not have entered into the contract, damages may be recoverable.[38]

19.8 Mitigation

A party who has suffered loss as a result of a breach of contract is under a duty to mitigate their losses. In other words, the law requires that they take reasonable steps to keep their losses to a minimum. What is reasonable will depend on the circumstances of each case.[39] In *Gul Bottlers (PVT) Ltd v Nichols Plc* a licensee had not acted unreasonably in refusing an offer for a new licence where the offer was a 'legal stratagem' to protect the breaching party's liability,[40] and in *Wroth v Tyler* the claimant was unable to mitigate his loss as he did not have the money to make an alternative purchase.[41] This failure to mitigate was not unreasonable in the circumstances.

The claimant further cannot take any steps to increase or enhance the losses suffered as a result of the breach of contract. In *Banco de Portugal v Waterlow* the defendant's breach of contract resulted in a large amount of forged Portuguese currency circulating in Portugal.[42] The claimant agreed to honour the face value of the forged currency despite being able to detect which ones were forgeries. The claimant's action increased the losses that it sustained; however, this was held to be reasonable as to do otherwise would have undermined confidence in the currency and the banking system. It was further held in this case that the assessment of whether the action is reasonable or not is to be judged at the time that the action is taken and not with the benefit of hindsight. The same reasoning has been applied in Irish cases. In *Bord Iascaigh Mhara v Scallan* the court held that the owners of a fishing vessel were required to take possession of a ship which

---

36 Unrep, High Court, 10 March 1983.
37 Unrep, High Court, 5 March 1985.
38 See *KBC Bank Ireland Ltd v BCM Hanby Wallace* [2012] IEHC 120.
39 This has been affirmed by the court in *Rosbeg Partners Ltd v LK Sheilds (a firm)* [2016] IECA 161 and *Hyland & Ors v Dundalk Racing (1999) Ltd* [2017] IECA 172.
40 [2014] EWHC 2173 (Comm).
41 [1974] Ch 30.
42 [1932] AC 452.

had been abandoned due to a repudiatory breach by the hirers rather than leave the ship deteriorate and claim damages for such.[43]

If the action in mitigation taken by the innocent party has the effect of removing all losses, they will still be entitled to damages for breach, but the amount will be nominal. The general position is that the claimant should not be in a better position financially than he would have been had the contract been performed. In *British Westinghouse Electric and Manufacturing Co Ltd v Underground Electric Railways Co of London* the defendant supplied the claimant with turbines which, in breach of contract, were deficient in power.[44] The claimant later replaced the turbines with others from another manufacturer which were much more efficient, resulting in savings being made. The claim for the cost of replacing the turbines was rejected by the House of Lords. The claimant had been so effective in mitigating its loss that it was not entitled to damages other than for the period in which the original turbines were running inefficiently.

The issue of receiving a further benefit as a result of mitigation was considered further by the Supreme Court in *Globalia Business Travel v Fulton Shipping*.[45] This case concerned a charterparty which was due to expire in November 2009. In breach of this, the ship was returned two years early in 2007 and the owners immediately sold the ship for $23.7 million. If the ship had been returned at the specified time, the impact of the global financial crisis meant that the ship would likely have been worth approximately $7 million. The question before the court was whether the owners had to give credit for the increase in profit. Initially, the court held that the decision to sell was to be looked at independently from the breach of contract, but the Court of Appeal disagreed. The Supreme Court then reinstated the initial decision, holding that the test was whether there was a causal link between the breach and the benefit. In this case, the Court found that a causal link was not present, and the sale of the vessel could not mitigate for the loss of income suffered by the breach of contract.

These matters have also come before the Irish Courts. In *O'Brien v White Spunner* the plaintiff was awarded a decree of specific performance in relation to the purchase of a house.[46] The defendant's who refused to complete were ordered to pay the rental value of the property from the original date of completion until the date that the plaintiff entered

[43] Unrep, High Court, 8 May 1973. See also *Cullen v Horgan* [1925] 2 IR 1 which held that the claimant must act within a 'reasonable point after the breach'.

[44] [1912] AC 673.

[45] [2017] UKSC 43.

[46] Unrep, High Court, 23 November 1979.

into possession of the property. However, the amount of interest that had accrued to the plaintiff while having the completion funds in his account was offset against this award.

Where an injured party has received compensation from another source (an insurance policy for example) these cannot be deducted from an award of damages for breach of contract. In *Irish Leathers Ltd v Minister for Labour and Foley* the court would not allow social welfare payments to be deducted from an award of damages for breach of contract.[47]

19.9 Contributory Negligence

As a general rule in contract law, damages are not reduced where the non-breaching party has contributed to the breach, unless they have either broken the chain of causation or failed to mitigate their loss.

In England, The Law Reform (Contributory Negligence) Act 1945 was enacted to reduce damages where the claimant has also been at fault. This Act is generally restricted to claims in tort and strict breaches of contract do not fall within the scope of the Act. There is one exception where there is concurrent liability for breach of contract and in the tort of negligence.

The position in Ireland is somewhat different. Section 2 of the Civil Liability Act 1961 defines wrong to include 'a tort, breach of contract or breach of trust'. In *Lyons v Thomas* the purchaser sought damages for deterioration of a property between the time the contract for sale was entered into and the completion date.[48] While it was held that the vendor was at fault, the purchaser knew of the deterioration and did not bring it to the attention of the vendor, resulting in a 10% reduction in damages.

19.10 Interest

Under the Debtors (Ireland) Act 1840, as amended by the Courts Act 1981, s 19(1) the defendant is obliged to pay 11% interest accruing from the date of judgment until the final payment is made. This was amended in 1989 to 8%.[49] Whether interest can be recovered between the date of the breach and the date of the judgment is down to the

47 Unrep, High Court, 12 March 1986.
48 [1986] IR 666.
49 SI No 12 of 1989.

discretion of the courts and will depend on the facts of each particular case.

The Supreme Court has examined the issue of interest in two important decisions. In *Reany v Interlink Ireland Ltd* O'Donnell J opined that if a wronged party is to obtain a realistic award of damages, then interest ought to be awarded.[50] He stated:

> It is a rudimentary economic theory that money has a time value. The person who has a sum of money over a period can obtain a benefit either in interest on that sum if invested, (or other return on investment) or interest avoided because that sum does not have to be borrowed. By the same token a person who has not received money incurs a cost, in particular if they have had to borrow.

This sentiment recognises the financial reality of many cases. For example, let us say that Mark undertakes work to decorate Edward's house. Edward agrees to pay €2000 on completion, but does not. Mark can obviously take his case to court for breach of contract to recover that money – but what may happen in the meantime? Say that Mark now cannot pay his rent or his employees, or but new equipment for another job and needs to borrow money for this. Awarding the €2000 is not going to sufficiently compensate Mark and interest ought to be recoverable in these cases.

Further, in the case of *First Active Plc v Cunningham*, the Supreme Court set down what the court ought to consider when determining whether or not to award interest as:

- The nature of the case
- The reasons why the debt was not discharged at an earlier date
- The conduct of each party to the litigation
- The reason for the passage or time or delay in the processing of the litigation
- The absence of a contract clause dealing with interest in the circumstances where its existence might be expected
- The desire to achieve full restoration, but no more, for the judgement creditor
- The avoidance of penalising the judgment debtor.[51]

19.11 Agreed Damages Provisions: Penalty Clauses and Liquidated Damages Clauses

It is not uncommon, particularly in commercial contracts, for parties to

---

50 [2018] IESC 13.
51 [2018] IESC 11.

stipulate in their contract the amount of damages that will be payable in respect of a breach. Generally, where this has been included, and given that both parties have freely entered into the contract and agreed to the term, the amount specified in the contract will be enforced over whatever damages might be assessed at common law. There are obvious advantages to this approach in that it makes claims for compensation relatively straightforward. However, as the purpose of damages in contract law is not to punish a wrongdoer, the courts have been reluctant to enforce these clauses where the amount of damages could be seen as punitive.[52]

A penalty clause is one that threatens to compel performance of the contract by stipulating exorbitant damages for breach, far in excess of the loss that would be suffered.

The traditional test for determining whether a clause was penal was set down in *Dunlop Pneumatic Tyre Co Ltd v New Garage and Motor Co Ltd*.[53] In this case, the appellant sold materials to the respondent who agreed not to resell them at a price below the appellant's sale price and to pay the sum of £5 for every breach of this clause. When this clause was breached, the appellant sued for liquidated damages. The House of Lords held that this was a genuine pre-estimate of loss and not a penalty clause. Lord Dunedin set down the following rules in determining whether the clause was penal or not, which can be summarised as:

(1) It will be held to be a penalty if the sum stipulated for is extravagant and unconscionable in amount in comparison with the greatest loss that could conceivably by proved to have followed from the breach. In *Durkan New Homes v Minister for the Environment, Heritage and Local Government* a clause which provided for damages on an increasing scale from the closing date to the date of transfer was held to breach this provision.[54]

(2) It will be held to be a penalty if the breach consists only in not paying a sum of money, and the sum stipulated is a sum greater than the sum which ought to have been paid. The Irish Supreme Court in *O'Donnell & Co Ltd v Truck and Machinery Sales Ltd* stated that where the breach consists of a failure to pay a sum, the damages will be that sum plus

---

52 Jeffrey Horahan, 'The Rule Against Penalties and the Enforceability of Default and Surcharge Interest Clauses in Loan Agreements' (2018) 25(5) Commercial Law Practitioner 107.

53 [1914] UKHL 1.

54 [2012] IEHC 265. See also *Irish Telephone Rentals Ltd v Irish Civil Service Building Society Ltd* [1991] ILRM 880.

interest.[55] Where the clause provides for a sum in excess of this formula, it will be classed as penal.

(3) There is a presumption (but no more) that it is a penalty when 'a single lump sum is made payable by way of compensation, on the occurrence of one or more or all of several events, some of which may occasion serious and others but trifling damages'. In *Schiesser International (Ireland) Ltd v Gallagher* a clause in a training contract provided that the defendant would repay all training and travel costs should he leave the employment of the plaintiff within three years of the training.[56] This clause was struck down as penal as it would require the same amount of damages whether the defendant left one day after the training was completed, or one day before the three years employment ended.

On the other hand:

(4) It is no obstacle to the sum stipulated being a genuine pre-estimate of damage, that the consequences of the breach are such as to make precise pre-estimation almost an impossibility.

The test for determining whether a clause is penal or not was reformulated recently by the Supreme Court in the conjoined appeals of *Cavendish Square Holdings BV v Makdessi; ParkingEye Ltd v Beavis*.[57] The Supreme Court rejected the contention that these clauses ought to be abolished or restricted to commercial cases only, but it did restrict the operation of the clauses to breach of primary contractual obligations. It held that even where a stipulated sum is not a genuine pre-estimate, it will not be deemed to be a penalty where it is not disproportionate and protects a legitimate interest:

> The true test is whether the impugned provision is a secondary obligation which imposes a detriment on the contract breaker out of all proportion to any legitimate interest of the innocent party in the enforcement of the primary obligation.

The approach taken by the UK Supreme Court has been criticised for being vague, particularly around the issue of protecting a legitimate interest.[58] The Irish Courts have preferred to remain with the tradition

---

55 [1998] 4 IR 191.

56 (1971) 106 ILTR 22.

57 [2015] UKSC 67. See Shivprasad Swaminathan, 'A Centennial Refurbishment of Dunlop's emporium of contractual concepts: Cavendish Square Holdings BV v Talal El Makdessi and ParkingEye Ltd v Beavis' (2016) 45(2) Common Law World Review 248.

58 Conor McEeaney, 'Penalty Clauses and Liquidated Damages: The Divergence in English and Irish Jurisprudence' (2020) 27(3) Commercial Law Practitioner

test set down in Dunlop with McKechnie J stating in *Launceston Property Finance Ltd v Burke*:

> I shall take this opportunity and say, although clearly obiter, that I am not immediately convinced that any change to the test is necessary, nor that the route taken by the UK Supreme Court is necessarily a superior one. I stress that the live debate must be left over for a more suitable case if and when that should arise.[59]

The court had an opportunity to reassess this position the following year in *Sheehan v Breccia* and again affirmed that the test as set down in *Dunlop* is the appropriate approach to be taken by the court.[60]

If the clause is determined as penal, it will be unenforceable. If the amount of damages claimed under this clause is a genuine estimate of damages likely to be suffered as a result of the breach, it will be enforceable as a liquidated damages clause. The question of whether it is penal or not will depend on the construction of the contract at the time it was entered into and will only be deemed penal where the damages sought are extravagant, exorbitant or unconscionable. It does not matter what the parties label the clause in the contract. For example, a clause labelled as a liquidated damages clause may still be found to be penal and unenforceable.

Where the clause is deemed to be a valid liquidated damages clause, the innocent party will be restricted to the amount of damages stipulated, even where the loss may be greater. In *Cellulose Acetate Silk Co Ltd v Widnes Foundry* the appellant agreed to pay 'the sum of £20 per week for every week we exceed 18 weeks' in a contract which required them to deliver and install a recovery plant.[61] The work was completed 30 weeks late which meant that the damages payable were £600, although the actual loss amounted to £5,850. It was held that the parties were restricted to the amount that they had provided for in their contract.

Where the clause is a penalty clause and therefore unenforceable, damages will be calculated by the court in the normal way.

Test Your Knowledge

Sharon owns a factory that produces orange juice. She has contracted

---

43; Solene Rowan, 'The 'Legitimate Interest in Performance' in the Law on Penalties' (2019) 78(1) Cambridge Law Journal 148.

59 [2017] IESC 62.

60 [2018] IECA 286.

61 [1933] AC 20.

with Basic Fruit Company to deliver 500 tonnes of fresh oranges to produce this juice and to fulfil her orders with various supermarkets. The oranges are due to be delivered on the 15th April. On the 10th April Basic Fruit contact her and tell her that the delivery is going to be delayed by two weeks. Sharon is obviously very unhappy with this clear breach of contract as it means that she will not be able to meet her deliveries. She is contacted by another company Fruit Heaven who tell her that they have a surplus of oranges and while they cannot provide the 500 tonnes, they can provide 100 tonnes which would mean that she will be able to meet her first orders. However, Sharon says no. She believes that as she has already contracted with Basic Fruit it is up to them to deliver on time. By the time Basic Fruit deliver, Sharon is well behind on her orders. The supermarkets fine her a combined late fee of €15,000. Sharon is suing Basic Fruit Limited for breach of contract and has included the late fee in her claim. Can Sharon:

A. Recover all of her losses?
B. Recover for breach of contract but not the late fee?
C. Recover none of her losses?

The correct answer here is B. While there has been a clear breach of contract that Sharon can claim for, she also has a duty to mitigate her losses. When the other company offered to provide some of the fruit which would have allowed her to meet her initial orders and avoid the late fee she should have taken this opportunity.

Stretch and Challenge Question

Analyse the UK Supreme Court's test set down in Makdessi and Parking Eye. Do you believe that the reformulated test is better?

CHAPTER 20

EQUITABLE REMEDIES

20.1 The Role of Equity

In the 12th century, the crown (or royal) courts were not fixed, but rather the King travelled the length and breadth of the country accompanied by his Lord Chancellor, who was usually a highly educated ecclesiastic man. Smaller cases were heard by local courts headed by the feudal lords. Over time the system of law began to solidify. The King would, through the Chancellor, issue legal writs, which were directions on how particular cases would be decided. This was the beginning of the common law system as we know it today. By the early 14th century, the form of the writ and the common law had become well established and particularly rigid. As far back as The Provisions of Oxford 1258 it was established that no new writs could be issued without the King's prior and express approval, meaning that should a claimant want to bring a case, that claim had to fall within a recognised and established writ. Thus, petitions to the King became a regular occurrence, and the King delegated to the Lord Chancellor the power to grant remedies and exercise mercy. The Lord Chancellor then established the Courts of Chancery which had the sole function of hearing cases that could not be heard in the common law courts due to its rigid rules.[1]

The establishment of the chancery courts was based on medieval thought; the King was accountable to God, and the Chancellor as keeper of the King's conscience would act to ameliorate the harshness of the common law, thereby ensuring that the King's conscience was clear. Petitions to the chancery courts increased, as the court was empowered to act by virtue of conscience and did not adhere to

[1] George Burton Adams, 'Origins of English Equity' (1916) 16 Columbia Law Review 87.

strict rules of law. The new body of rules coming from the courts of chancery were known as equitable principles or remedies. The court would not allow a person to insist on their legal rights where to do so would cause an injustice, and where damages (compensation) was the only remedy available in common law courts, equity fashioned new remedies, such as the injunction, to ensure that justice would be served. Equity was all about the fair and just outcome of the case, thus ensuring that the King's conscience before God was clear.

The position of having two separate systems – one based on rigid legal principles, and one based purely on discretion – resulted in inevitable conflict between the two. This came to a head in *The Earl of Oxford's Case*.[2] Here, judgment had been awarded in the common law courts against the defendant, who then applied to the Court of Chancery for an injunction preventing the enforcement of that judgment on the grounds that the judgment had been obtained through fraud. The head of the common law courts indicted the defendant, with the Lord Chancellor granting the injunction, leaving the two courts at an impasse. This dispute was finally referred to the King, who decided that where there was a conflict between the two, equity should prevail. This was placed on a statutory footing by the introduction of the Judicature Acts (see below).

With its status affirmed, equity began to develop a consistent body of law – never seeking to disregard or diminish the common law, but rather intervening when the common law was particularly harsh and unjust. The courts, though, became increasingly unable to deal with the sheer level of cases arriving at their door. As time went on, the courts of chancery began to fill with lawyers rather than spiritual judges, bringing with them their common law training, and the rules of equity equally started to become systematised. It was declared in *Re Telescriptor Syndicate Ltd* that 'this Court is not a Court of Conscience',[3] and in *Re National Funds Assurance Co* that it 'is not, as I have often said, a Court of Conscience, but a Court of Law'.[4]

While the rules of equity became clearer, its relationship with the common law did not. The intricacies of the relationship was illuminated in Charles Dickens' novel, *Bleak House*: 'Equity sends questions to law, law sends questions back to equity; law finds it can't do this, equity finds it can't do that; neither can so much as say it can't do anything, without this solicitor instructing and this counsel appearing for A, and that solicitor instructing and that counsel appearing for B, and

---

2 (1615) 1 Ch Rep 1.
3 [1903] 2 Ch 174.
4 (1878) 10 ChD 118.

so on.'[5] The need to strike a balance was clear, and in the 18th century legislative measures were introduced to reform the system. From the mid nineteenth century legislation was enacted to alleviate some of the issues associated with having two distinct legal systems. First, the Common Law Procedure Amendment Act (Ireland) 1865 which allowed the common law courts to grant equitable remedies was introduced. Then the Chancery Amendment Act 1858 (Lord Cairns Act) gave the Courts of Chancery the power to grant damages.

Major reform came when the Supreme Court of Judicature Acts 1873 and 1875 were enacted in the UK, followed in Ireland by the Supreme Court of Judicature (Ireland) Act 1877, which had the effect of replacing the existing structure of two separate court systems with one which would exercise both common law and equitable jurisdiction. The purpose behind these acts was twofold; to fuse the administration of equity and the common law which Lord Watson explained as 'to enable the parties to a suit to obtain in that suit and without the necessity of resorting to another court, all remedies to which they are entitled in respect of any legal or equitable claim or defence properly advanced by them, so as to avoid the multiplicity of legal proceedings'[6] and to reorganise the court structure. The new court structure consisted of a High Court which was subdivided into divisions,[7] and a Court of Appeal.

In placing the *Earl of Oxford's case* on a statutory footing, s 28(11) of the Judicature (Ireland) Act 1877 confirmed that where there is a conflict between the rules of the common law and equitable principles, the equitable principle was to prevail. The application of this rule was explained by the English Court of Appeal in *Walsh v Lonsdale* which involved the lease of a mill from Lonsdale to Walsh for a period of seven years.[8] The lease was not executed by deed which was (and still is under s 52 of the Law of Property Act 1925) required by law, however the agreement for lease contained a term which allowed for a years rent up front to be payable on demand. When Walsh fell into arrears on his rent, Lonsdale made the demand for the years rent. When this was not paid Lonsdale seized property to recover the rent. The issue before the court was whether Walsh could stop Lonsdale from demanding the years rent and seizing his property given that the deed was not executed. Under the strict application of

---

5 Charles Dickens, *Bleak House* (Cambridge University Press 1887).

6 *Ind, Coope & Co v Emmerson* (1887) 12 App Cas 300, 308.

7 Initially this was divided into Chancery, Queens Bench, Common Pleas, Exchequer and Probate and Matrimonial. After time these divisions were merged together and now what remains is the Chancery and Queens Bench Divisions.

8 (1882) 21 Ch D 9.

the common law, given that the lease was not executed the landlord the clause allowing the landlord to demand the years rent would be invalid and therefore the subsequent seizing of the property illegal. However, the court in applying the principle that equity regards as done what ought to be done found that the agreement for lease could be constituted as a lease in equity, thereby making the demand and subsequent seizure legal. Jessel MR commented 'There is only one court and equity rules prevail in it'.[9]

Equity initially developed on an ad hoc basis, intervening where the justice of the case so required, but over time became more solidified. Its impact on all areas of law can be keenly felt, and it has had a considerable impact in the realm of contract law.

Contract law, built on the foundations of the freedom to bargain and the assumption of equality of bargaining power, resulted in many parties being held to bargains that were ultimately unfair or unjust. The common law did allow for contracts to be set aside, but the threshold required could sometimes be unattainably high. Here equity intervened. Equity found that even where the common law threshold had not been met, equity could rescind the contract on the grounds of justice and fairness, in addition to creating new grounds not established previously. In addition, the only remedy available in the common law courts was damages, which were not appropriate in all cases. Equity created new remedies, and of particular importance to contract law are the remedies of rectification and specific performance.

20.2 Rescinding the Contract in Equity

In Part III of this book, we examined various vitiating factors that may arise in contract. As we saw in those chapters, the contract could be voided under common law (eg for mistake) or rescinded in equity (eg for misrepresentation or duress). The result is the same regardless of which one applies; however, as we have seen, the grounds for equitable rescission are wider than those under the common law. In particular, the equitable intervention of undue influence and unconscionable transactions as grounds to rescind a contract (see Chapter 14) gave the courts a wider scope to bring a contract to an end where it was just and fair to do so.

20.3 Rectification

This is a discretionary equitable remedy which seeks to rectify a legal

9 ibid, 14.

instrument where that instrument fails to correctly record the actual agreement made between the parties. The remedy does not rectify the agreement itself, rather the record of that agreement. Say, for example, that we are entering into a contract for the sale of land. You are selling the property that you own at 23 Duke Avenue, and I agree to buy that property. I have inspected the house; I know that I am buying 23 Duke Avenue. The subsequent agreement to sell and conveyance incorrectly record this (and we do not realise before signing). These reflect the property as being 32 Duke Avenue. You do not own this property and cannot sell it, and it is not the property that I have agreed to buy. In these circumstances, the court can rectify the conveyance to reflect our true agreement.

In *Pitt v Holt* the remedy was described as being 'a closely guarded remedy, strictly limited to some clearly established disparity between the words of a legal document and the intention of the parties to it'.[10]

The general rule for a claim for rectification to be successful is that the error must be common to both parties. In other words, that the written document does not truly reflect the intention of both. It must be shown that there was a common intention on the part of both parties and that there was an agreement to that effect, although not necessarily an enforceable contract. Further, that common intention must have continued up until the execution of the document in question. Then it can be said that if the instrument is rectified, it will reflect the true intention of the parties.

Only the actual agreement is relevant; rectification does not operate where the parties are operating under a common misapprehension. In *Frederick E Rose (London) Ltd v William H Pim Jnr & Co Ltd* a claim for rectification was unsuccessful.[11] Here the parties had agreed to buy and sell horsebeans and the written contract referred to horsebeans. However, both parties believed that these were the same as feveroles, which they were not. The parties here were both operating under a misapprehension, and rectification was not possible as the contract actually reflected their agreement.

Traditionally, rectification was not available where only one party was mistaken, as in these circumstances it could not be said that there was a meeting of the minds or a true agreement between the parties. This position was changed in the case of *A Roberts and Co Ltd v Leicestershire CC* where the court found that rectification could be awarded in such circumstances where it could be shown that:

---

10 [2013] 2 AC 108.
11 [1953] 2 QB 450.

(a) one party, A, mistakenly believed that the document contained (or did not contain) a certain provision;
(b) the other party, B, was aware of that mistake;
(c) B failed to draw this mistake to the attention to A; and
(d) the mistake is one that benefits B or detriments A.[12]

In Ireland, the proposition that an instrument could be rectified on the basis of unilateral mistake was first espoused by Kenny J in *Lucey v Laurel Construction Co Ltd* as:

> The court has the jurisdiction to rectify a written agreement made between two parties only when either there is a mutual mistake made by the two parties in the drafting of the written agreement which is to give effect to a prior oral agreement or when one party sees a mistake in the written agreement and when he knows that the other party has not seen it and then signs the document knowing that it contains a mistake.[13]

This has been adopted *Irish Life Assurance Co* where the Supreme Court stated that it would grant rectification for unilateral mistake where it would be inequitable to allow the other party to retain a benefit derived from a mistake.[14] This is also seen in the more recent Court of Appeal case *Slattery v Friends First* where it was determined that in order to succeed the claimant would need to show that he entered into the contract under a mistaken belief; that the other party was aware of the mistake; and that there was an element of sharp practice or other circumstances that would make it unconscionable for the court to enforce the contract as executed.[15]

20.4 Specific Performance

Specific performance is a discretionary equitable remedy whereby the court compels a person to perform their duties under the contract. Unlike general injunctions, specific performance is only applicable to contractual obligations and not those imposed by, for example, tort or public law.[16] The likelihood of a successful claim for specific performance can depend on the type of contract and the type of obligation.[17] We will look at these in turn.

---

12 [1981] 1 WLR 505.
13 Unrep, High Court, 18 December 1970.
14 [1989] IR 253.
15 [2015] IECA 149.
16 Paul S Davies, 'Being Specific about Specific Performance' (2018) 4 Conveyancer and Property Lawyer 324
17 Olivier Moreteau, 'Remedies for Breach of Contract: A Theoretical and Practical Approach to Specific Performance in International Commercial Law (2017) 6 International Business Law Journal 639.

20.4.1 Contracts for the Sale of Land

A person seeking to have an obligation enforced under a contract for the sale of land will first need to ensure that there is a valid and enforceable contract in place. This means that not only does the contract have to be properly formed (see Chapter 2) but also that all statutory formalities have been complied with. Section 51(1) of the Land and Conveyancing Law Reform Act 2009 states that the contract must be in writing, or that there must be a note or memorandum in writing signed by the parties or their authorised agent, or (as equity will not allow a statute to be used as a weapon of fraud) good reason as to why these formalities have not been complied with.[18] Barron J explains that 'where the agreement is a verbal one, the plaintiff must establish not only the concluded agreement but also the existence of a note or memorandum of the agreement signed by the defendant or his agent'.[19]

20.4.2 Contracts for the Sale of Personal Property or to Pay Money

The court will not order specific performance where damages are adequate, as they will be for contracts to pay money or generally for contracts for the sale of personal property. But, exceptionally, the property may be rare or of unique distinction and as such money will not be adequate compensation. Thus, from the case law, we can see that where the personal property is one of ordinary commercial value that can easily be replaced, damages will be an adequate remedy. In *Phillips v Lamdin* the court awarded specific performance of a contract for the purchase of leasehold premises and for the restoration of an Adam door that had been removed between the date of contract and completion.[20] Croom-Johnson J opined:

> But this is a case in which the defendant, in the teeth of his contract, has removed something which is not a mere trifle. I entertain no doubt at all that the defendant is liable to replace the door and to bring it back. You cannot make a new Adam door. You cannot in these times re-fashion a door or make a copy. It seems to me that this is a proper case in which the defendant should be ordered to return the door to where it belongs and to pay the expense of taking it down from where it is, bringing it back to where it ought to be …, and re-fixing it, and paying any expenses that there are

---

18 Previously this provision was contained in s 2 of the Statute of Frauds (Ireland) Act 1695. See Darius Whelan, 'The Existence or Non Existence of an Enforceable Contract for The Sale of Property: The Statute of Frauds Revisited' (2001) 8(5) Commercial Law Practitioner 103; Mark Tottenham, 'Statute of Frauds – Contracts for the Sale of Land' (2003) 8(4) Conveyancing and Property Law Journal 109.

19 *Jodifern Ltd v Fitzgerald* [2000] 3 IR 321, 330.

20 [1949] 2 KB 33.

> about it. I do not see how damages can be an adequate remedy in that case …

Again, in *Cohen v Roche* the court said that such an order would be refused in relation to an 'ordinary article … of commerce and of no special value or interest'.[21] Here the plaintiff sought specific performance of a contract for the sale of eight Hepplewaite chairs. In circumstances where the plaintiff purchased the chairs for resale at a profit, it was held to be appropriate to restrict him to damages.

The type of property in question is not the only issue; rather the availability of the goods is also of concern. In *Sky Petroleum Ltd v VIP Petroleum Ltd,* the claimant entered into a contract whereby the defendant would supply the petrol for its garages.[22] The defendant, in breach of the contract, purported to terminate at a time where petrol supplies were limited and the claimant would not be able to find an alternative source. The court awarded an injunction to restrain the withholding of petrol. Goulding J acknowledged that this in fact amounted to specific performance of the contract, and that in these circumstances damages would not be adequate as the claimant company could go out of business.

In terms of contracts to pay money, specific performance will likely not be granted as damages will be an adequate remedy. The one exception to this general rule is where the contract is to pay periodic amounts, as seen is *Beswick.*[23]

20.4.3 Contracts Requiring Supervision

The general rule here is that the court will not order the specific performance of a contractual obligation where the performance of that obligation would require the constant supervision of the court. One of the earliest authorities for this proposition is *Ryan v Mutual Tontine Westminster Chambers Association,* where the residents of a block of flats failed to enforce a covenant in the lease which required the landlord to provide a porter who was constantly in attendance.[24] A more relaxed approach was taken by the court in *Posner v Scott-Lewis* where it was found that supervision by the court was one thing to be taken into account in coming to a determination.[25] Here, the obligation was to provide a resident porter who would have responsibility for cleaning common areas, look after the heating and take rubbish to the

21 [1928] 1 KB 169.
22 [1974] 1 WLR 576.
23 *Beswick v Beswick* [1968] AC 58.
24 [1893] 1 Ch 116.
25 [1987] Ch 25

bins. In granting the order sought, Mervin J set out the following test to determine whether specific performance for these types of contracts should be awarded:

> Whether or not a specific performance order should be made seems to me to depend on the following considerations:
> (a) Is there sufficient definition of what has to be done in order to comply with the order of the court?
> (b) Will enforcing compliance involve superintendence by the court to an unacceptable degree?
> (c) What are the respective prejudices or hardships that will be suffered by the parties if the order is made or not made.

The issue came before the House of Lords in *Co-Operative Insurance Holdings Ltd v Argyll Stores (Holding) Ltd*.[26] The case concerned an action for specific performance to require a supermarket to remain open during business hours. The business concerned had been trading at a loss and there were 19 years remaining on the lease. Initially granted in the Court of Appeal, the House of Lords overturned this decision where Lord Hoffman analysed the rationale. He stated that the adequacy of damages was not the sole reason for granting or denying such a claim. Further, he explained the reason behind the court's reluctance to involve itself in continued supervision is that the only recourse open to it to enforce the order is to find the defendant in contempt of court, which is wholly unsuitable. In addition, due to the imprecise nature of such orders, they are likely to result in lengthy and repeated applications to the court, resulting in wasteful litigation. Also, in this particular case, it was highlighted that the result would cause the injustice of allowing the claimant to enrich itself at the expense of the defendant who would be forced to continue running a business at a loss. Lord Hoffman was of the opinion that none of these things alone would be determinative, but a cumulative effect of all of them would be taken into account. The court concluded that while damages in this case may be difficult to quantify, they were an adequate remedy.[27]

However, the Irish Supreme Court came to a different conclusion in *Wanze Properties (Ireland) Ltd v Five Star Supermarkets*.[28] Here the claimant sought to enforce a covenant in the lease that premises in a shopping centre would be used as a supermarket and would open during normal business hours. Here the case was distinguished from *Co-Operative Insurance* as the defendant in this case was not trading

---

26 [1998] AC 1.

27 Emma Hatfield, 'Is Specific Performance an Option for Landlords?' (2012) 156(42) Solicitors Journal 12.

28 Unrep, High Court, 24 November 1997.

at a loss and rather was making a commercial decision to relocate to a new shopping centre which promised to be more profitable.[29]

20.4.4 Contracts to Build or Repair

As a rule, the court will not make awards for specific performance relating to contracts to build and repair, primarily due to the imprecise nature of such contracts. However, there are exceptions. In *Wolverhampton Corp v Emmons* the law in relation to these contracts was established by Romer LJ as follows:

> [T]he first requirement is that the building work of which he seeks to enforce the performance is defined by the contract; that is to say that the particulars of the work are so far definitively ascertained that the court can sufficiently see what is the exact nature of the work of which it is asked to order the performance. The second is that the claimant has a substantial interest in having the contract performed, which is of such nature that he cannot adequately be compensated for breach of the contract by damages. The third is that the defendant has by the contract obtained possession of the land on which the work is contracted to be done.[30]

Further, in *Rainbow Estates Ltd v Tokenhold Ltd,* Lawrence Collins QC explained, in a case where the claimant sought specific performance of contractual obligations against a tenant for repairs to the building, that:

> Subject to the overriding need to avoid injustice or oppression, the remedy should be available where damages are not an adequate remedy, or, in the more modern formulation, when specific performance is the appropriate remedy. This will be particularly important if there is substantial difficulty in the way of the landlord effecting the repairs, the landlord may not have a right of access to the property to effect the necessary repairs since (in the absence of contrary agreement) a landlord has no right to enter the premises, and the condition of the premises may be deteriorating.[31]

20.4.5 Contracts for Personal Service

This type of contracts requires the performance of a personal service and are rarely specifically enforced. There are a number of reasons for this position, the fact that it would require extensive supervision of the court, that mutual trust and confidence between the parties may have broken down and that 'the courts are bound to be jealous, lest they

---

[29] See also the Judgement of Peart J in *Dakota Packaging Ltd v APH Manufacturing BV* [2005] 2 IR 54.

[30] [1901] 1 KB 515.

[31] [1999] Ch 64.

should turn contracts for service into contracts of slavery'.[32] However the refusal to grant specific performance for these types of contracts is not rigid and there may be times when the order is warranted.[33] This was explained by Megarry J as follows:

> I do not think that it should be assumed that as soon as any element of personal service or continuous service can be discerned in a contract the court will, without more, refuse specific performance… As is so often the case in equity, the matter is one of balance of advantage and disadvantage in relation to the particular obligation in question; and the fact that the balance will usually lie on the one side does not turn this probability into a rule.[34]

The difficulty in awarding specific performance in contracts of employment was again considered by the court in *Carroll v Dublin Bus* where the plaintiff sought a mandatory injunction in relation to his contract of employment.[35] In explaining the holistic approach that the court must take in making this decision it stated that 'even if such a jurisdiction exists, it seems to me that it could, in principle, only arise in circumstances where it was clear that no other difficulties could reasonably be expected to arise by virtue of making the order'.[36]

In *Ahmed v Health Service Executive* Laffoy J states that there were a variety of reasons why orders of this nature were refused and in this particular case she stated that she was not satisfied that an order could reasonably be complied with and further the consequences of such were unforeseeable.[37]

In the UK, s 236 of the Trade Union and Labour Relations (Consolidation) Act 1992 prohibits the awarding of specific performance in contracts of employment, however there are still certain exceptions to this. Where the contract is not one of employment and rather an independent contractor the award may still be made.[38]

20.4.6 Defences to an Action for Specific Performance

Although the remedy of specific performance is discretionary in itself, where the claimant has met all of the requirements, there are listed defences that the defendant can call to his aid. Successfully invoking

---

32 *DeFrancesco v Barnum* (1889) 45 Ch D430.
33 *Lift Manufacturers Ltd v Irish Life Assurance Co Ltd* [1979] ILRM 277.
34 *C.H Giles & Co v Morris* [1972] 1 WLR 307, 318.
35 [2005] 4 IR 184.
36 ibid, 210.
37 [2007] IEHC 312.
38 Jamie Glister and James Lee, *Hanbury and Martin Modern Equity* (20th edn, Sweet and Maxwell 2015) 729.

a defence here does not mean that the defendant will be absolved from all liability. It means that the defendant will not be ordered to specifically perform their obligations, but will have to pay damages for breach of contract.

20.4.6.1 Lack of Mutuality

This is the principle that the court will not grant the award of specific performance to one party where it would not be granted at the suit of the other – the remedy must be mutual.[39] In *Flight v Bolland*, the remedy was not available to the claimant because as he was below the age of majority, it could not be equally awarded against him.[40]

20.4.6.2 Mistake and Misrepresentation

As we have seen in Part III, these factors may be grounds to have the contract voided in common law or rescinded in equity. However, where they do not reach the severity for the contract to be set aside, they may still provide a defence to an action for specific performance. For example, in *Malins v Freeman* an estate was purchased at auction in circumstances where the bidder was mistaken as to the lot for sale.[41] Specific performance of the contract for sale was refused, even though the mistake was entirely the defendant's fault and the defendant waited until the auction was over before declaring the mistake.

20.4.6.3 Hardship

Generally, specific performance will be refused where to grant it would cause undue hardship to the defendant. In *Patel v Ali* the court was petitioned for an order of specific performance compelling the sale of a property.[42] After the contract was entered into, a series of unfortunate events befell Mrs Ali. Her husband went bankrupt and spent some time in prison, she contracted bone cancer and had one leg amputated. Also, she had two more children, she spoke almost no English and relied heavily on her neighbours for support. In these circumstances, the court found that granting the award of specific performance would cause considerably hardship for Mrs Ali and found that damages would be the more appropriate award.

A more modern approach to the defence can be seen in the case of

---

39 George Russell Northcote, *Fry: A Treatise on the Specific Performance of Contracts* (6th edn, Universal Law Publishing Co 2012) 219.
40 (1828) 4 Russ 298.
41 (1837) 2 Keen 25.
42 [1984] Ch 283.

Aranbel v Darcy.[43] The purchasers agreed to purchase an apartment in Dublin 'off the plans'. When it came time to complete the transaction two years later they were unable to do so. In 2006 Ireland was in the midst of a property boom which had collapsed by 2008 and saw prices of properties falling by up to 50%. The usual remedy of keeping the deposit and selling to another purchaser was not feasible and so developers began to seek the remedy of specific performance. Clarke J dealt with this case as a matter of impossibility, noting that even if the purchasers were to sell existing properties they would not be able to raise the amount of money required to go through with the sale, therefore damages were the adequate remedy in this case. Notwithstanding this, Clarke J did discuss some elements of the hardship defence and stated that the purchasers actions since the completion date would be instrumental in the court's determination; where a defendant was reducing his assets so that he would not be able to comply with the order that the court would be more likely to make that order, as distinct from a situation where the defendant was doing all within his power to meet his contractual obligations

20.4.6.4 Delay

Generally, time is not of the essence for equity, and specific performance may be granted where the contract has expired. Failure to complete on time may result in damages for breach of contract separately. Equity does not impose a statutory limitation period in bringing a claim, and therefore time limits imposed by legislation to bring a claim for damages for breach of contract do not apply here. Given that there is no statutory time limit, the defence of delay is available to the defendant where the claimant has delayed in bringing their case. The delay must be unreasonable, and rather than setting down rules, the determination of whether or not the delay was unreasonable will depend on the facts of each specific case. The modern approach is to look at whether or not it would be unconscionable in the circumstances to allow the claimant to succeed with their claim for specific performance given the lapse of time.

20.4.6.5 Conduct of the Claimant

As noted earlier, equity came into being as a court of conscience. It was based on discretionary principles, and the Chancellor determined whether or not the claimant was entitled to a remedy based on concepts of morality, justice and fairness. This resulted in equity developing some guiding principles, known as the maxims of equity, which the court could have regard to when determining whether it ought to

---

43 [2010] IEHC 272. See also *Titanic Quarter Ltd v Rowe* [2010] NI Ch 14.

use its discretion and award the remedy. The conduct of the person seeking the remedy became a pivotal consideration and still remains a strong element today. Essentially, if you are asking the court to exercise fairness and justice, it will consider if you have behaved in a just and fair manner. Therefore, 'He who comes to equity must come with clean hands' and 'He who seeks equity must do equity': the claimant must show that they have either performed their own obligations under the contract or that they are willing to do so.[44] Where a claimant has taken advantage of the other party, the remedy will not be available to them.

20.4.6.6 Illegality

A contract which is illegal will be void at law and therefore the obligations contained therein cannot be specifically enforced. Further, where the underlying purpose of the contract was illegal, it will equally not be enforced. Where the defendant is relying on an illegal purpose to defeat a claim of specific performance, it is for the defendant to prove.

20.5 Injunctions

An injunction is an equitable remedy which can be categorised by the type of obligation it imposes. A prohibitory injunction prevents a person from doing something, while a mandatory injunction compels positive action.

An injunction may be granted in circumstances where the court would not award specific performance. This is particularly the case where the injunction sought is prohibitory. For example, in *Metropolitan Electric Supply Co Ltd v Ginder Ltd,* a clause in the contract whereby the defendant promised to take all of its electricity supply from the claimant was interpreted to include a negative clause that the defendant would not take any from elsewhere, and an injunction was granted to prohibit it acquiring supply from any other provider.[45]

Whether this in fact amounts to indirect specific performance is a question that has been raised, particularly in terms of contracts for personal performance. In *Lumley v Wagner*, for example, the defendant had entered into an exclusive contract to sing at the claimant's theatre.[46] She then entered into a contract to sing elsewhere. While not ordering specific performance that would compel her to sing with the claimant, the court did enforce the negative obligation in prohibiting her from

---

44 See Claire-Michelle Smyth, *Principles of Equity and Trusts in Ireland* (Clarus Press, 2019) Chapter 2.

45 (1901) 2 Ch 799.

46 [1852] EWHC (Ch) J96.

singing elsewhere. However, an injunction of this kind will not be granted where its effect is to compel performance.

Test Your Knowledge

Leonard and Penny are a married couple and enter into a contract for sale with Brighton Developments in 2019 to purchase a 2 bedroom property in the Brighton Marina. The property was not yet ready and they purchased from the plans, paying a £5,000 deposit. They were expected to pay the balance of €210,000 on completion. The property was expected to be completed in 2021, but due to delays was not completed until 2023.

In 2020 Leonard lost his job, but Penny was still working and earning a good salary. Penny also owned additional property and under pressure from Leonard she agreed to draw down the mortgage to complete the sale, using this property as security. This money is drawn down in 2023 and held in an account for several months until the sale is ready to be completed. In June 2023 having examined the contracts Penny notices that there is an error in the details of the property and refuses to sign the contract.

The following events then transpire: Brighton Developments take an action against Leonard and Penny jointly requiring them to complete the sale of the property, on the basis of their earlier agreements, accepting that there is an error in the final contract. The bank, being concerned about the situation generally tries to enforce its security and take Penny's previous property to secure the mortgage. Penny then claims that she did not want to sign the documents using her existing property as security and only did so as Leonard threatened to leave her if she did not.

What are the Equitable Remedies available in the above situation?

There are three separate remedies available. Brighton Developments could pursue a claim of specific performance against Penny and Leonard to force them to complete the sale. They may be able to argue the defence of hardship as Leonard has lost his job. In relation to the contract itself, both parties agree that there has been an error in the final document. The equitable remedy of rectification will be available to both parties to rectify the defect. Finally, Penny may be able to claim undue influence in relation to signing the documents. It is unlikely that this will succeed if the bank can show that they have taken all reasonable steps to ensure that she was aware of the repercussions of using her second property as security.

Stretch and Challenge Question

Consider whether the prohibitory injunction is effectively being used to award specific performance in circumstances where specific performance is not in fact awarded.

INDEX